MEMORY IN VERGIL'S *AENEID*

Tracing the path from Troy's destruction to Rome's foundation, the *Aeneid* explores the transition between past and future. As the Trojans struggle to found a new city and the narrator sings of his audience's often painful history, memory becomes intertwined with a crucial leitmotif: the challenge of being part of a group that survives violence and destruction only to face the daunting task of remembering what was lost. This book offers a new reading of the *Aeneid* that engages with critical work on memory, and questions the prevailing view that Aeneas must forget his disastrous history in order to escape from a cycle of loss. Considering crucial scenes such as Aeneas' reconstruction of Celaeno's prophecy and his slaying of Turnus, this book demonstrates that memory in the *Aeneid* is a reconstructive and dynamic process, one that offers a social and narrative mechanism for integrating a traumatic past with an uncertain future.

AARON M. SEIDER is Assistant Professor of Classics at the College of the Holy Cross.

MEMORY IN VERGIL'S *AENEID*

Creating the past

AARON M. SEIDER

CAMBRIDGE
UNIVERSITY PRESS

CAMBRIDGE
UNIVERSITY PRESS

University Printing House, Cambridge CB2 8BS, United Kingdom

Published in the United States of America by Cambridge University Press, New York

Cambridge University Press is part of the University of Cambridge.

It furthers the University's mission by disseminating knowledge in the pursuit of education, learning and research at the highest international levels of excellence.

www.cambridge.org
Information on this title: www.cambridge.org/9781107031807

First published 2013

Printed in the United Kingdom by CPI Group LTd, Croydon CR0 4YY

A catalogue record for this publication is available from the British Library

Library of Congress Cataloguing in Publication data
Seider, Aaron M., 1980–
Memory in Vergil's Aeneid : creating the past / by Aaron M. Seider.
pages cm
Includes bibliographical references and index.
ISBN 978-1-107-03180-7 (hardback)
1. Virgil. Aeneis. 2. Memory in literature. 3. Epic poetry, Latin – History and criticism. I. Title.
PA6825.S47 2013
873′.01 – dc23 2013009532

ISBN 978-1-107-03180-7 Hardback

To ERIN, Noah, and Lailah

Contents

Acknowledgements

I was fortunate to benefit from the support and generosity of many people while researching and writing this book. This work began as an idea for my dissertation at the University of Chicago, and I am very grateful to the members of my committee, Shadi Bartsch, Ralph Johnson, Michèle Lowrie, and David Wray, for their critiques and encouragement as it progressed from one draft to another. A particular debt of gratitude is owed to my chair, Shadi, who saw this project through from its proposal in fall 2007 to its defense in fall 2010 and then continued to offer invaluable guidance all the way through to its publication. As a graduate student at Chicago I also benefited from discussion with many other faculty members, including Cliff Ando, Liz Asmis, Helma Dik, Chris Faraone, Jonathan Hall, Sarah Nooter, Mark Payne, and Peter White, as well as with my fellow students, Nick Houlahan, Tobias Joho, and Alex Lee. I also thank those involved with running the Rhetoric and Poetics Workshop at Chicago, a venue where I enjoyed delivering several talks to an engaged and receptive audience.

During my last year of work on the dissertation, I was fortunate to receive a *Memoria Romana* International Doctoral Fellowship, an award that offered financial assistance along with the splendid opportunity to discuss topics related to Roman memory at an October 2010 colloquium. I gained much from my conversations with the other fellowship recipients, Susan Blevins, Lauren Donovan Ginsberg, Lucy Jones, Sebastian Modrow, Shreyaa Patel, Maggie Popkin, Emmanuelle Raymond, and Stefano Rebeggiani, as well as Anna Anguissola, Reinhold Glei, and Wolfgang Polleichtner, who also participated in our meetings. I am especially grateful to Emmanuelle, who, along with her insightful feedback on my ideas, generously shared her own work on memory in the *Aeneid*. My greatest thanks in regard to the *Memoria Romana* project go to Karl Galinsky. Not only did he organize and oversee our meeting in Rome as well as many other aspects of the project, but he has been unstintingly generous with his time and advice, beginning with his support of my application to the fellowship and extending through to his feedback on later drafts of the book and assistance with the process of publication. In fact, the publication of this book is supported by a generous subvention from the *Memoria Romana* project, for which I am deeply grateful.

As the dissertation was being revised into a book, I began teaching at the College of the Holy Cross. Since that time, I have enjoyed being a member of a Classics department marked by its collegiality and vibrancy. My colleagues, in spite of their numerous commitments both inside and outside the classroom, have always been generous with their support and advice. I am particularly grateful to Tom Martin and Mary Ebbott, who, in their roles as successive department chairs, encouraged me to bring my own research interests into the classroom and allowed me to develop courses that did just that, and to Tim Joseph, who was kind enough to discuss many aspects of this book with me as it went through its final stages before publication. Outside of the Classics department, I thank Mark Freeman, who generously took time to discuss his own rich work on memory with me. I gladly acknowledge my Holy Cross students as well, who have heartily engaged with many of the ideas about memory and the *Aeneid* contained in this book.

In addition to all those mentioned above, I have also profited from the comments and suggestions of many others. Audiences at two meetings of the Classical Association of the Middle West and South (2009 and 2010) offered feedback on talks related to this book. Antonia Syson sent drafts of her work on the *Aeneid* along with feedback on this project, and Richard Tarrant was kind enough to share his commentary on *Aeneid* 12 with me before its publication. Two of my professors from my undergraduate days at Brown University, Joe Pucci and Michael Putnam, have offered their unstinting support and encouragement. Lastly, I am deeply grateful to the Press's anonymous readers for their extensive and thoughtful feedback on the book. The work has been vastly improved by their critiques, and the same can be said for the suggestions of all others named above. All errors and deficiencies that remain in the work are, of course, my responsibility. In regard to the book's production, I offer my gratitude to my editors at Cambridge, Laura Morris and Elizabeth Hanlon, who shepherded my book through the entire publication process with pleasant efficiency.

Last, but certainly not least, I thank my family, who has encouraged me throughout my study of the Classics. My parents have always supported my interest in this topic, even going so far as to read and comment on chapters of the dissertation and entire drafts of the book. Just as the dissertation was moving through its final stages, my wife and I welcomed our son Noah into the world, and, as the book was coming to an end, we were fortunate enough to see our family grow once more, as our daughter Lailah was born. Both children have been wonderful companions for late-night revisions. My deepest and most heartfelt debt of gratitude goes to my wife, Erin. She has read and discussed this work with me time and time again, offering her wonderful blend of insightful commentary, hearty encouragement, and charming humor. This book is dedicated to her and to our two children.

Introduction

The *Aeneid* begins and ends with deeds provoked by memory. The epic's action opens with Juno's devastating attack on the Trojan fleet, an assault that springs from the goddess' "unforgetting anger" (*memorem . . . iram*, 1.4).[1] Eleven books later, when Aeneas stands over Turnus in the poem's final lines, remembrance drives him to act. Turnus pleads for his life and seems to succeed, but his fortune changes when Aeneas sees that he wears as spoils the baldric that once belonged to Pallas. Characterized by the narrator as a "monument of violent grief" (*saevi monimenta doloris*, 12.945), the baldric spurs Aeneas on to slay Turnus in a sudden and savage rage. These bookends to Vergil's poem showcase the traumatic energy and narrative fashioning that mark the characters' engagement with memory in the *Aeneid*. Juno and Aeneas both react with fury to their recollections of earlier suffering (Juno to wrongs associated with the Trojans, Aeneas to Pallas' death), and both seek to avenge their remembered losses (Juno by casting the Trojans into oblivion, Aeneas by reshaping the memory of Pallas' defeat).

That remembering elicits an active response is not surprising in the epic genre. The heroes of the *Iliad* and *Odyssey* frequently act upon their recollections, such as when Achilles returns Hector's body after Priam prompts him to think of his father (*Il.* 24.456–7 and 507–12) and when Odysseus decides to leave Calypso's island behind for Penelope (*Od.* 5.214–24). Vergil, though, endows memory with a unique role in his epic, intertwining the process of recollection with a crucial leitmotif: the challenge of being part of a group that survives traumatic events only to face the daunting task of remembering what was lost. A tincture of pain and hope, disbelief and certainty, attends many of the characters' interactions with memory as they reimagine their own and their societies' stories.

Complementing and complicating the characters' engagement with memory, Vergil figures the song of the *Aeneid*'s narrator as an act of

[1] The text of Vergil is from Mynors 1969. All translations are my own, unless otherwise noted.

recollection and commemoration. The narrator creates a vast social memory for his Roman audience, a fashioning that simultaneously showcases his own mnemonic power and reveals the challenges he faces in controlling his story's emotional ramifications. The narrator makes his control of memory apparent at the poem's beginning, when he heralds his own artistic production. The words "Arms and the man I sing . . . " (*Arma virumque cano* . . . , 1.1) open the epic, and the narrator's first-person verb stakes an aggressive claim to the creation of his song and, thereby, of a commemoration of Aeneas' story.[2] The rest of the epic explores the repercussions of this commitment. Continuing to characterize himself as deeply invested in constructing a memory of what he sings, the narrator focuses on his ability to control how his song is remembered in his rhetorical questions, apostrophes of characters, and invocations of the Muse.

Vergil's epic explores the movement between past and future and, above all, the question of how individuals and groups negotiate that perilous journey: the Trojans face the task of founding a new city after their old one is destroyed, and the narrator strives to represent age-old deeds which sometimes show uncomfortable similarities to Rome's recent civil wars. Memory governs these transitions from past traumas to future paths, but, in spite of memory's prominence in the *Aeneid*, its role in the poem has not received a commensurate level of attention. Scholars consider that topic only occasionally, and, for the most part, their evaluations take too rigid an approach.[3] In a series of studies that offers numerous insights, and is perhaps the most influential exploration of memory in Vergil's epic, David Quint argues that the *Aeneid* "elevates the therapeutic effects of forgetting into one of its explicit themes."[4] Quint's essential claim, though, sets too strict an opposition between remembering and forgetting. He writes that remembering is an unproductive process while forgetting allows the Trojans to escape from a cycle of loss, yet this book will show that the process of memory in the *Aeneid* typically blends remembering and forgetting, as characters simultaneously emphasize certain aspects of the past and

[2] Vergil links memory and song together in the programmatic beginning to *Georgics* 3: "I will sing of you also, great Pales, and you, shepherd from Amphrysus, who must be remembered, and you, woods and streams of Mount Lycaeus" (*te quoque, magna Pales, et te memorande canemus | pastor ab Amphryso, vos, silvae amnesque Lycaei, G.* 3.1–2). Here, song is depicted as an art form appropriate for responding to the need for something or someone to be commemorated. See a similar statement at *Aen.* 10.793.

[3] The most significant recent studies of memory in the *Aeneid* are Quint 1982, 1989, and 1993 E. Henry 1989; Hardy 1991; Most 2001; and Scarth 2008.

[4] Quint 1989, 28. Most 2001 picks up on these arguments and writes that the Trojans' need to forget their past is "condensed within the development of their leader Aeneas, who . . . must learn . . . that he must forget the past in order to remember his future" (162).

leave others behind, forgotten.[5] Just as Quint's work suffers from the stark opposition it poses between forgetting and remembering, the studies of Elisabeth Henry and Robert Hardy are likewise hurt by their adherence to a binary approach. The opposition they explore is set along a political axis: although each advances perceptive readings of individual passages, both figure memory's role as part of the epic's approval or disapproval of the nascent Augustan principate and the idea of empire, a perspective that deprives memory of much of its complexity and nuance.[6]

This book aims to move beyond these dichotomies. Along with engaging with Vergilian scholarship open to considering the epic's multiple perspectives, it also joins in the ongoing discussion of memory in the humanities and social sciences. Offering terms and concepts that help to articulate crucial moments in the *Aeneid*, current investigations of memory argue that it is a complex and multi-layered process.[7] These studies' broadest conclusions – that memory "is socially and culturally constructed,"[8] a product of a person's own characteristics and present circumstances as well as the society to which he or she belongs – allow for a richer engagement with many of the questions raised by memory's role in the *Aeneid*.[9] Although this understanding certainly does not match the Roman's so-called art of memory,[10] an example of the "static model of recollection" which was

5 Scarth 2008 also does not view memory as a constructed process. Instead, she argues that the epic's characters avail themselves of the "art of memory" in their interactions with the past (see n. 10 for a description of the "art of memory"). According to Scarth, the characters' recollections are not "consolidated from key elements of their experiences and prone to distortion, like our memories, but were intended, in the manner of elite mnemonic training, to be retrieved and viewed like a photograph and then translated into a form of verbalized expression" (2008, 5).

6 E. Henry 1989 argues that the epic presents us with a hero who is in control of his emotions and whose actions foreshadow later Roman success, while Hardy 1991, building on the arguments of Parry 1963 about the epic's different voices, claims that memory's role in the epic contains traces of praise for empire but also raises questions about the human cost of establishing and maintaining rule.

7 The early twentieth-century writings of Frederic C. Bartlett and Maurice Halbwachs were foundational for much of this later work, and excerpts from their writings, along with dozens of other important treatments of memory ranging from the eighteenth century to the present day, can be found in the collection of Olick, Vinitzky-Seroussi, and Levy 2011. Erll and Nünning 2010 present a compilation of articles providing an overview of major areas in memory studies.

8 Küchler and Melion 1991, 7.

9 These questions concern not just the role of memory in the epic's action, but also how the epic positions itself as a social memory. Vervliet and Estor 2000 and Grabes 2005 offer collections that explore different methods of studying literature as social memory.

10 Utilized by orators to recall topical subjects (*res*) and exact words (*verba*), this art consists of memorizing a real or imagined building and then placing images associated with whatever needs to be remembered in each of the building's niches. When the appropriate time arrives, the orator moves through the building in his mind and sees images that remind him of the necessary information. The major ancient illustrations of this technique are *Ad Herr.* 3.16–24; Cic. *de Or.* 2.86.351–4; and Quint. *Inst. Orat.* 11.2.17–22. For more on the "art of memory," see Blum 1969; Yates 1974; Favro 1996, 7; Knape 1997, 11–13; Small 1997; Sorabji 2006, 22–34; and Möller 2009, 224–31. For a critique of the practicality of this sort of mode of recollection, see Eco 1988, 259.

the dominant conception of memory's operation all the way to St. Augustine,[11] the manner in which memory functions in a society need not be the manner in which that society thinks memory functions.[12] Current approaches open up problems and complexities of remembrance and commemoration, an opening which leaves behind the unproductive binarism of remembering versus forgetting. The willingness of this recent work to recognize ambiguity complements the general shift in Vergilian studies away from the overly simplified rubric that sets the *Aeneid* as either optimistic or pessimistic, pro- or anti-Augustan.[13] Instead of viewing memory chiefly through the lens of these uncomplicated but ultimately false oppositions, this book explores more open-ended issues related to how individuals represent the past and what impact those representations have on larger groups.

By combining a literary study of the *Aeneid* with the careful application of these new analyses of memory, this book aims to enrich our interpretation of memory's function in the epic and increase our appreciation of the *Aeneid*'s engagement with larger dialogues about the role of the past in Augustan Rome. Its main argument is that memory in the *Aeneid* acts as a social and narrative mechanism for integrating a traumatic past with an uncertain future. For both the narrator and characters alike, remembering and commemorating the past and present are painful but necessary ways to move forward, a process that comes to challenge the epic's audience as well. The book's first three chapters analyze memory's role within the epic's action, concentrating on the Trojans' transition to Italy (Chapter 1), Aeneas' relationship with Troy (Chapter 2), and his interactions with Dido (Chapter 3). Chapter 4 treats the narrator's characterization of his own relationship with memory, and Chapter 5 focuses on the issue of mnemonic control in *Aeneid* 12 as it relates to the epic's characters, narrator, and audience. The Conclusion argues that there are several properties associated with recollection and commemoration throughout the epic, properties that invite the epic's characters and narrator to engage with memory at the same time as they frustrate that engagement.

11 Alcock 2002, 2. Ancient beliefs, beginning with Plato and Aristotle, envisaged "memory as a storage receptacle from which images can be retrieved at will" (Küchler and Melion 1991, 3). Casey 1987, 3–7, offers a brief overview of the shift in the theoretical understanding of memory over time.

12 Farrell 1997 shows that, in at least one instance, the Romans' engagement with memory did not match up with their theoretical beliefs about its reproductive quality. He argues that one of the very passages that describes the "art of memory," Cic. *de Or.* 2.86.351–4, actually reveals the sort of dynamic changes and manipulation of an anecdote that fit in well with a modern understanding of remembering.

13 For an overview and evaluation of these two different schools of criticism, see Johnson 1976, 8–16; Stahl 1990, 179–82; Galinsky 1996, 4–5; and P. Hardie 1998, 94.

The boundaries and character of memory

An outline of what the words "memory" and *memoria* designate in English and Latin shows a considerable amount of range, and, as a prelude to this study, it is necessary first to consider what those words may signify and then to establish how the process of memory is characterized in Vergil's epic. The English word "memory" has a wide and varied array of meanings.[14] Excepting its technical uses,[15] it can designate both the process of remembering and what is remembered.[16] The process of remembering may be either conscious or unconscious, and an individual may remember something either because he experienced it (natural memory) or learned it (learned memory).[17] The Latin word *memoria* shows a similar expanse of meanings, though its denotations are specific to Roman culture. Uwe Walter's excellent overview of the different uses of *memoria* shows that the word can denote both the content and process of memory. An illustrative list of its reference points might include memories passed down by earlier generations; the practice of *damnatio memoriae*; the memorization of literature as a school exercise; and the conception of the *mos maiorum* as a sort of memory.[18] And, outstripping the meanings associated with "memory" and *memoria* in English and Latin, the number of subjects studied under its heading is expanding at a rapid pace, moving beyond an individual's recollection of the past to include, for instance, areas of social history and literary interaction.[19]

14 As Fentress and Wickham 1992, x, note, the word "memory" "can include anything from a highly private and spontaneous, possibly wordless, mental sensation to a formalized public ceremony."

15 Such as uses that describe electronic storage and the properties of material goods; in *Webster's Third New International Dictionary* (Gove 1993), these are definitions 6 and 7, respectively.

16 In Gove 1993, definitions 2a and 4a concern the process of memory; and definitions 2c and 4b concern the contents of memory. In *The Oxford English Dictionary* (Simpson and Weiner 2009) definitions 2a, 2b, 6a, and 7a all relate to the process of remembering, while 2c and 3a relate to the thing or person remembered. (The same range can be seen for the words "remembrance" [in Gove 1993 definitions 2a and 3 concern the act of remembrance or the ability to remember, while 4 concerns the content that is remembered] and "recollection" [in Gove 1993 definition 2a relates to the action or ability to recall something to mind, while 2b denotes the contents that are recalled].)

17 See definitions 1–4 in Gove 1993 for this range. See Casey 1987, ix; Fentress and Wickham 1992, xi; and Bergmann 1994, 226, on the expansiveness of what is indicated and impacted by the process of memory.

18 Walter 2004, 26–35. *OLD* 1, 2, and 3 concern the process or faculty of remembering; and *OLD* 4, 5, 7, and 8 concern the contents of memory. In the *TLL*, IB2 generally relates to the process of memory, while IB1 generally relates to the contents of memory (specifically thought of as a part of the spirit).

19 For an idea of what can be studied under the rubric of memory, see Olick, Vinitzky-Seroussi, and Levy 2011, and for a discussion of the recent increase in memory studies in the past several decades (sometimes termed the "memory boom"), see ibid., 3–62, as well as Davis and Starn 1989 and Van

The capaciousness of memory's significance is a boon to this project, as is recent scholarship in the burgeoning field of memory studies.[20] A study of memory in the *Aeneid*, however, which tried to encompass all the subjects related to "memory" and *memoria*, would be far too diffuse and, just as importantly, potentially alien to how the *Aeneid*'s characters and narrator think about and engage in recollection and commemoration. The characters' and narrator's use of the vocabulary of memory offers a foundation for the analysis of the *Aeneid*'s representation of these processes.[21] A survey of the *Aeneid*'s vocabulary of memory yields a nine-word set of nouns, adjectives, and verbs that unequivocally refer to either remembering or forgetting and together articulate a set of precise characteristics for the process of memory. These words, designated here as the *Aeneid*'s core vocabulary of memory, are *immemor*, *meminisse*, *memor*, *memorabilis*, *monimentum*, *oblivisci*, *oblivium*, *recordari*, and *reminisci*. Taken together, they appear a total of sixty-seven times in the epic, with their occurrences ranging from a low of three in a book (*Aeneid* 10 and 12) to a high of ten (*Aeneid* 4).[22] While they vary in their significance, the six words linked with remembering (*meminisse*, *memor*, *memorabilis*, *monimentum*, *recordari*, and *reminisci*) are all connected with the process of bringing something that would otherwise be absent to the forefront of a person's mind. These words typically denote the process of remembrance, the person who remembers, or that which is remembered.[23] Turnus' pre-battle exhortation to his troops in *Aeneid* 10 offers a characteristic example: "Now let each man remember his wife and his house" (*nunc coniugis esto | quisque suae tectique*

Dyke and Alcock 2003, 19–21. See n. 62 for scholarship that considers subjects related to Roman memory.

[20] See pp. 21–23 for a more detailed discussion of the aspects of this new critical work that will be utilized here.

[21] This focus excludes other subjects sometimes studied under the rubric of memory, such as generic memory or reception history, whose links are tenuous at best with the actual interactions with memory that occur within the *Aeneid*. (See Herzog 1993 for an example of an article that largely focuses on generic memory and the *Aeneid*; Most 2001 considers generic memory alongside examples of memory within the *Aeneid*'s action.) Scholars have shown connections between intertextuality and the theme of memory within a text (see J. Miller 1993 and Barchiesi 2001, 130), and, while this book does not study Vergil's allusions under the heading of memory, it does consider instances where intertextual "remembering" and remembering within the action of *Aeneid* occur at the same time.

[22] These totals are calculated from Wacht 1996. J. Miller 1993, writing on Ovid's poetry, considers a similar group of words under the heading of the "vocabulary of memory."

[23] This characterization of memory does not depart far from the conception of memory in ancient Rome. Similarly, a survey in the *OLD* and *TLL* of Late Republican usage for the nine words listed above shows a focus on the process of remembering someone or something which would otherwise be absent along with the content of that memory.

memor, 10.280–1).[24] Turnus tells his men to turn their attention to people and things which are not present, indicating that their wives and houses should be at the forefront of his men's minds in order to inspire valor. The three words associated with forgetting (*immemor*, *oblivisci*, and *oblivium*) describe an opposite process, whereby something is lost from a person's mind that would otherwise be able to be recalled. An example comes during Aeneas' trip to the underworld, when Anchises explains to him how certain souls "drink in long oblivion" (*longa oblivia potant*, 6.715) from the Lethe River, a drink that causes the souls to lose any memory of their earlier existence.

The *Aeneid*'s vocabulary of memory characterizes remembering as a mental process that makes present something that would otherwise be absent. This process can be differentiated based on what is remembered. A remembrance can bring to a character's mind content that is either temporal or non-temporal. A temporal recollection carries something from the past, while a non-temporal memory concerns an obligation or a simple piece of information. No absolute divide exists between these two categories, as the moral weight of an obligation is sometimes attached to an action that occurred in the past.

Non-temporal recollections take place less frequently and are generally less complex than temporal recollections. These non-temporal engagements occur when an obligation or piece of information comes to the front of a person's mind. For instance the word *memor*, used temporally in the epic's fourth line to denote Juno's anger as unforgetting of past incidents,[25] later signifies that Cupid is "mindful of his Acidalian mother" (*memor ille | matris Acidaliae*, 1.719–20).[26] In this latter instance, *memor* signifies that Cupid remembers his obligations to his mother, not an earlier incident such as when Venus gave him this specific order.[27] Another example of non-temporal memory appears in *Aeneid* 4, where Jupiter notices that Aeneas and Dido, "because of their love, have forgotten their better reputation" (*oblitos famae melioris amantis*,

[24] Harrison 1991, ad loc. compares this passage with a number of "similar exhortations of troops evoking home and family," including a passage in the *Iliad* (15.662–3) where memory governs the mental action.

[25] "Unforgetting anger" (*memorem . . . iram*, 1.4). See *OLD* 5: "(of actions, feelings, etc.) Showing remembrance, unforgetting."

[26] See *OLD* 2: "Mindful of one's obligations, grateful." *immemor* shows a similar branching of temporal and non-temporal meanings: it can mean "Not remembering, forgetful" (OLD 1) or "Not remembering one's obligations, etc." (*OLD* 2a).

[27] As Servius remarks, "'But mindful of his mother' means that Cupid is mindful of his mother's orders" (AT MEMOR ILLE MATRIS *hoc est praeceptorum matris*).

4.221). Here again, the memory-word refers to an obligation, not a past incident.[28]

The majority of characters' interactions with memory in the *Aeneid* are temporal in nature. In these cases a person remembers something from the past or thinks about how future generations will remember the present. The *Aeneid*'s opening book offers examples of both sorts. Juno's "unforgetting anger" (*memorem . . . iram*, 1.4) shows how the goddess remembers events from earlier times, an interpretation confirmed by the subsequent list of such incidents in 1.25–8. Not too much later, after Aeneas has barely survived the sea storm caused by Juno, he tells his men that "perhaps one day it will be pleasing to remember even these things" (*forsan et haec olim meminisse iuvabit*, 1.203). Here, Aeneas ventures to think of a time in the future when his men will recollect with pleasure incidents they are suffering through now. These two examples hint at the range of people or events that may be remembered, as well as the different sorts of interactions one may have with memory. Juno's thoughts on the past are a private mental sensation, while Aeneas shares his ideas about the function of memory in a public speech. Moreover, as later examples will show, the person or event that is remembered or envisaged as remembered may be real or imaginary. What binds these instances together is that they focus on a different time period.

Within this range of interactions that characters have with temporal memory, one motif consistently repeats itself: the events a character remembers are presented as something that he or she personally experienced in the past. Aeneas' speech to his men upon landfall, quoted above, shows this feature, as do Dido's words to Aeneas shortly after meeting him (1.619; 623–6):

> atque equidem Teucrum memini Sidona venire . . . 619
> . . . tempore iam ex illo casus mihi cognitus urbis 623
> Troianae nomenque tuum regesque Pelasgi.
> ipse hostis Teucros insigni laude ferebat 625
> seque ortum antiqua Teucrorum a stirpe volebat.

> And I indeed remember that Teucer came to Sidon . . . Already from that time Troy's fall was known to me, along with your name and the Pelasgian kings. Teucer himself, although an enemy, used

[28] Although a sense of obligation is usually felt, this non-temporal use of memory sometimes focuses solely on the retention of pieces of information. Examples include Palinurus' inability "to remember the way" (*meminisse viae*, 3.202) to Italy in the midst of rainstorm. See 5.25 for a similar instance of Palinurus setting his ability to sail somewhere as dependent on his memory, although here the memory could be either of information or of past experience, since he refers to the route to Sicily; in the example at 3.202, though, Palinurus must be referring to his memory of information about the way, not his experience of the way, since the Trojans have never before sailed to Italy.

> to say that the Trojans were of noteworthy renown, and he maintained[29] that he had been born from the Trojans' ancient race.

Dido introduces her speech as a representation of a recollection (*memini*) and then proceeds to describe something that she witnessed at an earlier time. As C. J. Fordyce notes, Vergil greatly prefers the present infinitive to the perfect as the object of *meminisse*, with that tense making a past event "live again" both for the speaker and audience.[30] The vitality of the present infinitive brings Dido's past experience into the present and transforms this prior event into something that she experiences once more.

The nine words listed above, all explicitly linked with memory, establish the sort of mental operations this book studies. This vocabulary characterizes memory as a process that makes present something that is absent, a process generally temporal in nature and closely connected with one's own past. The consistency of this characterization allows for the book to consider passages that describe a mnemonic process without using any core memory words. Some of these instances are not linked by any commonalities and must be considered individually as they arise, but a significant number have their mnemonic associations highlighted by what is here termed secondary vocabulary of memory. This secondary vocabulary is not as firmly defined as the core vocabulary described above, for there are a number of words that have the potential to sometimes, although not always, be connected with the process of memory. The four words considered here (*abolere*, *memorare*, *monere*, and *repetere*) often occur in the context of words from the *Aeneid*'s core vocabulary of memory.[31] In a text as multivalent as the *Aeneid*, where Vergil manipulates and plays with the meaning of words,[32] such associations add to the mnemonic undertones of these four words and increase the possibility that they may indicate on their own that a process of memory is occurring.

29 For this interpretation of *volebat*, see Conington 1884, ad loc.; Austin 1971, ad loc.; and *OLD* 18.

30 1977, ad 7.206.

31 *Fama*, *imago*, and *nomen* could easily be included in this list as well, although they relate to memory less frequently than the four words listed above. For examples of these words' association with memory in the *Aeneid*, see pp. 58, 82–3, 120, 130, 135, 137, 142, 144, and 183 (*fama*), pp. 47–8, 62, 89, and 178 (*imago*), and pp. 63, 97–8, 114, 147, and 173 (*nomen*). For consideration of the goddess *Fama* and the concept *fama* in the *Aeneid*, see P. Hardie 2012, 78–149.

32 See Lyne 1989 for some of the techniques through which Vergil grants poetic force to ordinary words, often through employing them in surprising combinations or exploiting the expected sense of a word. Vergil's expansion of his vocabulary of memory can be regarded as a somewhat similar phenomenon, as he brings out further significations from these four words both through their context and through their juxtaposition with words from the epic's core vocabulary of memory. For an ancient critique of Vergil's practice of using standard words in a new way, see Donatus' *Life of Vergil* 44 and Lyne 1989, p. 18 n. 65 on Donatus. See O'Hara 1996 for a consideration of Vergil's etymological wordplay.

Examples involving *abolere* and *repetere* are representative of how words from this secondary vocabulary are linked with memory and thereby become able to indicate on their own that memory is in play. The verb *abolere* generally means to destroy something,[33] but another meaning comes to the fore in *Aeneid* 4. As Dido nears her suicide, she says, "It helps to destroy all the monuments of that wicked man" (*abolere nefandi* | *cuncta viri monimenta iuvat*, 4.497–8). Here, *abolere* could mean simply "to destroy," but the presence of *monimenta* as its direct object brings out a mnemonic resonance.[34] When it occurs at 11.789, this same resonance appears even without the presence of any word from the core vocabulary of memory: "Allow, father, for this disgrace to be destroyed by my arms" (*da, pater, hoc nostris aboleri dedecus armis*, 11.789). Spoken by Arruns, who goes on to deny his wish for any commemorative "trophy" (*tropaeum*, 11.790) for himself, *abolere* hints that he wants not just to destroy his enemy, but also to make any memory of his foe's battlefield exploits disappear.

An example involving *repetere* reinforces how the *Aeneid*'s core memory vocabulary can bring out implications of remembering in a secondary vocabulary word, thus enabling that secondary word to designate the process of memory on its own elsewhere. In *Aeneid* 12 Aeneas addresses his son: "Since you will soon become a man, take care to remember and let both your father Aeneas and your uncle Hector rouse you as you seek examples of your people with your mind" (*sis memor et te animo repetentem exempla tuorum* | *et pater Aeneas et avunculus excitet Hector*, 12.439–40). *Memor* introduces the idea of remembrance in this passage, and *repetentem* echoes it, indicating that Ascanius ought to use his memory to look back for examples of Aeneas and Hector's actions.[35] Earlier in the epic *repetere* brings in the idea of remembering on its own: "For my father Anchises (now I remember) left such secrets of fate for me" (*genitor mihi talia namque* | *(nunc repeto) Anchises fatorum arcana reliquit*, 7.122–3). Here, as part of Aeneas' introduction to his recapitulation of his father's words, *repeto* communicates to Aeneas' audience that he is currently remembering something from the past.[36]

33 See *OLD* 1 and *TLL* 116.46–117.33.

34 The *TLL* denies this meaning here, instead cataloguing 4.497 as the first entry under the more typical meaning of "to destroy" and taking care to comment that Servius makes his gloss (*a memoria tollere*) wrongly (see *TLL* 116.46–8). Vergil innovates in introducing this mnemonic use of *abolere* at 1.720 (for discussion of this example, see pp. 99–100).

35 Tarrant 2012, ad 439 also interprets *repetentem* as indicating the process "of calling to mind past events or persons."

36 Mnemonic associations come to the fore in the other appearance of *abolere* in the epic, and the same can be said for about a quarter of the instances of *monere* and *repetere*. The other use of *abolere* occurs at 1.720 (where it appears in the context of *memor*). *Monere* occurs twelve times in the epic and it takes on a possible mnemonic resonance (see *OLD* 1 and 3; and *TLL* 1406.76–1410.10) in

Out of the four words from the secondary vocabulary of memory discussed here, *memorare* has the greatest potential to influence the understanding of the basic characteristics of memory in the epic, as it further links personal narrative with the act of recollection. Of the words in this secondary vocabulary *memorare* occurs the greatest number of times in the epic (twenty-seven). Its dominant meaning is "to speak of" or "to narrate,"[37] and in the *Aeneid* it is most frequently used to signify that a character is either about to begin speaking or has finished doing so.[38] The verb can also mean to "to remind"[39] or "to remember,"[40] and explicit memory cues not infrequently allude to one of these significations.[41] In the epic's eighth line, for instance, the narrator addresses the Muse: "Muse, tell me the causes . . . " (*Musa, mihi causas memora . . .* 1.8). Two factors here imply that *memorare*, even though its surface meaning is "tell," also indicates that memory is at stake: the Muse is Memory's daughter and the narrator asks her to remind him of the reasons for Juno's unforgetting anger.[42] The meaning is again brought to the fore in a later invocation, when the narrator pairs *memorare* with *meminisse*: "You, goddesses, both remember and are able to remind" (*et meministis enim, divae, et memorare potestis*, 7.645). The narrator describes the Muses as possessing a mastery over two different aspects of memory: *meministis* indicates the Muses recollect the past themselves and with *memorare*, defined through its opposition with *meminisse*, shows that they can make others remember these events as well through reminding them. Furthermore, there are other instances, outside of apostrophes of the Muses, when *memorare* is explicitly connected with memory.

three of those instances: at 3.188 (where it is linked with a search for a new home already associated with memory, see 3.102, 107, 182, 184, and 187; Mynors prints *moveret* at 187 and there is manuscript support for that reading as well as *moneret*); 7.41 (where it is used in the context of an invocation to a Muse); and at 7.110 (where it appears in the general context of Aeneas' recollection of the tables prophecy, a mnemonic crux discussed below at pp. 28–31 and 41–6). *Repetere* has fifteen appearances in the epic, and it takes on a possible mnemonic resonance (see *OLD* 6) three times: at 7.123 (discussed in a passage also associated with the tables prophecy); 10.36 (where Venus uses it as part of her recapitulation of all the Trojans have suffered); and 12.439 (discussed on p. 10).

37 See *OLD* 1, 2, and 3, and *TLL* 686.52–691.60.

38 The verb is used in this way eleven times: 1.631, 2.650, 3.182, 5.641, 5.743, 6.699, 8.79, 8.532, 9.250, 9.324, and 10.680.

39 *OLD* 4; Ernout and Meillet 1932; and *TLL* 691.61–73. The examples of this meaning in the *TLL* are later than Vergil, but the *OLD* has one example earlier than Vergil (Sal. *Jug.* 33.4) and one contemporaneous with him ([Tib.] 3.7.19).

40 The *TLL*, unlike the *OLD*, includes the meaning of "to remember" for *memorare* (*TLL* 691.74–692.34), but all of these entries are post-Vergilian.

41 The *TLL* (686.37) also notes that *memorare* is derived from *memor*, an etymological link that may hint at the potential mnemonic implications of the verb.

42 See Hes. *Th.* 53–5 and 915–17 and M. L. West 1966, ad 54 for the Muses' parentage. Livius Andronicus 12 M describes a Muse in the same way: "For the goddess, daughter of Moneta, taught" (*nam diva Monetas filia docuit*). See Hinds 1998, 60 n. 14 on this passage from Livius.

As Lausus nears his death, for instance, the narrator apostrophizes him: "I will not be silent about you, a youth so worthy to be remembered" (*nec te, iuvenis memorande, silebo*, 10.793). The narrator's song in the *Aeneid* is characterized as something that creates memory, and the link here between *memorande* and his vow not to be silent draws out the verb's less typical meaning of "to remember."[43]

In addition to these three examples involving the core vocabulary of memory, strong mnemonic cues of other sorts bring out the secondary connotations of *memorare* another eight times in the epic.[44] This frequent association allows those connotations to rise to the surface in some of the word's sixteen other appearances where no explicit memory cues are present. Two examples from *Aeneid* 2 show how a character's verbalized personal history may be framed as a recollection. In the second and more straightforward of these instances, Anchises tells Aeneas that he will not flee Troy, even as the city is in the midst of being destroyed. The gods are against him, he says, and he is lame, a condition he has suffered since the time when Jupiter "blew on me with the winds of his thunderbolt and touched me with fire" (*fulminis adflavit ventis et contigit igni*, 2.649). Anchises' closing words refer to the punishment he suffered at Jupiter's hands for speaking of his affair with Venus.[45] Aeneas marks the end of Anchises' speech thus: "Saying such things he was standing still and remaining fixed on the spot" (*talia perstabat memorans fixusque manebat*, 2.650). The primary meaning of *memorans* indicates that Anchises was speaking, but the word's secondary meaning lurks in the background as well, implying that Aeneas regards his father's story as a recollection of a personal experience, a memory that Anchises believes justifies his decision to stay.

The more complex and significant example of *memorare* comes earlier in Aeneas' story of Troy's downfall, as he narrates how the Trojans caught Sinon on the shore.[46] The Trojans surround their Greek prisoner and

[43] See the remarks on the meaning of the gerundive of *memorare* at *TLL* 693.61–694.23. This specific example is cited at 693.66–7.

[44] 1.631 (occurs immediately after Dido references her own past experiences); 3.182 (see remarks on 3.188 in n. 36); 5.392 (occurs in the context of a discussion of Entellus' past experience; also note use of *fama* in same line); 6.716 (occurs as part of an explanation of soul's oblivion before rebirth; note *oblivia* in 6.715); 7.564 (in the same line as *fama*); 8.339 (in the larger context of the narrator's description of various ancient sites of Pallanteum and the structures now occupying those sites in present-day Rome, the verb is used in close context with *nomine* in 8.338 to indicate the history of the name of a gate); 9.250 (immediately following a speech that mentioned the complete destruction of Troy, designated by *delere* at 9.249, which itself can have mnemonic connotations – see *OLD* 1.c); and 10.680 (following a speech of Turnus, which closes with his hope in 10.679 that neither his followers nor *fama* may follow him).

[45] See *HHAphr.* 281–90 and Faulkner 2008, ad 53–199 and 286–8.

[46] See pp. 44, 96–97, and 107–11 for further discussion of this passage.

compel him to speak: "We urge him to state what trust there is for a captive" (*hortamur* . . . | . . . *memoret quae sit fiducia capto*, 2.74–5). The primary meaning of *memoret* is surely the significance felt most strongly here, as Sinon is ordered by his captors to reveal specific pieces of information. Yet, when Sinon spins a false but believable story of his escape from the Greeks and the Trojans are convinced that he experienced what he says he had, the seemingly personal nature of Sinon's story combines with the secondary meaning of *memorare* to situate his words as a memory.[47] Having been deceived by this false tale that masqueraded as a personal experience, Aeneas now selects *memorare* to introduce Sinon's story to Dido, a choice that hints that he sees memory as closely linked with the Trojans' deception. These two uses of *memorare* in *Aeneid* 2 associate the concept of memory with a character's representation of his past, and similar examples occur six other times in the epic.[48] This association elaborates on the characterization of memory outlined by the *Aeneid*'s core vocabulary of memory and allows for the possibility that when characters speak or think about their personal past, even when no word from the core or secondary vocabulary of memory appears, they do so through the process of memory.

Context

A consideration of the *Aeneid*'s literary and historical context reveals the singular depth and relevance of its engagement with memory. Written at a moment when Romans were gravely concerned about a loss of regard for their history and standing as the culmination of a poetic corpus that explores the interplay between past and future, the *Aeneid* presents a complex portrait of memory's role in a time of transition for individuals and societies alike. In comparison with earlier epics, the poem is remarkable for its awareness of the complexities of remembering and forgetting; its engagement of its audience in the experience of a vast social memory; and its vivid depiction of characters driven by their past and deeply concerned with how future generations will remember them.

[47] Servius ad loc. entertains the possibility that *memoret* indicates an act of memory, although in his understanding *memoret* signals the recollections of a non-temporal obligation as much as it does an accurate recollection of one's past: "Or surely 'let him say' means 'let him remember,' so that it means that he remember that there is faith for a captive in speaking truly of his life. From this there is such a response as 'I will tell true things'" (*aut certe 'memoret' est meminerit, ut significet, meminerit in captivo per veriloquium vitae est fiduciam. unde et responsio talis est 'fatebor vera'*). Also, see pp. 11–13 on the meaning of *memorare*.

[48] These instances are 1.631, 3.182, 5.392, 5.641, 6.699, and 8.532.

When any epic is considered as an act of communication between narrator and audience, memory holds an important function for both parties. As Philip Hardie writes, "Memory is the ground and goal of the epic, a narrative received as a gift from the daughters of Memory by the human poet who in turn offers it to posterity as a memorialization of great deeds."[49] The *Aeneid* makes significant innovations within these generic conventions. While Homer and Vergil's poems alike memorialize great deeds for posterity, only the *Aeneid*'s audience listens to events that account for its very existence.[50] Since the narrator imagines his audience as the Romans to whom Aeneas' actions lead, the foundation story he tells becomes a recollection of their communal origins.[51] A Trojan victory in the *Iliad* or Odysseus' death in the *Odyssey* would result in a different Greece and Ithaca,[52] but neither epic depicts the sequence of events necessary for its audience's existence and neither records a social memory of its audience's origins.

Along with the *Aeneid*'s aetiological character, the particular nature of the Trojans' mission likewise emphasizes memory. Self-consciously journeying between past and future, Aeneas and his followers interact with memory from two temporal perspectives. The Trojans are compelled time and time again to consider both how they remember their earlier home now and how generations to come will remember them in the future. In contrast, the characters in the *Iliad* and the *Odyssey* generally take up only one of these two perspectives. Exceptions exist,[53] but the *Iliad*'s heroes chiefly concern themselves with how they will be remembered in the future.

49 Hardie 1990, 263. See also Fantuzzi and Hunter 2004, 117–22 on the relationship between epic and memory.

50 The *Aeneid*'s narrator consistently links his hero's actions with the existence of Rome and the epic's audience. This begins in the proem, where Aeneas' journey from Troy to Italy culminates in "the Latin Race and the Alban fathers and the walls of high Rome" (*genus*... *Latinum* | *Albanique patres atque altae moenia Romae*, 1.6–7), and it continues throughout the poem, such as when Anchises addresses Aeneas as "Roman" (*Romane*, 6.851) and when Aeneas receives a shield from his mother emblazoned with Rome's future history (8.624–728). Horsfall 1991 notes that "The whole poem . . . is a meditation on Roman history from 1.5–7 . . . onwards" (203–4) and argues that "Historical continuity . . . is a fundamental theme of the poem, integrated deeply into its structure and very being" (205). See also Mack 1978, 85–6 on this point and Rea 2007, 13–14 on how Vergil makes his audience's "encounter with the past personal."

51 Berlin 1998, 12 also notes that the *Aeneid* "constructs a kind of collective memory" for its audience. See Mack 1978, 85–6; Feeney 1991, 185; Hardy 1991, 2; P. Hardie 1998, 63–6; Horsfall 1991; and Rea 2007, 13–14 on the epic's aetiological nature.

52 Dougherty 2001, 161–76, makes the argument that Odysseus' return to Ithaca is characterized as a colonial settlement of that island, but this theme is nowhere as overt as the *Aeneid*'s focus on the foundation of Rome and the *Odyssey*'s audience is nowhere figured exclusively as Ithacans.

53 Examples include Achilles' remembrance of his father at 24.456–7 and 507–12 and his dedication to not forgetting Patroclus after his death (e.g., 22.385–90), yet even with Patroclus, there is an emphasis on how Patroclus will be commemorated for the future, and, in particular, on how Achilles' bones will one day be buried alongside his (23.80–92, 23.125–6).

Achilles' choice lies between a short life with eternal fame and a lengthy, but anonymous, existence, and Hector is preoccupied with what men will one day say of him.[54] The *Odyssey*, meanwhile, largely explores how the past is remembered in the present. Odysseus' memories of his family motivate his desire to return home, and this orientation persists even after his arrival in Ithaca. When Penelope tests her husband's identity by claiming that she moved their marriage bed, she plays upon Odysseus' remembrance of his long-ago construction of that bed around a tree.[55]

Beyond these factors that distinguish the *Aeneid* from other examples of its genre, the poem also provides a remarkably detailed exploration of some of the most fundamental qualities of remembering. A glance at memory's emotional resonance in several scenes shows the range of effects that occur when a character thinks of the past and, particularly, of his or her own experiences. Andromache, for instance, remembers her dead husband and son with a mixture of mournful pain and wistful yearning,[56] while Aeneas, in a speech given shortly after he and his men escape death, holds out future recollection as a potential balm, even though he doubts his own words.[57] The narrator, too, is bound up in this process: he displays anger, pride, and astonishment as he transforms the story of Rome's origins into a social memory for his audience to share.[58]

At the same time as the *Aeneid* shows the emotional reactions characters have to their recollections, the epic questions the link between a character's representation of the past and the events he experienced. The characters' remembrances rarely show a straightforward relationship with what actually occurred. Many times when a character recollects a past deed, the narrator hints at the possibility of manipulation. He describes, for instance, how Juno will not let certain past events be forgotten, and the tenacity of her memory implies that she tendentiously reconstructs those events as grievous wrongs in order to fuel her rage.[59] And, when Aeneas attributes a certain prophecy to Anchises in *Aeneid* 7, it is impossible to miss the discrepancy between this recollection and Aeneas' narration of Celaeno's nearly identical prophecy in *Aeneid* 3.[60] As will be discussed in greater detail below, such representations share many features with the process of memory elucidated in modern scholarship.

[54] Martin 1989, 130–45.

[55] 23.174–204. For commentary on other episodes in the *Odyssey* where forgetting the past is a central concern, see Weinrich 2004, 13–16.

[56] See 3.310–12, 3.321–43 and p. 88 for discussion.

[57] See 1.198–207 and pp. 79–82 for discussion.

[58] See pp. 125–35 and 167–7 for examples and discussion of this range of emotions.

[59] See 1.4–29 and pp. 67–75 for discussion.

[60] See 3.255–7 and 7.120–34 and pp. 28–31 and 41–6 for discussion.

Beyond its singularity within its genre and its challenging depiction of memory's nature, the place of the *Aeneid* in both Vergil's career and late Republican Rome draws attention to its depiction of recollection and commemoration. The *Aeneid* stands as the capstone to a body of poetry deeply concerned with temporal boundaries. Several scholars have shown the significance of memory in the *Eclogues* and *Georgics*, works where Vergil explores the remembrance of songs, the relationship between politics and memory, and the results of devotion to the past.[61] Because of the *Aeneid*'s genre and subject, it offers the poet his most ample opportunity to contemplate the nature of memory and, in truth, demands that he do so.

Vergil took up this exploration of memory in a society where remembrance and commemoration were central to people's beliefs and identity. Memory was an integral part of the Romans' everyday life, cultural expression, and political maneuvering, from funeral processions and reverence for the *mos maiorum* to citations of *exempla* and construction of monuments.[62] Alongside this regard for the past, Romans were also extraordinarily concerned with how the future would remember the present. There was a general belief that men wished not to "pass through life in obscurity" (*vitam silentio transeant*, Sal. *Cat.* 1.1), an attitude evident in Roman literature as well as in the aim of the punitive memory sanctions (*damnatio memoriae*) intended to excise the memory of those who had offended Roman power.[63] Alongside their speeches and actions, the Romans also viewed buildings and images as closely connected with memory. A variety of constructions designed to commemorate specific events and people, Rome's monuments sought to define the past and ensure that it be remembered in the future in a particular way.[64]

[61] Hardy 1991, 46–99; Hubbard 1998, 120–7; Most 2001, 156–9; Gale 2003, 332–3; and Meban 2009.

[62] The monographs of Walter 2004, Gowing 2005, and Flower 2006 demonstrate the importance of memory in Republican and Augustan Rome. See also Hölkeskamp 2006 and the collection of essays in Hölkeskamp and Stein-Hölkeskamp 2006. Rea 2007, *passim* and esp. 9 and Scarth 2008, 7–43 discuss the extensive role memory played in everyday Roman life, and Beard 2007, 18–31 and 36–41 details the role memory plays in the Roman triumph.

[63] See Earl 1961, 28–40 for more on this topic in regard to literature (and for more examples of this attitude in Sallust, see *Cat.* 1.3, 2.9, 9.2 and *B.J.* 2.1–2). On memory sanctions in Roman culture, see Flower 2006.

[64] See Zanker 1988 on Roman buildings and images and Bergmann 1994 for a more narrowly focused study of the memories prompted by a particular series of paintings. Larmour and Spencer 2007, 1–22 comment in general about the endurance and dynamism of the past in Rome's urban space. See Earl 1961, 18–27 and Flower 2006, 44–55 on the goal of the Roman aristocracy to control how the past is remembered in the future through monuments and other means. Rodgers 1992 provides examples of such an orientation in grave engravings and literature, and Häusle 1980, 29–40 and Hölscher 2006 write on the relationship between memory, monuments, and inscriptions.

Roman etymological beliefs reflect the idea that memory serves as a conduit both from the past to the present as well as from the present to the future. Varro's etymologies depict memory as something that can both move back to the past from the present and also look toward a future where the present is remembered.[65] According to Varro, "memory" (*memoria*) comes from "remaining" (*manendo*, *L.* 6.49), a derivation indicating that events both remain in one's memory from the past and remain to be remembered by others in the future. This implication is borne out by two other related Varronian etymologies. The forward-looking aspect of memory is visible in the etymology of the words "to remind" (*monere*) and "monument" (*monimentum*):

> ab eodem monere, quod is qui monet, proinde sit ac memoria; sic monimenta quae in sepulcris, et ideo secundum viam, quo praetereuntis admoneant et se fuisse et illos esse mortalis. Ab eo cetera quae scripta ac facta memoriae causa monimenta dicta. Varro *L.* 6.49
>
> "To remind" is derived from the same word [i.e., "memory"], because he who reminds is just like a memory; the same is true for monuments, which are on graves and, for this reason, along streets, so that they might remind those going by that they themselves were mortal and so are the readers. For this reason, the other things which are written and done to preserve their memory are called monuments.[66]

If these explanations consider how a recollection can carry information to the future or how someone or something can remind a person about an obligation or a potentially uncomfortable fact of life,[67] the complement to this is visible in the etymology for the verb "to remember" (*meminisse*). Varro derives "to remember" (*meminisse*) from "memory" (*memoria*), since "there is a motion again toward that which remained in the mind" (*id quod remansit in mente rursus movetur*, 6.49). Here, the backward-looking aspect of memory is expressed, as the mind moves back to what remained from before.

To put it broadly, as shown by the Romans' etymologies as well as by their everyday activities, cultural practices, and physical constructions, they conceived of memory as a central link between past and future, one that was of crucial importance to themselves and their society. More specifically, memory was a vehicle to preserve both themselves and the state. As Alain Gowing writes, the "Romans viewed memory as an essential means of

[65] See Maltby 1991 for more on the following etymologies.
[66] Translations of Varro are adapted from Kent 1938.
[67] Feldherr 2000, 219 discusses the implications of Varro's etymology of *monimentum*.

connecting with the past, and thereby of preserving their sense of self and identity."[68] Underpinning this idea was the notion that recollection performed a vital function within Roman society: it preserved the past as a means to achieve stability and prosperity in the present.[69] Some of Rome's earliest literature associates memory with the city's success. Ennius asserted that "Rome rests upon its ancient customs and men" (*moribus antiquis res stat Romana virisque*, Skutsch 156),[70] and Cicero, Polybius, and Livy all followed him by pointing out the necessity of building the present on memories of the past.[71]

In Vergil's lifetime the Romans increasingly worried that their link with the past was dangerously frayed. During periods of general upheaval, societies tend to become concerned with their connections with earlier times, and the Romans were no exception.[72] Cicero, Sallust, and Livy all lamented that a breakdown in memory was both a cause and result of Rome's turmoil.[73] In a passage that hearkens back to Ennius, Cicero marked the current failure to remember as an instance of moral decline:

> quid enim manet ex antiquis moribus, quibus ille dixit rem stare Romanam? quos ita oblivione obsoletos videmus, ut non modo non colantur, sed iam ignorentur. *Rep*. 5.1.2
>
> For what remains from the ancient customs upon which Ennius said Rome stands? We see that they have fallen into such oblivion that not only are they no longer cultivated, but they are already unknown.

Ironically remembering Ennius at the same time as he wonders at the failure of Rome's tradition of drawing upon the past, Cicero offers a dispiriting picture of the present. His final two clauses emphasize the depth of the

[68] Gowing 2005, 152.

[69] See Meban 2009, 101, who notes the connection that Romans made "between smoothly functioning memory and social and political success."

[70] While the hypothetical context for this verse (the consul Manlius Torquatus' speech justifying the execution of his son) may not be the most sanguine, this statement can nevertheless stand as evidence for the existence of a belief espoused by some part of Rome's population. On this fragment's context, see Skutsch 1985, 316–18.

[71] Cicero *Rep*. 5.1.1, Polybius 6.54.3, and Liv. *praef.* See Meban 2009, 101–2 for discussion of Cicero and Polybius, and Galinsky 1996, 58–9 for discussion of Ennius and Cicero as well as of Livy, which (59) "link the ineffectiveness of republican government to a lack of adherence to the old principles and mores."

[72] See Fentress and Wickham 1992, 122–3 and Meban 2009, 102. Nora 1989, 7 explores "sites of memory" ("lieux de mémoire"), namely places "where memory crystallizes and secretes itself" when there is a sense that society's relationship with the past has been ruptured and its memory of earlier times lost.

[73] These texts are Cic. *Brut.*, Cicero *Rep*. 5.1.2, Sal. *Jug*. 3.1, and Liv. *praef.* (Meban 2009, 103–6 discusses the last three works; Stem 2007, 435–6 comments on Livy and Gowing 2000 treats Cic. *Brut.*

Romans' forgetfulness. If past customs are "not cultivated" (*non colantur*), the chance still remains for them to be reinvigorated. Yet if ancient customs "are already unknown" (*iam ignorentur*), that reflects a deeper state of oblivion from which they may never be recovered. Cicero's emphasis on the totality of this forgetfulness hints at a concern that Rome's future, which relies on its link with the past, may be similarly imperiled.

Seeking to gain and consolidate power in the midst of this turmoil, Augustus presented both himself and Rome as holding a consequential and far-reaching relationship with the past. Whether through his extensive reconstruction of physical monuments[74] or, later on, his *Res Gestae*,[75] Augustus influenced how Rome's past was remembered and what those memories signified.[76] Geoffrey Sumi has shown how Augustus' manipulation of Roman monuments set his ideology as the "filter" through which memories of the past "were communicated to the Roman people,"[77] an argument that echoes Eric Orlin's claim that Augustus used buildings to "reshape Roman memory" and identity alike.[78] Taking advantage of the opportunities at hand in a culture where the past was prized, Augustus turned to the memory tradition to construct his own and Rome's values.

There is no shortage of specific examples illustrating this behavior. Augustus' rededication of the Temple of Castor in the names of Tiberius and Drusus, for instance, turned early national history into part of his family's story.[79] This same tendency is apparent in the unbroken lines of statues of Julian ancestors and Roman heroes in the *exedrae* to the Temple of Mars Ultor, an arrangement that melded Augustus' lineage with Rome's.[80] Aeneas figured prominently in this series of Augustus' forefathers, and the inclusion of his statue vividly advertised Augustus' personal connection with Rome's illustrious history and the myth of its Trojan foundation.[81] By reaching back to earlier times and presenting a cohesive image of the past which overcame competing mnemonic narratives, Augustus constructed a

[74] Favro 1996, 218 remarks that Augustus' monuments and buildings generally portray him as continuing the Republic's "traditional morality and beliefs" even as they imply that the current time surpasses the past. See Favro 1996, 79–142 and Norden 1901 for a broad overview of Augustus' cultural activity along with a bibliography on this subject; Zanker 1988, 101–263 on imagery in Augustan Rome and its ties to the city's past; and Rea 2007, 21–63 on Augustus' attempts to manipulate memory via monuments on the Palatine and Capitoline.

[75] See Galinsky 1996, 49 on Augustus' "conscious appeal to an earlier tradition and precedents" in the *Res Gestae*.

[76] On this topic, see Gowing 2005, 18–19, 152–3, 156; Flower 2006, 115–32; Orlin 2007; and Meban 2009, 106–7.

[77] Sumi 2009, 168. [78] Orlin 2007, 84. [79] Sumi 2009, 186. [80] Zanker 1988, 210–13.

[81] Horsfall 1987, 23–4 and Erskine 2001, 18, and see Erskine 2001, 15–43 for a detailed discussion of the place of the Trojan myth in Late Republican and Augustan Rome.

compelling story in which he and his rule were shown to be preserving Rome's intrinsic values and mores, carried over from the Republic's glory days.[82]

Augustus' manipulation of memory and society's concern about its connection with the past form part of the larger dialogue about memory in which the *Aeneid* participated.[83] Scholars such as Denis Feeney and David Wray have offered productive ways to consider Roman literature as an active participant in a cultural conversation, rather than as a passive product of its context.[84] From this perspective, we may regard the importance of memory in Roman culture not as a phenomenon mandated by Augustus, but rather as something that arose out of consideration between a number of different people with unique points of view.[85] With this in mind, it can be useful to evaluate the *Aeneid* within its cultural context, especially since certain aspects of Vergil's epic so easily map onto its surroundings. The *Aeneid*'s characters and Vergil's countrymen, for instance, both find themselves struggling with their relationship with the past in the midst of vast upheaval, and Aeneas and Augustus both play a sizeable role in a societal transition.[86] These similarities, however, exact as they may appear at times, ought not to turn the poem into a political allegory or a veiled endorsement or critique of Augustus' mnemonic policy.

[82] Flower 2006, 131 notes how Augustus' "new constructions of the past... logically also reinforced the new politics of the present. At the same time, he tended to remove the gaps and scars of these erasures by celebrating his own magnificent constructions and status rituals." Rea 2007, 4–7 comments specifically on how Augustus showed the strength of the community and its values by restoring ancient sites and evoking the memories attached to them. As other scholars have shown, though, different memories can stand alongside and contend with those that a new ruler promotes. Alcock 2002, 16, writing in regard to memory in Greece, argues that "subversive 'counter-memories'" can co-exist and even "forcibly challenge master narratives."

[83] The *Aeneid* was published in 19 BCE, before the construction of the memorials mentioned above (Temple of Mars Ultor, 2 BCE; Temple of Castor, 6 CE) and the publication of the *Res Gestae* (14 CE), yet the gap between Vergil's epic and Augustus' commemorative acts is not so great that they cannot be considered as part of the same political and cultural milieu.

[84] Feeney 1998, 1–2 and Wray 2001, 27–8.

[85] Lowrie 2009, 21 writes that the very term "Augustan program" could lead to a false conclusion, since it "makes it appear the message came from the top and that there was cohesion," even though univocality is not found among the various artists of the time. J. Miller 2009, 5 offers a useful model in lieu of a program or ideology. Pointing out the experimental nature of Augustus' initiatives, Miller moves away from envisioning an "utterly fixed ideology" to thinking of an "Augustan discourse" which challenges the poets and invites their participation. See also White 1993 on the relationships between Augustus and the poets; Galinsky 1996, 8, 37, 57, 71, 73, 225 on the substantial role of the individual artist in Augustan culture; and Beard 2007, 4 on the possibility, shown by their consideration of the triumph, for the Romans to critically consider some of their society's central values.

[86] Barchiesi 2002, 1 notes that Augustus "mans and controls... a double temporal boundary: he is the one who stands between the old Republic and a new order, and between the present and a potential return of civil wars."

Instead, they offer an opportunity to regard the *Aeneid* as actively engaging in the ongoing discussion of memory's role in individual life and societal development.

Methodology

In this work, I augment a philological approach[87] to the *Aeneid* with recent critical work on memory as well as with aspects of narratology suited to a consideration of personal stories about the past. Recent work in the humanities and social sciences offers insight into the processes of recollection and commemoration. As mentioned above, this scholarship broadly argues that people reconstruct memories of the past under the influence of their present surroundings and concerns. These general findings, along with some specific terminology and ideas concerning trauma and identity, are of assistance to this project. Indeed, the outlines of many of these theoretical constructions are already visible in the action of the *Aeneid*. Three of these concepts are especially useful: individual memory, social memory, and oikotype.

The categories of individual memory and social memory help to broadly characterize different sorts of recollection in the *Aeneid*. It is only individuals who can perform the mental action of remembering the past; however, in the twentieth century, scholars increasingly began to explore how memories are impacted by and "attached to membership of social groups."[88] While a variety of names have been applied to this type of memory,[89] James Fentress and Chris Wickham's term "social memory" is particularly well suited to describe the memory an individual shares with a larger group.

[87] I use the term philology to signify a detailed attention to the text, perhaps best encapsulated in Calvert Watkins' phrase "the art of reading slowly" (Watkins 1990, 25, who attributes the phrase to Roman Jakobson). This is more in the European sense of the word, namely to indicate a commitment to literary criticism and close reading, than in the American sense, which signifies an engagement with textual criticism. For three relatively recent explorations of the question "What is philology?" see Hexter and Selden 1992; Fowler and Fowler 1996, 871; and Edmunds 2005, 1–13.

[88] Fentress and Wickham 1992, ix. See also Rea 2007, 8–9 for a brief overview of the topic. For a description of the various areas of research involving social memory, see Kirk 2005. A. Assmann 2011 offers an extensive introduction to the concept.

[89] Maurice Halbwachs, who initiated the study of such memory, described it by the term "collective memory." By its name alone, though, "collective memory" divorces memory from the individual to an extreme extent and, in Halbwachs' conception is associated with a near compete dismissal of the individual's relationship with memory (for examples, see Halbwachs 1992, 38, 49, and 51). For a critique of the term "collective memory" on account of its use as a catch-all to stand for many other ideas related to history, see Gedi and Elam 1996; for a less hostile consideration of some repercussions of using the term, see Olick 1999 and Alcock 2002, 15.

In this book, the term "social memory" designates a memory that is spoken aloud by an individual member of a group, is relevant to and shared by the group, and is in some way influenced by the individual's place within his or her social framework.[90] An individual memory, on the other hand, may be thought of as a recollection mainly concerned with an individual's life, which the person who remembers reflects on himself, sharing it with no other.

With this having been said, as useful and necessary as the terms "individual memory" and "social memory" are for evaluating the recollections of characters in a variety of social settings, the clear categorization their names imply is slightly misleading. Research has shown the influence that group membership exercises on a person's remembrance,[91] and there is a constant tension within the *Aeneid* between the memories that individuals voice and the mnemonic needs of the group to which they belong. Within the *Aeneid*, any character's memory is influenced by his membership in a larger group, and any social memory is likewise shaped by the singular nature of the person who remembers.[92] The two terms are best thought of as descriptions of a recollection's general character rather than as closed-off categories whose members never approach one another. Juno shares her memories of the Trojans' wrongs with no other, for instance, and they represent an example of individual memory even though they are powerfully influenced by the goddess' knowledge that she belongs to the society of immortals; and Aeneas' two-book-long narration of Troy's destruction and the Trojans' wandering represents an example of social memory, even though he narrates substantial portions of those events from his own perspective.

For the Trojans in particular, remembering and commemorating the past are often interpersonal experiences, as they speak about and act upon their memories of past traumas and hopes of future commemoration. The present continually reminds them of their past, and they seek to ensure that they and Troy are remembered in the future. These challenges raise

[90] These characteristics contain elements of what Olick 1999 identifies as the "individualistic" and "collectivistic" perspectives on social memory.

[91] See Fentress and Wickham 1992, 7; Halbwachs 1992; Irwin-Zareka 1994, 4; Olick 1999, 346; and J. Assmann 2006, 2–3.

[92] Irwin-Zareka 1994, 4 captures well the tension between an individual's memory and larger cultural forces when he writes that every memory is produced by an individual who, even though he is capable "of making sense of the past on his own," is nonetheless influenced, consciously or not, by the larger group to which he belongs. Fentress and Wickham 1992, 7; Olick 1999, 346; and J. Assmann 2006, 2–3 also remark upon the mixed individual and social nature of every memory.

the question of how individuals reconstruct a version of the past that enables them to engage with the present, and Aeneas in particular faces this issue head on in his interactions with his fellow Trojans. The concept of a standardized version of the past helps to evaluate the goals, failures, and frustrations of these sorts of interpersonal interactions. Referred to by anthropologists as an oikotype, a standardized version of the past arises out of a community's decisions about which account of the past "is acceptable and which is not."[93]

Over the course of the *Aeneid*, various characters aspire to make their representation of the past an oikotype for the group at large. This process verges between unconscious action and conscious intention and arises from a complex set of interactions among individuals as part of a larger group. Aeneas, for instance, often attempts to form the Trojans' oikotype, such as when he promises his men that they will one day look back with pleasure upon their current trials.[94] Other characters make similar efforts in their commemorations of the dead. The narrator, too, takes part in this process; his entire song is an attempt to influence the oikotype his audience possesses.[95] What all of these oikotypes, or attempts at oikotypes, share is an engagement in selective remembering, a representation of the past that leaves certain aspects behind to be forgotten and brings others forward to be remembered.

Through this combination of remembering and forgetting, an oikotype can offer a palatable story about the past, and a great deal of the process of remembering involves fashioning stories about the past or imagining stories that the future will tell about the present. In light of this, narratology – through its focus on the construction and narration of a story – productively supplements these critical approaches to memory.[96] It offers assistance both in evaluating specific acts of memory and in demarcating the epic's

93 Fentress and Wickham 1992, 74. R. Thomas 1992, 109, writing on the transmission and evolution of oral traditions, shows that this process shares similarities with the formation of a community's memories. Traditions "do not get passed on accidentally: the reasons for remembering them and passing on are fundamental. [The people involved] select the tradition and may well change it in the process: the reasons for change can be cultural, social, political, or ideological." See also Yerushalmi 1982, 95, who notes that social memory "is drastically selective. Certain memories live on; the rest are winnowed out, repressed, or simply discarded by a process of natural selection." See Confino 1997, 1390 for more on this topic.

94 See 1.203 and p. 80 for discussion.

95 See pp. 135–54 for discussion of the other characters and the narrator.

96 I am most interested in applying some of the work done by those who focus "on the narrow core of narratology," namely "the intermediary structures of story construction and narration" (Onega and Landa, 1996, 28). Wheeler 1999 illustrates the benefits of combining philological analysis with a narratological approach.

discourse levels so as to allow for an analysis of memory's role within each level.[97]

While not all memories appear in narrative forms, characters often present their recollections as stories from the past. A character's remembrance is supposedly grounded in actual experience,[98] and narratology offers a productive way to evaluate the relationship between representation (a voiced remembrance) and reality (past experience).[99] The narratological term "fabula" describes the sequence of events represented by a story.[100] When, for instance, Aeneas remembers his father telling him a prophecy, his narrative represents a fabula of Anchises' speaking to the Trojans in the past.[101] Yet, as Jonathan Culler notes, it is possible to question whether a fabula necessarily comprises actions that the actors experienced. Culler argues that there are two mutually contradictory ways of regarding a fabula: either it is "a sequence of events which is prior to and independent of the given perspective on the events [i.e., the narrator's story]" (in this case, Aeneas really did hear his father deliver a prophecy) or "the events [of the fabula] are justified by their appropriateness to a thematic structure [i.e., the narrator's story]" (in this case, Aeneas constructs a story, based on his current needs, that represents something that never actually occurred).[102] The former belief holds that the events of the fabula "are prior to their narrative representation," while the latter regards the fabula as "a tropological product of narrative requirements."[103] In this instance, the speaker's story represents the fabula as something that happened, yet one may suspect that the fabula is merely a scheme of events that the speaker fashions for reasons of his own. In other words, the speaker may use his story to represent a fabula that he never experienced.

It is not always possible to ascertain whether a fabula did or did not happen. For instance, when Sinon first tells the Trojans how Odysseus tried to kill him, they believe that the fabula his story represents was something Sinon experienced: Odysseus truly attempted to have Sinon killed. It is only later, after the Greeks' treachery comes to light, that Aeneas realizes

97 For an overview of narratological approaches to the *Aeneid*, see Fowler 1997b.

98 Irwin-Zarecka 1994, 18.

99 Bal 1997, 147 considers the relation between narrative and memory: "Memory is an act of 'vision' of the past, but, as an act, situated in the present of the memory. It is often a narrative act: loose elements come to cohere into a story, so that they can be remembered and eventually told. But as is well known, memories are unreliable . . . and when put into words, they are rhetorically overworked so that they can connect to an audience . . . Hence the 'story' the person remembers is not identical to the one she experienced."

100 See Fludernik 2009, 4 on the history of this term.

101 See 7.120–34 and pp. 28–31 and 41–6 for discussion.

102 Culler 1980, 32.

103 Culler 1980, 31.

that Sinon constructed a fabula that fitted his mission's requirements. When Aeneas narrates the story of Troy's fall in *Aeneid* 2, his discourse presents Sinon's story as false, since he knows that Sinon never experienced the fabula his story implied. From a mnemonic perspective, Sinon's story represented something as a memory that he never experienced.[104]

Just as the Trojans, when they were in the midst of listening to Sinon's story, lacked the evidence necessary to assay the veracity of the fabula it represented, the *Aeneid*'s audience is often unable to judge the fabula seemingly at the root of a character's memory. For instance, it is difficult to say with certainty whether Dido's memory of Teucer's visit to Phoenicia represents a event she experienced or is something she invented in order to secure the Trojans' goodwill and trust.[105] No other account of this visit exists for the sake of comparison.[106] There is even another option: namely that Dido's story revolves around a visit that actually did occur, but that she embroiders it with details to fit her present purposes, emphasizing certain aspects of it, leaving others forgotten. A great portion of characters' interactions with memory comes in the form of stories, and narratology helps to describe and analyze the relationship these stories construct between representation and reality.

The communication of a memory, along with representing a particular past as having been experienced, sets that past event as having been experienced from a particular perspective. Here, the narratological concept of focalization may be of particular use. As defined by Mieke Bal, the "focalizer" in a particular stretch of narrative is "the point from which elements are viewed."[107] By differentiating the one who tells (the narrator) from the one who sees an event or feels its impact (the focalizer), it becomes possible to notice moments in the *Aeneid* where the two diverge.[108] Vergil frequently illuminates the same event from multiple perspectives, and the concept of focalization allows for a comparison of how two characters create varying memories of the same event. Euryalus' death prompts one such moment.

104 For discussion of the story of Sinon, see pp. 44, 96–7, and 107–11.

105 See 1.619–26 and p. 98 for discussion.

106 Beard 2007, 171, writing in regard to evidence about ancient Rome, notes how "Nothing can contradict a single account; more often than not two accounts of the same events prove incompatible or at least different in significant details."

107 Bal 1997, 146.

108 Although Lyne 1987 does not use a narratological approach, his work shows many moments in the *Aeneid* when different perspectives are offered on events. See Galinsky 2003, 277 on this technique of illuminating a single event from different and often conflicting points of view and its connection with Greek tragedy.

Fowler 2000, 40–63 offers a very "open" view of focalization in the *Aeneid*, claiming that the reader decides the answer to the question "Who sees?" largely depending on his own interpretive goals.

Immediately after the boy is killed, the narrator calls the dead Nisus and Euryalus "a fortunate pair" (*fortunati ambo*, 9.446) whose memory will be kept alive by song. In contrast, the narrator's subsequent description of Euryalus' mother occurs from her point of view, and it reveals the excruciating pain she feels in remembering her earlier relationship with him.[109] This exploration of two views of the same event affords insight into the different purposes memory is used for and the different ways in which an event can be remembered and commemorated for the future.

Along with its assistance in analyzing individual examples of memory, narratology also aids in understanding what role memory plays on each of the epic's discourse levels. Narratological concepts, in particular those advanced by Wayne C. Booth and Gérard Genette, offer a productive framework for separating a text's discourse levels. From the perspective of the text's production, the levels move from the author (Vergil) to the implied author (he who creates the *Aeneid*, "an implicit picture of an author who stands behind the scenes")[110] to the narrator (the "I" of "I sing" (*cano*) in the epic's first line).[111] There are corresponding levels of discourse from the vantage point of the text's recipient: the actual audience (anyone who reads the *Aeneid*), the implied audience (the audience figured in the text), and the narrative audience (those who listen to the narrator sing).[112] Since this book is largely centered on literary questions and, even when considering the *Aeneid* within its historical setting, focuses on the ideas advanced by Vergil the *Aeneid*'s author, not Vergil the historical figure, I collapse the distinction between the terms "author" and "implied author."[113] Thus, I only differentiate between Vergil and the narrator, a separation that leaves the narrator as a distinct figure and enables the consideration of how Vergil constructs the narrator's relationship with

109 See pp. 142–5 for more discussion of these two reactions to Nisus and Euryalus' deaths.

110 Booth 1961, 151. On the same page Booth further defines the implied author: He "is always distinct from the 'real man' – whatever we may take him to be – who creates a superior version of himself, a 'second self,' as he creates his work." Chatman 1978, 148 writes on the same concept: The implied author "is not the narrator, but rather the principle that invented the narrator, along with everything else in the narrative, that stacked the cards in this particular way, had these things happen to these characters, in these words or images. Unlike the narrator, the implied author can *tell* us nothing" (emphasis original).

111 I follow terms pointed out by Booth 1961, 73 and use "narrator" to mean "the speaker in the work who is . . . created by the implied author and who may be separated from him by large ironies."

112 For more on these concepts (although with slightly different terminology), see Booth 1961, 138; Genette 1980, 259–60; and Fludernik 2009, 26.

113 Alongside this reason, since the ancient biographical tradition was quick to construct a life for an author based on his work, it can also be debated what we securely know about Vergil the historical figure and how that knowledge would differentiate him from the *Aeneid*'s implied author (see Horsfall 1995 on Vergil's life and Lefkowitz 1991 on the Greek biographical tradition).

memory. From the perspective of the text's reception, I focus mainly on the *Aeneid*'s implied audience, whose origins spring from Aeneas' actions.

This discourse framework also proves useful for elucidating the characteristics of further narrators within the *Aeneid.* Numerous characters tell stories in the epic, spinning tales that range from several lines to two books. The contents of such stories occupy another discourse level within the *Aeneid*'s narrative framework. As Genette notes, "any event a narrative recounts is at" a new discourse level, separate from "the level at which the narrating act producing the narrative is placed."[114] When Aeneas tells Dido his story in *Aeneid* 2 and 3, he acts as the narrator and she as the narrative audience, and the content of his story occupies a new level of discourse in the epic. By separating these levels of discourse, it is possible to evaluate how memory functions on each level of the epic and what influence, if any, one level has on another. At the same time, this delineation helps to reveal the variety of voices, beliefs, and attitudes present within and between these levels and, in doing so, shifts the interpretation of the *Aeneid* away from unsubtle binarisms and toward a view of the sum of these parts as an intentional construction that presents complex and challenging views about memory.

[114] Genette 1980, 228. See Fludernik 2009, 28 for an overview of various terms used to describe these "embedded narrative acts."

CHAPTER ONE

Turning toward Rome

A lighthearted remark signals the turning point in the Trojans' quest to found a city in Italy. It also occasions one of the epic's most confounding acts of memory. Having sailed up the Tiber River for a stretch, Aeneas and his men disembark for a meal, some food spread over wheaten cakes. When they devour the food and turn their attention to the cakes below, Aeneas' son Iulus asks in jest: "Hey, are we even eating our tables?" (*heus, etiam mensas consumimus?* 7.116).[1]

The boy's remark is playful, but the response it prompts from his father is anything but (7.120–9):

continuo "salve fatis mihi debita tellus
vosque" ait "o fidi Troiae salvete penates:
hic domus, haec patria est. genitor mihi talia namque
(nunc repeto) Anchises fatorum arcana reliquit:
'cum te, nate, fames ignota ad litora vectum
accisis coget dapibus consumere mensas,
tum sperare domos defessus, ibique memento
prima locare manu molirique aggere tecta.'
haec erat illa fames, haec nos suprema manebat
exitiis positura modum."

Straightaway Aeneas says, "Hail, land owed to me by the fates, and hail, you, o faithful gods of Troy: this is our home, this is our country. For my father Anchises (now I remember) left such secrets of fate for me: 'When, son, you are carried to unknown shores and hunger forces you to eat your tables after your food has been devoured, then, exhausted, remember to hope for a home, and to place your first buildings there with your hand and to build them up with a mound.' This was that hunger, this was the last thing waiting for us, about to put a limit on our ruin."

[1] See Horsfall 2000, ad loc. on this line's "markedly colloquial and colourful . . . tone."

Aeneas' words project a state of joyful recognition as he announces to the Trojans that they have fulfilled Anchises' prophecy and finally arrived at the location of their new city.[2]

The satisfaction Aeneas' speech offers, however, is matched by the magnitude of the crux it creates. The same prophecy that he here attributes to Anchises was, according to his narrative in *Aeneid* 3, spoken by the harpy Celaeno. There, she details just what the Trojans will suffer in return for their attempts to despoil her cattle (3.255–7):

> sed non ante datam cingetis moenibus urbem
> quam vos dira fames nostraeque iniuria caedis
> ambesas subigat malis absumere mensas.

> But you will not encircle your given city with walls before dread hunger and the wrong of our slaughter drive you to devour your tables with your jaws.

The scene Aeneas describes in *Aeneid* 3 is at odds with his attribution of this prophecy to Anchises in *Aeneid* 7. In *Aeneid* 3, Celaeno utters the tables prophecy and the only thing Anchises says is a desperate prayer in response: "Gods, hold off the Harpy's threats; gods, turn aside such a calamity and graciously preserve the pious" (*di, prohibete minas; di, talem avertite casum* | *et placidi servate pios*, 3.265–6). Anchises' words in *Aeneid* 3 are in no way similar to the ones Aeneas remembers him having said in *Aeneid* 7.

The conflict between these passages draws our focus to a set of issues central to Vergil's epic: the relationship between past, present, and future; Aeneas' role as a leader of a group in transition; and the challenge of surviving traumatic incidents while facing the threat of more devastation. This chapter argues that in this instance, as well as in several others, Aeneas turns to the process of memory in order to structure and understand his transition from a known past to an unknown future.[3] With regard to the different recountings of the tables prophecy in *Aeneid* 3 and 7, it will be claimed that this inconsistency arises from Aeneas' creative reconstruction of the past with an eye to present needs. Instead of the Trojans' foundation in *Aeneid* 7 being based on a dreadful threat from Celaeno, it rests on the words of Aeneas' beloved father. Although Aeneas' efforts to manipulate the past are not always so clearly marked as they are here, his interactions

[2] Primmer 1994/95, 397 also notes the pleasure and gratitude evident in this scene.

[3] Smith 2005, 61 sets out a similar claim for vision's importance: "Visions from the past deepen a character's understanding of the present and can even anticipate that character's vision of the future." Novara 1986, 67, writing in regard to *Aeneid* 8, also argues that Aeneas uses his memories to frame his actions in the present and accomplish his mission.

with memory consistently reshape the Trojans' past into a positive force for the present.[4] When Aeneas looks to the Trojans' history, his present surroundings matter just as much as what occurred in the past.

As he shares his memories, Aeneas' version of the past becomes the Trojans' standardized version of their history or, in other words, their oikotype. Through his construction of his community's oikotype, Aeneas claims leadership over the Trojans' transition to Italy and builds a future on an edited version of the past that passes on his own cultural values and worldly outlook.[5] Aeneas' choice to remember, though, does not mean that oblivion is absent from his world. Rather it is present in two distinct ways. On a micro-level, forgetting is inscribed in every individual recollection, since the process of remembering is necessarily selective and leaves certain aspects of the past behind. When Aeneas remembers Anchises as the speaker of the tables prophecy, for instance, he consigns Celaeno's role to oblivion. On a macro-level, a more threatening oblivion confronts the Trojans. In the transitional episodes occurring in *Aeneid* 6–10 considered in this chapter,[6]

[4] This argument, that Aeneas attempts to manage his memory, contradicts a widely held view that he and the Trojans must forget the past in order to embark on a new beginning. While I agree with Quint that Aeneas needs to gain "some control over his psychic history" in order to construct a satisfying narrative for his life (Quint 1993, 51), I argue that Aeneas creates a new version of his past through remembering, not forgetting. Along with Quint, many other scholars argue that Aeneas leaves the past behind, largely forgotten. A good number locate this reorientation from past to future either in *Aeneid* 6 or early on in *Aeneid* 7 (Pöschl 1970, 37–9; Rutledge 1971, 2, 112; Lyne 1987, 214; MacDonald 1987, 31; Hardy 1991, 219; P. Miller 1995, 229; Gale 2003, 340; and Smith 2005, 82), and some set it in or around *Aeneid* 3 (Holt 1979/80, 111, 116; Cairns 1989, 117; Hershkowitz 1991, 69; Syed 2005, 175). Galinsky 1996, 125 and Most 2001, 162 argue that the transition extends over the entire epic. From a more general perspective, arguments of this sort, which set the past as something that most be forgotten in order to live a productive life in the present, have much in common with Nietzsche's influential comment that "the past has to be forgotten if it is not to become the gravedigger of the present" (Olick, Vinitzky-Seroussi, and Levy 2011, 74). An examination of that comment's larger context shows, though, that Nietzsche does not view the need to forget as necessary for everyone, but as something that varies depending on people's ability to incorporate the past into their lives. Wiltshire 1988, 70–80; Berlin 1998; and Reed 2007, 170 are some of the few who recognize Troy's importance to Aeneas throughout the *Aeneid.*

[5] The power Aeneas gains by molding the past into an oikotype may be brought out by considering the distinction post-colonial studies makes between space and place: "A space becomes a place once it is defined – by the imposition of boundaries or its inclusion on a map – and, most importantly, when it is named. To name a place is to assert discursive control, so what was previously an unmarked and unseparated space is now a site quilted into a fabric of meaning" (Larmour and Spencer 2007, 11; for an illustration of this from the *Aeneid,* see 6.773–6). This is similar to the formation of a standardized version of the past, wherein an unmarked and unshaped length of earlier time becomes a significant and coherent episode, imbued with a particular meaning and set within the fabric of a larger story about the group's past and identity.

[6] This cohesive group of books describes Aeneas' arrival in Italy and its immediate aftermath. *Aeneid* 6–7 stretches over a small, but imprecise number of days, and *Aeneid* 8–10 lasts three days (for the chronology of *Aeneid* 8–10, see Duckworth 1938, 135–44 and S. J. Harrison 1991, xxiii–xxxiv). The twelve-day peace treaty struck by the Trojans and Latins at 11.133 establishes a natural break between 6.1–11.132 and the epic's conclusion.

Rome and its foundation are associated time and again with the need to move forward by forgetting, a link that reveals the challenges Aeneas faces in metaphorically founding this unique city.

Remembering the future

Shortly after Aeneas arrives in Italy in *Aeneid* 6, he voices a tension he feels between past and future. In an address to the Sibyl, the Trojan leader expresses a particular hope: "May Troy's ill-fortune have followed us only this far; it is lawful also for you [gods and goddesses] to spare Pergama's race already" (*hac Troiana tenus fuerit fortuna secuta; | vos quoque Pergameae iam fas est parcere genti*, 6.62–3).[7] The separation between *Troiana* and *fortuna* embodies the overlong measure of time Aeneas feels he has been followed by Troy's bad fortune.[8] At the same time though, even as Aeneas voices his desperation to escape this ill-fortune, he still identifies himself and his men with the adjective *Pergameae*, a reference to Troy's citadel.[9] The challenge he and his men face, Aeneas implies, lies in pivoting from destruction to prosperity even while retaining their link to Troy. As he shifts from searching the Mediterranean to settling in Italy, Aeneas must figure out what role his past identity will play in his future and how that future can be marked by success, not failure.

A bit later, when Aeneas asks the Sibyl for permission to settle in Latium, her answer hints that his past will play a sizeable role. Apollo's priestess offers an intimidating prophecy (6.88–97):

> non Simois tibi nec Xanthus nec Dorica castra
> defuerint; alius Latio iam partus Achilles,
> natus et ipse dea; nec Teucris addita Iuno
> usquam aberit, cum tu supplex in rebus egenis
> quas gentis Italum aut quas non oraveris urbes.
> causa mali tanti coniunx iterum hospita Teucris
> externique iterum thalami.
> tu ne cede malis, sed contra audentior ito,
> qua tua te Fortuna sinet. via prima salutis
> (quod minime reris) Graia pandetur ab urbe.

The Simois and Xanthus rivers will not be absent for you, and neither will the Greek camps; already a different Achilles has been

[7] See Austin 1977, ad loc. and Kristol 1990, 175 on *fortuna* and Conington 1884, ad loc. and Austin 1977, ad loc. on *fuerit*.

[8] Conington 1884, ad loc. notes the bitterness of the phrase *Troiana fortuna*; Austin 1977, ad loc. remarks upon its forceful alliteration.

[9] Aeneas is not the only one to identify himself thus; the Sibyl describes him as Trojan at 6.52, 126, and 403.

> born in Latium, he himself also a goddess' son; and nowhere will Juno fail to plague the Trojans, while you, a supplicant in dire circumstances, will beg all the races and towns of Italy for help. The cause of such hardship to the Trojans will once again be a foreign wife and once again an alien marriage. Do not yield to these troubles, but rather go forward more boldly in whatever way your fortune allows. The first route of salvation (something which you least expect) will open from a Greek city.

As William Fitzgerald notes, "the Sibyl's response to [Aeneas'] prayer is by no means encouraging."[10] Yet it does offer him an avenue for gauging his surroundings. The Trojans' future in Latium is figured as a repetition of their past, and such a framing compels Aeneas to remember.[11] For instance, when the Sibyl mentions the birth of a different Achilles, she forces Aeneas to think about the Greek Achilles and to use his memories to imagine how he will proceed against this new foe. The same can be said for her references to Troy's two rivers, the Greek camps, Juno, a foreign wife, and an alien marriage. These last two references, in fact, only strengthen the theme of repetition, as they evoke Helen and Dido alike, bringing two past experiences into Aeneas' future. With the distant past (Helen) having already repeated itself once in the years immediately preceding (Dido), now it will intrude into his future. Each of the Sibyl's citations compels Aeneas to recognize the utility of his memories and the necessity of carrying them into the future.

Yet if these repetitions hint that Aeneas' past will always be a part of his future, they also show that it will return with significant changes. Even the statement that expresses strict repetition in lines 88–9 contains the seed of alterity. Line 88 promises dissimilarity with the past, only to have the enjambed verb in 89, "will be absent" (*defuerint*), emphatically dismiss the idea that the future will be different from the past. After difference is at first denied, true changes begin to appear. It is not *the* Achilles who will be in Latium, but "another Achilles" (*alius . . . Achilles*, 6.89). Likewise, even though the insistent doubling of "once again" (*iterum*, 6.93 and 94)

10 1984, 58.

11 Anderson 1957 argues that the repetition of the past in these verses "constructs a new *Iliad*" (19) in *Aeneid* 7–12 that will eventually see the Trojans become the victors, parallel to the Greeks. Anderson is right that the parallels between the past and future are not perfect, but he misses Aeneas' determination to remain Trojan. Quint 1993, 67 picks up on Anderson's arguments and claims that the Sibyl's speech signals that the Trojans will "now reach their new beginning not simply by forgetting and repressing [the past], but by reversing and 'undoing' the past as they repeat it." The Trojans do in fact repeat particular elements of their history, but I will argue below that they do not reverse and undo their past so much as they fold it into their present and future.

portends nothing short of another Trojan War, the surprise help of a Greek city reveals an undeniable distinction between past and future.[12] The future, according to Apollo's priestess, will be both similar to the past but simultaneously different from it, a state that requires Aeneas to apply his memories creatively to his current environment. Although this prophecy is daunting at first, it actually makes the future less threatening; instead of being confronted with entirely unfamiliar difficulties that are threatening in "their bewildering specificity," Aeneas learns of events that are potentially terrible but nonetheless comprehensible because they are set "within old patterns."[13]

The Sibyl's words are the first prophecy Aeneas receives upon his arrival in Italy, and, as such, they are a key text. Aeneas' response shows his confidence in meeting these challenges (6.103–5):

> non ulla laborum,
> o virgo, nova mi facies inopinave surgit;
> omnia praecepi atque animo mecum ante peregi.
>
> Not a single type of labor, virgin, arises unfamiliar or unexpected for me now. I have anticipated all these things, and I have thought them over in my mind with myself.

Aeneas points to his earlier contemplation as a route to success in the future.[14] It is not immediately clear how Aeneas was able to anticipate and think over these trials. He could be referring to the knowledge he gained in earlier prophecies about his tasks in Italy, but these prophecies proved misleading, sometimes devastatingly so.[15] It is more likely, coming so soon after the Sibyl's repeated references to the Trojan War, that Aeneas refers to the thought he has given to his battles at Troy.[16] Having been through one war, Aeneas believes that nothing will surprise him in Italy, and this yields a degree of self-assurance far from the desperation embodied by his earlier prayer to the gods.[17]

[12] Anderson 1957, 19 also notes how the help of a Greek city undermines the prophecy's "apparent parallelism."

[13] Yerushalmi 1982, 36. This quote is taken from Yerushalmi's analysis of Jewish memory and history, where he writes about how memory can help one approach the future.

[14] Conington 1884, ad 6.103 and Austin 1977, ad 105 offer a similar interpretation of these lines.

[15] For one example, see Aeneas' bitter comment on his father's death (3.712–3). Mack 1978, 55–67; O'Hara 1990; and J. Miller 2009, 103 discuss the prophecies Aeneas receives and their frequently misleading nature.

[16] Joseph 2010, 168 sees an appeal on Aeneas' part to earlier prophecies as well as his experiences at Troy.

[17] J. Miller 2009, 138 notes that the hero here is "as self-assured as he has ever appeared."

Forgetting the past

No sooner does Aeneas discover that he must draw upon his past to survive than he learns of a type of progress that is enabled by forgetting. Shortly after the Sibyl delivers her prophecy, she helps Aeneas descend to the underworld in order to speak with his father. When Aeneas finds Anchises in Elysium, he is reviewing the souls who now flock about the Lethe River but one day will become Roman. It is in this setting, as Anchises explains why so many souls surround Lethe, that Aeneas begins to learn how forgetting enables progress (6.713–15):

> tum pater Anchises: "animae, quibus altera fato
> corpora debentur, Lethaei ad fluminis undam
> securos latices et longa oblivia potant."
>
> Then father Anchises said: "The souls to whom another body is owed by fate drink in carefree waters and long oblivion at the bank of the River Lethe."

These souls are engaged in a cycle of reincarnation, and an oblivion-inducing drink from Lethe is part of their return to life.[18] When Anchises' description associates this drink with a lack of concern, forgetting becomes a pleasant prospect.

Aeneas, though, still wonders about what motivates the souls' return to life. He asks his father why any shade would desire to live once more.[19] Anchises answers his son's question by setting the movement of these souls within the universe's larger structure.[20] "A fiery energy and a heavenly origin" (*igneus . . . vigor et caelestis origo*, 6.730), he says, animate the entire universe and every creature within it. This force is present in earthly bodies, but it is blunted by its containment therein and further sullied by the evil deeds people commit during their lives. Freed from the body after death, each soul nonetheless retains the taint of its terrestrial wrongs, and it is only after being sufficiently cleansed in the underworld's darker regions that a shade may proceed to Elysium. Upon its arrival there, Anchises says, a soul

18 The name Lethe comes from the Greek noun λήθη, meaning "forgetfulness" or "forgetting." Its earliest uses are not yet connected with death and the underworld (M. L. West 1966, ad 227; and *LSJ* I). Only after Homer does the Lethe River come to signify "a place of oblivion in the lower world" (*LSJ* II). The association between forgetting and the underworld, though, likely goes back to proto-Indo-European myth (Lincoln 1982).

19 As Catto 1989, 62 notes, "To the weary Aeneas the desire to live again seems . . . [an] inexplicable and blind desire."

20 For the varied philosophical strands of Anchises' speech, see Feeney 1986; Catto 1989; Braund 1997, 216–20; and Gill 2006, 436.

moves into one of two groups.[21] A few exceptional souls, Anchises among them, will return to their original ethereal state after having been purified still further. They will not be born again. The other, much larger group of souls, though, cannot become pure enough to revert to their earlier state. Instead, this group gathers about the Lethe River in order to return to life once more.

This larger group is the one Aeneas sees massed by the river's banks. Anchises now describes them in further detail (6.748–51):

> has omnis, ubi mille rotam volvere per annos,
> Lethaeum ad fluvium deus evocat agmine magno,
> scilicet immemores supera ut convexa revisant
> rursus et incipiant in corpora velle reverti.[22]

> All these souls, when they have rolled the wheel of time through a thousand years, a god calls to the Lethe River in a great throng, so that oblivious (you see) they may once again go back to the upper world and begin to wish to return to bodies.

Forgetting plays an essential role in reincarnation.[23] An anonymous god calls the shades down to the river to take a drink, the implication being that if they were allowed to make a decision based on their memories, they would choose not to be reincarnated. The particle *scilicet* emphasizes the obvious need for their forgetfulness,[24] and the insertion of the infinitive *velle* between *incipient* and *reverti* brings out how a loss of memory leads to a change in attitude and behavior. This imposition of forgetting answers Aeneas' original question about just what could motivate these souls to want

[21] For the argument that the souls divide into two groups upon arrival in Elysium, see Norden 1970, 16; Austin 1977, ad 743 ff. and 744; and Bews 1987, 93.

[22] I follow Conington 1884, ad 6.751 in placing no comma after *rursus*. The idea of repetition is already implicit in the two verbs *revisant* and *reverti*, and this punctuation allows the adverb to be understood with both. Mynors 1969 and Austin 1977 place a comma after *rursus* and limit its application to *revisant*, while Norden 1970 sets a comma after *revisant* and limits the application of *rursus* to *reverti*.

[23] In Plato's "Myth of Er" it is necessary for the dead to drink from the River of Forgetfulness, but the possibility exists for a soul to imbibe only one measure of water and thus not to forget everything (*Rep*. 621a). An inscription found in a grave in Petelia, Italy, also indicates a belief that a soul may be able to retain certain memories even after death. This inscription, likely from the fourth or third century BCE, was buried with the deceased, and it contains instructions for the afterlife detailing how to avoid the waters of oblivion and to instead drink from the waters of memory (for the inscription's text and further references, see Lincoln 1982, 21–4). For those about to return to life in the *Aeneid*, there is no chance to retain memories either of a previous life or of their time in Elysium: a drink from Lethe, enforced by a divinity, leads to complete oblivion.

[24] *OLD* 2.

to live once again.[25] There is a "melancholy" quality to their oblivion,[26] a state that spurs them on to willingly exchange their Elysian existence for an earthly life so dreadful that they would not return if they remembered it.

Mnemonic intimidation

Adding to the challenge Aeneas finds in contemplating the choice between remembering the past and forgetting it, the Trojans' enemies not infrequently taunt them with their earlier defeat in an effort at psychological intimidation. In *Aeneid* 9 and 10, Turnus twice brings up the notion of the Trojans' past repeating itself, and Numanus Remulus, Turnus' brother-in-law, references the Trojans' past and present besiegement in a derisive speech aimed at Ascanius. In their words, the only difference between the past and the present is that the Trojans now face a tougher enemy than the Greeks; all else is the same. The Italians claim that the Trojans cannot escape their past destruction, a threat that recalls Aeneas' opening prayer to the Sibyl and compels the Trojans to figure out a way to respond. Even when the Trojans are able to kill those who speak,[27] they still do not successfully define their relationship with their past, instead leaving it defined as a disastrous and dangerous memory, something to be silenced.

Turnus first addresses the past in a speech to his men outside of the besieged Trojans' camp. He begins with a reference to the anger that arises from the theft of a spouse and then moves on to the Trojans' futile defenses (9.138–45):

> nec solos tangit Atridas
> iste dolor, solisque licet capere arma Mycenis.
> 'sed periisse semel satis est.' peccare fuisset
> ante satis, penitus modo non genus omne perosos
> femineum. quibus haec medii fiducia valli
> fossarumque morae, leti discrimina parva,
> dant animos; at non viderunt moenia Troiae
> Neptuni fabricata manu considere in ignis?

That grief does not touch only Atreus' sons, and it is not permitted only to Myceneans to take up arms. 'But it is enough to have

[25] Gotoff 1985, 36 notes that Anchises' speech makes the implicit argument "that the desire to return in these souls is not *dira* precisely and only because they now have no memory or notion of what they are in for. There is the further implication (*incipient . . . velle reverti*) that, if they had any such memory, they might be justifiably reluctant to make the journey back to corporeality."

[26] Hardy 1991, 70.

[27] Ascanius does so in a scene discussed below, as does Aeneas in a passage outlined in n. 33.

> perished once.' Their previous sinning might have been enough for them, with a heartfelt hatred for all but the whole race of women.[28] They take courage from their trust in the intervening palisade and in the delay offered by trenches, small separations from death; but did they not see Troy's walls, built by Neptune's hand, collapse into the flames?

Turnus' words set up a structure and expectation of repetition. Looking out over his men, Turnus compares himself to Menelaus and reminds them of how the Trojans have already seen one set of walls fail them and, presumably, remember that terrible loss.[29] The Rutulian leader needs to stretch the facts to make these analogies (Lavinia is not his wife and the Trojans' hasty palisade cannot be compared with Troy's divinely constructed defenses),[30] but his purpose here is exhortation not accuracy. As Turnus proceeds, he says that the only difference between the Trojans' upcoming defeat and their previous one is the nature of the enemy. The Rutulians, he says, will not resort to shadowy tricks and hidden subterfuges, but will rather battle it out on the field, not allowing Aeneas and his men to stave off defeat for a full ten years.

Turnus' speech, with its focus on the Trojans' repetition of their past destruction at the hands of a fiercer enemy, sets out the basic building blocks for the taunts he and his men will utter to the Trojans' faces. Turnus follows this paradigm himself later that same day. Inside the walls of the Trojan camp, Turnus turns to Pandarus and invites him to fight: "Begin, if there is some virtue in your heart, and join battle. You will tell Priam that even here an Achilles has been found" (*incipe, si qua animo uirtus, et consere dextram, | hic etiam inventum Priamo narrabis Achillem*, 9.741–2).[31] Stating to Pandarus that he will soon be dead, Turnus likens himself to Achilles, the Trojans' most feared Greek foe. "Even here" (*hic etiam*) emphasizes the dogged burden of the Trojans' past, as Turnus keys into the Trojans'

[28] See P. Hardie 1994, ad 140–2: on the difficulties of the phrase *penitus modo non genus omne perosos femineum*; the above translation of *peccare . . . femineum* is taken from his note.

[29] Vision is often connected with recollection in the epic, whether one remembers an event viewed in the past or has a memory prompted by something seen in the present, and Turnus implicitly brings in the idea of memory by referencing the Trojans' sight. And, although some of the points of Turnus' comparison do not hold up under scrutiny (see n. 30 below), he is correct that Aeneas, at least, has seen the destruction of Troy's walls. *Aen.* 2.610–2 not only reveals that Aeneas remembers this act, but Aeneas' inclusion of his vision in his narrative of Troy's destruction commemorates this event and grants a memory of it to his audience as well.

[30] See P. Hardie 1994, ad 123–75, ad 138, and ad 145 on how Turnus misrepresents the present situation to force a parallel with the Trojan War.

[31] See P. Hardie 1994, 214 and ad 742 for how this verse and its larger context invoke different Homeric backgrounds that offer the potential for him to be seen as both Achilles and Hector.

memories of Achilles' fighting prowess to threaten them with the same sort of fury.

Numanus Remulus, who was likely part of the audience Turnus addresses at 9.138–45, expands further on what Turnus says and, moreover, speaks it directly to Ascanius. This episode describes Ascanius' initial foray into battle and stands as a marker both of his coming of age as well as of the maturation the next generation of Trojans, young men whose relationship with Troy may not be as strong as their fathers'.[32] Numanus addresses Ascanius from outside the walls of the Trojan camp (9.598–604):

> non pudet obsidione iterum valloque teneri,
> bis capti Phryges, et morti praetendere muros?
> en qui nostra sibi bello conubia poscunt!
> quis deus Italiam, quae vos dementia adegit?
> non hic Atridae nec fandi fictor Vlixes.
> durum a stirpe genus natos ad flumina primum
> deferimus saevoque gelu duramus et undis.

> Are you not ashamed, twice captured Phrygians, to be hemmed in again by siege and ramparts, and to hold off death with walls? And these are the ones who demand our wives for themselves by war! What god, what madness drove you to Italy? Neither the sons of Atreus nor Ulysses, the teller of tales, is here. Instead, we are an utterly hard race, as we first bear our infants to rivers and harden them with cruel cold and waves.

Intertwined with his intimidating references to the Trojans' past defeat, Numanus attaches a note of moral disapproval for the Trojans that complements his description of the tested strength of their Italian foes.[33] The past comes around again for the Trojans, with the sole difference being that they now fight an enemy that will conquer them with straightforward valor. As Philip Hardie notes, this depiction of repetition sets up a simple,

[32] J. Miller 2009, 152–4 writes on the importance of this scene to the conception of Rome in the *Aeneid.*

[33] This innate strength is alluded to again in Liger's taunt of Aeneas at 10.581–3, where he tells Aeneas that he does not fight against Achilles or Diomedes and that the end is near both for the Trojans' war with the Latins and for Aeneas' life. (See S. J. Harrison 1991, ad 581–2 on the Iliadic episodes to which Liger's words allude – two failed attempts to kill Aeneas.) Although his taunt is briefer than Numanus' or Turnus', Liger's words imply that Aeneas sees a near repetition of the past, with the one vital difference being that Aeneas now fights a harsher foe who will actually succeed in killing him. When Aeneas kills Liger, who lies before him begging for mercy, the Trojan specifically cites Liger's words (10.599–600), showing that it is just as important to him as it is to Ascanius to combat those who advance a view of the past that promises death for the Trojans in the present because of their past.

but difficult challenge for Aeneas: he "must find a different ending to the old story."[34]

Ascanius' response, with its focus on the necessity of combating Numanus' words, shows the danger such an attitude poses.[35] As soon as Numanus finishes his speech at 9.620, the narrator indicates that Ascanius will not let his foe's assertions stand: "Ascanius did not bear the one tossing out such boasts in speech" (*talia iactantem dictis ac dira canentem | non tulit Ascanius*, 9.621–2), but stretches out his bow.[36] After a prayer to Jupiter and a promise of future sacrifice, Ascanius strikes Numanus dead with his first shot, and now it is the young Trojan's turn to taunt his foe: "Go, mock virtue with proud words! The twice captured Phrygians send these responses to the Rutulians" (*i, verbis virtutem inlude superbis! | bis capti Phryges haec Rutulis responsa remittunt*, 9.634–5). Having successfully displayed his manly valor for the first time in battle, Ascanius sarcastically repeats Numanus' characterization of the Trojans as "twice captured" (*bis capti*, 9.599=9.635), a refutation of the claim that the Trojans' dreadful past will repeat itself in the present. Ascanius' devastating verbal and physical response reveals the threat posed by the possibility that the Trojans' past may repeat itself, that their memories of their previous defeat may become all too real in the present.

In a remarkable coda to this episode, Apollo remarks on Ascanius' success. The god's brief celebratory exclamation begins by praising the boy's present and future success but ends with a reference to Troy that sets the city as an emblem of past limitations that must be escaped (9.641–4):

> macte nova virtute, puer, sic itur ad astra,
> dis genite et geniture deos. iure omnia bella
> gente sub Assaraci fato ventura resident,
> nec te Troia capit.
>
> Bravo for your new virtue, boy, this is the way to the stars, born from gods and ancestor to gods. All wars fated to come will subside rightfully under the race of Assaracus, and Troy does not capture you.

34 Hardie 1994, ad 598.

35 Just as Ascanius' immediate response reveals the threat such taunts pose, the same attitude can be seen in Aeneas' swift dispatching of Liger (see n. 33).

36 The participle *canentem* brings out the potential mnemonic impact of Numanus' words, as *canere* is marked as an action that commemorates the past for the future through its use to describe the narrator's activity in the epic's first line. See p. 126 for further discussion. The verb's link with creating a strong and impactful commemoration of the past is also seen in Dido's description of Aeneas' narrative at 4.14: "What dreadful wars he survived to sing of!" (*quae bella exhausta canebat!*).

Assaracus was Anchises' grandfather, and Apollo's reference allows for the preservation of a familial connection to the past (one that links Ascanius, obliquely, with his divine heritage from Venus), but the god then decrees that Ascanius has already left Troy behind. Standing emphatically in a half-line of speech all their own, Apollo's last words state that Ascanius has escaped Troy's limiting confines. The god implies that Troy's destruction was the Trojan culture's final doom and that Ascanius can only flourish free from the city's literal and metaphorical bounds. Apollo offers a tidy picture of progress and of Rome free from the taint of Troy. Scholars have been quick to commend this view,[37] yet, as will be argued later, the god's beliefs do not necessarily equal those of Aeneas, and they may differ from those of the narrator as well.

From the perspective of Turnus and Numanus, the Trojans' memories of the past are a deadly threat, a reminder of a terrible loss which can never be undone and which marks the Trojans' core character. Ascanius refutes this picture by killing Numanus and implying through his sarcastic mimicry that the past will not influence the present; after all, he has just demonstrated as much through his physical actions. Apollo's words enforce this even more explicitly, emphatically placing Ascanius above and beyond Troy. The Latins represent the past as a promise of repeated destruction, Ascanius denies that the past can influence the present, and Apollo claims that Ascanius succeeds because he is free from that past. Together these various viewpoints stand beside the implications of the Sibyl's speech and beside Anchises' depiction of the soon-to-be reborn Romans, yet another portrayal of the past for Aeneas to evaluate as he searches for a way to make a new beginning in Hesperia.

Aeneas' choice

At Cumae the Sibyl shows Aeneas how to move forward by remembering, but in the underworld, he learns from his father how souls must forget in order to be reincarnated. Moreover, as if to further tempt the Trojans simply to forget their past, they will soon hear their enemies portray Troy's destruction as a lodestone around their necks, a dead weight that will drag them down to defeat time and time again.[38] In light of these possibilities,

[37] Jenkyns 1998, 581, writes that "Apollo's last words seem just and satisfying. Yes, Troy is not enough, and it is good news that Troy 'does not contain' the boy. Troy has 'contained' or 'captured' Helenus and Acestes, but we have felt in them some failure of nerve or enterprise. The doom of Troy's name and language, melancholy for the Trojans, is a healthy doom none the less."

[38] Aeneas hears neither the Latins' taunts, Ascanius' response, nor Apollo's words in *Aeneid* 9, so he would not be evaluating their specific claims as the narrator and audience do. He does, though,

it may appear natural for Aeneas to believe that he too should forget the past.[39] Many of the souls Aeneas sees waiting to be reborn in the underworld are the shades of future Romans, and if these Romans will return to life by forgetting, why should Aeneas, their ancestor, be any different? Aeneas' departure from the underworld may even be thought of as a metaphorical rebirth, and Aeneas could certainly conceive of himself as beginning a new phase of his life in Italy with Troy more distant than ever before.

Yet throughout his time in Italy Aeneas turns to his memories in order to understand his surroundings and formulate his decisions. This is not always a process that he actively controls. While Aeneas sometimes relates a past with purposely altered details, at other times he simply guides his actions by earlier experiences, and in certain situations an event triggers a memory that influences him to act in a particular way. Regardless of what sort of agency characterizes his interactions with the past, Aeneas strives to find success through memory and to establish a standardized version of the past for his followers. Simply put, forgetting does not figure into Aeneas' conception of his or his people's progress.

Returning to the tables prophecy in light of what Aeneas has learned in *Aeneid* 6 and what use his enemies will make of his history, it is possible to see how his behavior in *Aeneid* 7 constitutes an example of active engagement with the past. Coming at a crucial juncture in the Trojans' quest, Aeneas' reaction to Ascanius' remark reconstructs the Trojans' history with an eye toward the present and, specifically, toward blessing their city's foundation with a propitious atmosphere. The key to understanding this passage lies in acknowledging the consequential nature of the inconsistency that arises between Aeneas' representation of his father's prophecy in *Aeneid* 7 and his narration of Celaeno's prophecy in *Aeneid* 3.[40] Certain scholars downplay the need to account for this inconsistency as a meaningful element in the *Aeneid*'s story. Richard Heinze and Gordon Williams, for instance, argue that the contradiction between *Aeneid* 3 and 7 is the result of the epic's unfinished state.[41] James O'Hara persuasively shows, though, that such inconsistencies in Latin epic are often meaningful within their context.

face a similar diatribe from Liger in *Aeneid* 10 (see n. 33), and given the confluence of such taunts in *Aeneid* 9 and 10, it may be implied that Aeneas and the Trojans are well aware of the Latins' general attitude about their past.

39 For arguments along these lines, see Quint 1993, 64.

40 See E. L. Harrison 1986, 147–54 for a thorough overview of pre-Vergilian literary treatments of the tables prophecy and 159 for the history of this passage being cited as an inconsistency.

41 Heinze 1993, 72–3 and G. Williams 1983, 272. G. West 1983, 135 implies the same thing. Berres 1982, 212–39 argues that Celaeno's prophecy in *Aeneid* 3 is a late addition.

Moreover, as part of an argument against those who would attribute the *Aeneid*'s inconsistencies to Vergil's death, O'Hara demonstrates that the poet's earlier complete works also contain their share of contradictory passages, presumably fashioned with the poet's full intention.[42]

Other scholars explain these two passages as a product of Vergil's intentions but maintain that any contradiction between them is illusory. Nicholas Horsfall, for instance, claims that the narrator simply did not bother to record Anchises' prophecy.[43] This argument, though, is unconvincing. Firstly, Anchises' speech as Aeneas presents it in *Aeneid* 7 essentially repeats Celaeno's prophecy;[44] as such, there would be little reason for Anchises to ever deliver it. Furthermore, the prayer, which, according to Aeneas' narrative in *Aeneid* 3, Anchises does utter, also gainsays the idea that he verbalized this prophecy: "Gods, hold off the Harpy's threats; gods, turn aside such a calamity and graciously preserve the pious" (*di, prohibete minas; di, talem avertite casum* | *et placidi servate pios*, 3.265–6). Why would Anchises deliver a prophecy that he asks the gods to avert?[45] Yet, even assuming that Anchises did in fact repeat Celaeno's prophecy, why would Aeneas exclude this repetition from his narrative in *Aeneid* 3?[46] Aeneas makes reference to the terrible hunger Celaeno predicted at 3.365–7, and Helenus responds to this reference in his own revelation of the future at 3.394–5. If Aeneas was happy to represent Helenus' repetition, then why not Anchises'? After all, Anchises' appropriation of the Harpy's threats

42 O'Hara 2007, 77. Meban 2009, 112 shows how certain inconsistencies in the *Eclogues* can be understood with reference to the characters' memories. Also see Hubbard 1998, 120–7 on this point in regard to the *Eclogues*.

43 Horsfall 2000, 112. There are moments in the epic where characters refer to events that fall within the purview of the *Aeneid*'s story but that the narrator does not include in his song. Examples include the dream visitations that Aeneas alleges he received from Anchises (3.351–3) and a prophecy from Apollo about Palinurus which Aeneas says he heard (6.343–6). (See E. L. Harrison 1986, 159–62 on the topic of unnarrated scenes in the *Aeneid*.) Heinze 1993, 86–7 n. 12 also argues against the claim that Anchises' prophecy was unnarrated. Horsfall 2000, 112, advances another explanation for the two passages from a different perspective, arguing that the inconsistency is an artful allusion to two different traditions (see Horsfall 1986, 8–9 on this argument as well). Yet even if Vergil were alluding to conflicting traditions about the prophecy's speaker, this does not exclude the possibility for significance to arise within the action of the *Aeneid*.

44 Anchises does nothing to unravel the one ambiguous term (*mensas*) that exists in Celaeno's prophecy. Aeneas' recollection has Anchises using the same word himself.

45 None of the unnarrated scenes discussed in n. 43 would contradict the text of the *Aeneid* in the way that Anchises' unnarrated prophecy would.

46 Since Aeneas presents Anchises' speech as something he heard long ago (Conington 1884, ad 7.123; G. West 1983, 134; contra E. L. Harrison 1986, 160–1), it is unlikely that it was an unnarrated communication made by Anchises in *Aeneid* 4–6 (contra Primmer 1994/95, 405–15, who locates the unnarrated scene in *Aeneid* 6). E. Harrison 1986, 160 argues that "speculation about when and how [Anchises] delivered it is unnecessary"; yet the very fact that Aeneas cites this speech, unrecorded anywhere else, demands such speculation.

could have helped to calm the Trojans' fears,[47] the sort of reassuring behavior that would fit in well with Aeneas' characterization of his father as a venerable and helpful figure.[48]

If Aeneas attributes a prophecy to his father in *Aeneid* 7 that Anchises never delivered,[49] what could cause him to do this? O'Hara is one scholar who ventures a compelling reason: "Others might wish to read this passage in Book 7 more psychologically, and say that Aeneas has mis-remembered, has suppressed the dark episode involving the Harpy and attributed the prophecy to his father."[50] This is an intriguing notion to explore, but O'Hara does not seem to regard it as particularly promising.[51] He treats other reasons for the inconsistency as equally plausible, and he closes his discussion by disavowing the search for a single explanation: "The text is not clearly marked."[52]

Yet, the text is marked, and these markers lead toward a mnemonic explanation similar to the psychological reading O'Hara raises but ultimately does not embrace: that Aeneas purposely manipulates his memory and reattributes the prophecy to his father. Perhaps most significantly, it is hard to fathom that Aeneas, after already representing this prophecy in one way in *Aeneid* 3, would now unconsciously change it. Another telltale sign of manipulation comes in Aeneas' concerted effort to convince the Trojans that Anchises did in fact say these words. There is his introductory aside,

[47] J. Miller 2009, 126–9 and 363, points out how Aeneas' own references to Celaeno's prophecy at Buthrotum show how troubling her prophecy was to him.

[48] The short prayer of Anchises that Aeneas does record is consistent with this image. (Note Aeneas' introduction of Anchises right before his prayer as "father Anchises" (*pater Anchises*, 3.263), and see Horsfall 2006, ad 3.9 on this phrase.) For questions about the consistency of Aeneas' portrayal of Anchises between *Aeneid* 2 and 3, see G. Williams 1983, 274–6 and C. Lloyd 1995, 108.

[49] The alternative (that Anchises actually spoke the prophecy and that Aeneas' attribution of the prophecy to Celaeno is false) is far-fetched. The prediction of hunger is a threat perfectly calibrated for the Trojans' attempt to eat the Harpies' cattle. Furthermore, Aeneas confirms at 3.365–7 that Celaeno delivered *this* prophecy and says at 3.713 that she delivered *a* prophecy. (Of course it is possible to doubt the truth of these two offhand remarks, yet one would then need a sufficient motivation for Aeneas to fabricate the prophecy and confirm it twice in his story to Dido.)

[50] O'Hara 2007, 82. Block 1981 sets forth a claim along the lines of O'Hara's, as she argues that Aeneas has an "apparent lapse of memory" Williams 1972, ad. 7.107f. writes that Aeneas "incorrectly attributes" the prophecy to Anchises because of Anchises' guidance of Aeneas at the beginning of the mission. E. L. Harrison 1986, 131 writes that the tables prophecy is not an inconsistency, "but rather a fundamental element in Vergil's handling both of the Latium-based prodigies and of Anchises' role in the epic," Harrison looks back to Aeneas' reference to Celaeno's prophecy as "terrible to speak" (*dictu nefas*, 3.365) and sees this as an indication that her prophecy is "to be consigned to oblivion" (155). In a claim somewhat similar to Horsfall 2000, 112 and Horsfall 1986, 8–9, Harrison then writes that it is Vergil who fulfills our expectation that Celaeno not be referred to again by reverting to the tradition that Anchises delivered the table prophecy (156) and thus ensuring that the Harpy does not cast a "blight on the [Trojans'] new beginning" (158).

[51] Note the distancing effect of the introductory phrase "Others might . . ."

[52] O'Hara 2007, 82.

"now I remember" (*nunc repeto*, 7.123); the injunction within Anchises' speech, "remember" (*memento*, 7.126);[53] and Aeneas' recognition of the perfect match between his father's prophecy and the Trojans' current situation, "This was that hunger" (*haec erat illa fames*, 7.128).[54] Anchises' imperative sets his words as something to be remembered, and the remarks bracketing the prophecy in lines 123 and 128 present Aeneas as having done just that. As if he is a performer portraying a character recollecting the past, Aeneas works to create the image of himself dutifully remembering something that actually occurred. In the end, though, Aeneas' overdetermined presentation just focuses more attention on the contradiction his "memory" occasions and hints that his current recollection has been tailored to his present circumstances. He tries to cheer his men at this crucial point in their journey by framing the Trojan's foundation of a city as the reification of a benevolent promise instead of a dire threat.[55]

Earlier incidents in the epic demonstrate that Aeneas is capable of such manipulation. His narrative of the story of Sinon in *Aeneid* 2, for instance, shows that he recognizes the emotional leverage that comes from a narrative grounded in memory, even one that its speaker does not believe. In this episode, Sinon fabricates a story indicating that the Greeks have abandoned their siege of Troy, a tale that fulfills the Trojans' yearning to believe that the war is over and that grounds its credibility in its supposed status as a representation of Sinon's personal experience.[56] Later, when Troy's destruction shows Aeneas that Sinon's tale must be false, it only serves to underscore how a personal story of past experience can influence

[53] Anchises uses this same imperative in his speech to his son in the underworld at 6.851 (quoted and discussed on p. 55). The presence of this imperative here raises a number of questions. Since it has been shown to be a formulation of which Anchises is fond, should it serve as evidence for the claim that Aeneas is remembering something Anchises actually said? Or, more cynically, is the imperative a shrewd choice for Aeneas to put into Anchises' mouth, since the word not only implies that Aeneas is remembering now but also mimics his father's manner of expressing future obligations and thus makes the speech appear authentic? To complicate matters further, Aeneas never explicitly remembers anything from his visit to the underworld in *Aeneid* 6 (see Most 2001, 169–70). So could it even be argued that Aeneas would remember to use that language to validate a false memory? Ultimately, since other factors make it so unlikely that Anchises ever recited this prophecy to Aeneas, it must be concluded that Aeneas attributes this imperative to his father as a way to characterize his own speech as a recollection.

[54] Horsfall 2000, 7.107–47, notes these "back-references" in Aeneas' speech, but he does not connect them to memory. See also 7.110 and Horsfall 2000, ad loc. This is a verse where the narrator explicitly calls attention to *Aeneid* 3 and thus to the prophecy's two different speakers.

[55] G. Williams 1983, 272 remarks that "in Anchises' mouth, the prophecy takes on a totally different tone and denotes not suffering but hope."

[56] See Hexter 1990a, passim and especially 109 for the argument that the interaction between Sinon and the Trojans is better characterized as a collusion to fulfill the Trojans' desires than as straight-out trickery on the part of Sinon.

a speaker's audience. Moreover, *Aeneid* 7 would not be the only time that Aeneas presents a memory he does not believe for the purpose of satisfying a particular desire. In *Aeneid* 1 Aeneas turns to the idea of recollection in order to convince his men that their sufferings will one day lose their edge: "Perhaps one day it will be pleasing to remember even these things" (*forsan et haec olim meminisse iuvabit*, 1.203). This promise of future reminiscence makes the Trojans' present challenges seem less threatening.[57] Yet the narrator soon reveals that Aeneas does not believe his own words: "He says such things in speech and yet troubled with great worries he makes a pretense of hope on his face and presses his pain deep into his heart" (*talia voce refert curisque ingentibus aeger | spem vultu simulat, premit altum corde dolorem*, 1.208–9). Already having tried to raise the Trojans' spirits by attributing an ameliorative power to recollection that he doubts,[58] now, in *Aeneid* 7, Aeneas once more attempts to cheer his men, this time by constructing a memory of an event that he knows did not occur.

As a result of Aeneas' speech, the Trojans receive a fresh memory of the past, one that helps them enact a new beginning in the present and grant a positive meaning to a history otherwise composed of suffering. The interaction between the Trojans and their leader perfectly illustrates the formation of an oikotype. Instead of questioning Aeneas' recollection, the Trojans celebrate the fulfilled prophecy.[59] Even though the Trojans experienced Celaeno's threats themselves several years ago and heard Aeneas describe them to Dido recently, each decides that the version of the past acceptable to him is that with Anchises, not Celaeno, as the prophecy's author. In his position as the group's leader, Aeneas exerts a considerable amount of social pressure on his followers to make this decision. By not fighting this version of the past, the Trojans allow it to bind them together.[60] Communally, their celebration consecrates Aeneas' rendition of this incident.

By forming this oikotype, Aeneas uses his command of memory to claim leadership over the Trojans' transition to Italy and the meaning of their

[57] See further analysis of this episode on pp. 79–82.

[58] See pp. 81–2 for further discussion of this.

[59] Knapp 1989 considers at length the question of why it matters that a narrative "correspond to historical actuality." In this scene, it does not matter much at all; the Trojans are more than ready to act based on Aeneas' false memory.

[60] In presenting a memory that is in essence a lie, Aeneas follows in the epic tradition of Odysseus who spins a series of false stories upon his return to Ithaca in order to "keep his true identity concealed" and overthrow the suitors (Trahman 1952, 35). This similarity reveals a telling difference between the two heroes: while Odysseus presents false memories for his own gain, Aeneas constructs this memory primarily for the Trojans' sake, although it is possible that he may also come to believe and be comforted by his misrepresentation of the past.

past. Aeneas gains a further degree of influence due to the inchoate and evolving nature of his community. As Jan Assmann points out, people who found a new community are uniquely situated: they both experience their community's foundational events and have the chance in the future to relate those events as memories.[61] Aeneas and the Trojans are just such a group, and Aeneas' act of verbalizing his "memory" of the tables prophecy initiates and becomes such a foundational event. As the one who drives this foundation, he enjoys an unparalleled opportunity to shape how it will be remembered and passed down by members of this new community. Thanks to Aeneas' false recollection, this act of foundation and that event's relationship with the past have the potential to become a social memory of a smooth and prosperous process for future generations to share. The Trojans' past, present, and future productively interlace, as the grandson's words initiate the father's memory of the grandfather's prophecy. The foundation is one of continuity and success, a propitious event that Aeneas and his followers can now relate as a memory for the future, influencing the oikotype that the community will come to possess.[62]

Two episodes from *Aeneid* 10 show that Aeneas continues to use his memories to frame the Trojans' transition to Italy. Aeneas does not actively manipulate these memories to the extent that he does with the tables prophecy in *Aeneid* 7, but he still fits them to his current circumstances. In one case a memory of the past comes to him unbidden, and in the other he voices a simple and short memory of his own. The first example occurs when Aeneas battles a Rutulian soldier named Cydon. Under siege by Cydon's seven brothers, Aeneas shelters himself from their spears and plots a counter-attack. He tells his comrade Achates (10.333–5):

> suggere tela mihi, non ullum dextera frustra
> torserit in Rutulos, steterunt quae in corpore Graium
> Iliacis campis.

> Bring me the spears which stood in the bodies of the Greeks on the Trojan plain. Not one of them will my right hand hurl in vain at the Rutulians.

[61] J. Assmann 1992, 50–6. He uses the term "communicative memory" ("kommunikative Gedächtnis") for the period when a new community is still close to its origins and group members experience foundational events and then verbally relate them as memories. For a recent treatment of this and related issues, see Welzer 2007.

[62] An observation by Alcock 2002, 1 is especially germane to the Trojans' actions here: "People derive identity from shared remembrance – from social memory – which in turn provides them with an image of their past and a design for their future. What people remember of their past determines their sense of community." See Fentress and Wickham 1992, 7 and 30 on the connection between memory and identity.

Such an appeal to the earlier use of a weapon is not unheard of in the *Aeneid*, but Aeneas' vaunt is distinguished by his selective representation of the past. When Turnus, for instance, mentions his earlier use of a spear in *Aeneid* 12, there is no reason to think that his description of previous success hides the specter of past defeats: "Now, spear, never having frustrated my calls, now the time is here" (*nunc, o numquam frustrata vocatus | hasta meos, nunc tempus adest*, 12.95–6).[63] Aeneas, though, has more work to do with his past. Casting aside the result of the Trojan War, he focuses exclusively on the spears' deadly efficiency in battle. Aeneas likens his situation to one that he has faced before, but he now takes up the spears in a new war against new enemies. When Aeneas kills two brothers, his attack's success validates his use of the past and allows him to claim power over it via his memory: having stripped away any of the negative associations of the Trojan War, Aeneas' earlier use of the spears now stands solely as a helpful precursor to his present cause. Just like the literal spears that he takes up, his past becomes a metaphorical weapon, a source of strength to draw upon in the face of daunting challenges.

Later in *Aeneid* 10 another situation arises when Aeneas recalls the past; here, though, the memory that comes to him is unbidden and his reaction to it offers insight into how he strives to meet his present challenges by linking them with past action. As the battle between the Trojans and Italians continues, Aeneas wounds Mezentius, a one-time king of the Etruscans. About to be killed, Mezentius is saved when his son, Lausus, leaps to his defense. As Aeneas sees Lausus step in front of his father, he threatens him with sure death: "Where are you rushing to die, as you dare things greater than your strength? Your piety tricks you into being unwary" (*quo moriture ruis maioraque viribus audes? | fallit te incautum pietas tua*, 10.811–2).

Aeneas' words prove correct. As Mezentius escapes, Aeneas strikes Lausus with his sword and watches the boy's final moments (10.821–4):

> at vero ut vultum vidit morientis et ora,
> ora modis Anchisiades pallentia miris,
> ingemuit miserans graviter dextramque tetendit,
> et mentem patriae subiit pietatis imago.
>
> But when the son of Anchises looked upon the dying boy's face, a face growing pale in a remarkable way, he sighed deeply out of pity and stretched forth his right hand, and the image of his piety shown toward his father came into his mind.

[63] See Tarrant 2012, ad loc. on the confident tone of Turnus' boast.

Line 823 betrays the disturbance that Aeneas feels over killing Lausus, as he sighs and reaches out to touch the boy. While Aeneas earlier taunts Lausus with the consequences of his piety, the boy's valiant death leaves him experiencing pain. In a movement foreshadowed by the patronymic "son of Anchises" (*Anchisiades*) in line 822, a word which already shows that Aeneas' relationship with his father lurks in the back of his consciousness,[64] the image of Aeneas' piety toward his father comes to the front of his mind in line 824. Now, instead of being regarded as an attachment that leads Lausus incautiously to his death, Lausus' piety reminds Aeneas of his own devotion to his father, a nebulous memory of a dutiful emotion more general than any specific recollection.[65]

The mnemonic association between Aeneas and Lausus' filial piety would seem at first to open the door for Aeneas to experience greater pain, but he quickly steers its significance in a new direction.[66] The memory could give rise to more intense distress if Aeneas were to concentrate solely on Lausus' piety, leaving himself as the cold killer of a devoted son. Aeneas, though, shifts the interpretation of his action by claiming piety for himself: "What now, pitiful boy, what gift worthy of such excellence will pious Aeneas give to you for such praiseworthy deeds" (*quid tibi nunc, miserande puer, pro laudibus istis, | quid pius Aeneas tanta dabit indole dignum?*, 10.825–6). As part of his rhetorical question, Aeneas characterizes himself as "pious" (*pius*). Since Aeneas was just thinking of piety in filial terms, this marks his killing of Lausus as reflective of that same strand of piety. A statement Anchises made to Aeneas in the underworld reveals the grounds for this claim, as it figures Aeneas' larger goal of founding a city as part of his piety toward his father. Aeneas journeys to the underworld at the prompting of his father's shade, which tells him to go there so that he may learn of the people and city that will one day be his (5.737). Upon seeing his son approach him in Elysium, Anchises asks: "Have you come at last, and has the piety your father hoped for conquered the harsh journey?" (*venisti tandem, tuaque exspectata parenti | vicit iter durum pietas?*,

64 See S. Harrison 1991, ad 821–2 on the effect and placement of this patronymic.

65 The use of *imago* most similar to this occurs at 9.294. There Iulus is struck by Euryalus' devotion to his mother, and his thoughts move toward his own father: "The image of the piety shown by his father touched his mind" (*animum patriae strinxit pietatis imago*) (see p. 142 for further description of this passage). I follow S. J. Harrison 1991, ad 10.824 in regarding *patriae* as an objective genitive at 10.824 and a subjective genitive at 9.294, "a typically Vergilian innovation." The remarks of Conington 1884, ad 9.294 are also applicable to 824: "*Imago* may be merely the sight . . . but it is perhaps better to take it of the resemblance." See also *Aen.* 2.560, where *imago* denotes the image of a person that serves as a reminder (see *TLL* 409.23–5, 28–9). On *Aen.* 2.560, 10.824, and the use of *imago* as an indication that memory is at stake, see Berlin 1998, 12–8.

66 On the change in Aeneas' attitude, see Johnson 1976, 73; Putnam 1981; and Wright 1997, 181.

6.687–8). Anchises' greeting associates Aeneas' filial piety with his city's foundation, a goal that Lausus threatens when he stands before Aeneas in order to protect his father. When Aeneas calls himself "pious" in his speech to Lausus' corpse, he implies that he acts out of piety toward Anchises just as much as Lausus does toward Mezentius. This audacious claim, based on Aeneas' response to his memory of his relationship with his father, helps him to conceive of his present actions in a much more favorable light: his slaughter of an overmatched young boy protecting his father becomes the necessary killing of one who stands in the way of his mission, one that his own father urged him to complete.

In this example, similar to the two discussed above, memory offers both a challenge for Aeneas and a route around that challenge. The challenge is that Aeneas kills someone whose actions remind him of his dedication to Anchises. He escapes from this problem, though, by calling himself pious and thereby subsuming his current actions under his remembered paradigm of filial piety. Aeneas' interaction with memory here moves from passive to active, as he responds to the image that enters his mind by labeling himself with a word (*pius*) that keys into that memory. In doing so, he lessens the possibility that he will be adversely affected by the killing of a young boy much like himself. In this act, just as when he takes up his old spears or recapitulates his father's prophecy, Aeneas structures his actions in the present based on memories of his past. He has heard the Sibyl's prophecy well.

The distance to Rome

The events that Aeneas recollects are not far removed from his present. His feelings toward his father, his spear attack in the Trojan War, and the tables prophecy all fall within the last two decades of his life. The progress he makes via remembering these past incidents, following a paradigm adumbrated by the Sibyl in *Aeneid* 6, occurs on what might best be termed the human scale of time. This temporal scale measures out a day-to-day existence, where a tangible urgency paces mortal endeavors. This pressure is felt equally in the quick pacing of Aeneas' fight with Cydon as well as in the slow accretion of days that paces the Trojans' search for a new home.

What, though, is the place of recollection when progress must be accomplished on a decidedly larger scale of time, one which might best be termed cosmic?[67] A vast temporal gulf separates the Trojans from Rome's

[67] Novara 1986, 18–19 also writes on the differentiation between human and divine time in the *Aeneid*; Bews 1987, 97 and P. Hardie 1986 see a division in the *Aeneid* between cosmic and human/historical. For a different conception of the *Aeneid*'s levels of time, see E. Henry 1989, who argues that the

foundation. As Jupiter tells Venus in *Aeneid* 1, more than three centuries lie between Aeneas and Rome's beginning. The god marks out the time between the epic's present and Rome's beginning with his measurements gliding from the three years of Aeneas' rule in Latium (1.265–6) to the "thirty years" of Ascanius' sovereignty (*triginta magnos ... orbis*, 1.269) and, lastly, to the "three hundred entire years" of reign at Alba Longa (*ter centum totos ... annos*, 1.272). While the preservation of social memory is possible on this scale of time,[68] oblivion plays a pivotal and explicit role in the epic's most sustained consideration of how Aeneas' Roman race will come to be. There Aeneas visits his father in the underworld and learns that forgetting will enable Rome's great heroes to return to life. Souls must wait a thousand years to be born again, and a drink from the Lethe River initiates the journey's final step.

The mechanisms that enable progress on the human and cosmic scales of time, remembering and forgetting, respectively display a similar mixture of cyclical and linear characteristics, yet their effects diverge when the focus shifts to identity.[69] In the underworld, for instance, the souls gathered around Lethe are set to embark on a return to life, a cyclical movement which is joined by an opportunity for linear progress. If the souls lead a more virtuous existence in their coming life, then they might become pure ethereal matter after their next death, escaping the fate of having to live again.[70] Oblivion stands at the center of this process, and oblivion strips away the memories which form a person's core identity.[71]

Progress initiated by memory shows the same combination of linear and cyclical characteristics, but here identity and memory reaffirm one another.

epic depicts three interrelated temporal levels: (1) the short time span of the heroic narrative; (2) the thousand years of historical time; and (3) cosmic time. In the two-level conception of time used here, historical time is included within human time, as both are essentially different from cosmic time. See Feeney 2007 for a general overview of Greek and Roman constructions of time and Falkner 1990 and Bassi 2005 for analyses of other ancient literary treatments of time.

68 The epic itself stands as proof of this, as does the narrator's description in *Aeneid* 5 of how a concerted effort carries the performance of the Trojan games down to present-day Rome. See pp. 136–7 for consideration of these games.

69 Scholars' views about time and progress in the *Aeneid* fall into three camps: (1) Aeneas moves forward over the course of the epic and does not repeat the past; e.g., Cairns 1989. (2) The hero and his companions progress in a manner that is both linear and circular; e.g., DuBois 1982, 35–50; Quint 1982 and 1993; and E. Henry 1989. (3) The *Aeneid* demonstrates a circular conception of time; e.g., Knauer 1964, 83; P. Hardie 1998, 7; and Dyson 2001.

70 There is certainly a feeling of repetition to this cycle, but it is not the "endless repetitiveness of existence" (Mitchell-Boyask 1996, 297), since the souls' next life may finally allow them to return to their origins.

71 See Toll 1997, 41 on the link between amnesia and the loss of identity for individuals and nations alike and Gill 2006, 69–70 on the link between memory and identity in Lucr. 3.845–61. Gowing 2005, 2 remarks that, for the Romans, "to forget ... the past, at either the level of the individual or of the state, risked loss of identity and even extinction."

In *Aeneid* 10 for instance Aeneas takes up his spears from the Trojan War in battle against the Italians. As he does so, the past comes around again (the spears perform their function admirably) but in a different way (the weapons are used against Italian, not Greek, opponents).[72] In this pattern, Aeneas' identity influences what he remembers and how he interacts with those memories, and, in the process of interacting with his memories, he reinforces his identity by selectively fitting the past into the present.[73] Since Aeneas consistently attempts to move forward via memory, he draws upon and strengthens his identity time and time again.

These two levels of time, with their attendant mechanisms of progress and their identity-centered conflict, intersect at moments in the epic that center on Rome and its foundation. Seen in the *Aeneid* only in prophetic utterances, divine conversations, and the narrator's glances toward the far-off future, Rome also stands as the goal of Aeneas' nitty-gritty mortal labor. The city exists on both the cosmic and human scales of time,[74] and it is in doubt whether the Trojans can move toward Rome solely by remembering, and, accordingly, whether they will pass their Trojan identity down to Rome's citizens. After all, while Aeneas' mnemonic-dedication preserves his identity and grants him success in his transition to Italy, it contrasts with the complete oblivion imposed on the souls who will one day make Rome great as well as with Apollo's exultation that Troy does not hold Ascanius.

Three episodes in the epic, all connected with Rome's foundation, illustrate how humans conceive of connections between the past and present in terms of recollection, even as the limitations and failures of memory sometimes frustrate them. Aeneas' visit to Pallanteum, a city joined with Rome

[72] Another illustration of this tendency comes in Aeneas' remark after recollecting his father's prophecy, "This was that hunger" (*haec erat illa fames*, 7.129). An element of the past (a hunger so great that the Trojans eat their tables) appears again, but it occurs in a new way (the hunger is no longer an abstract prediction but an actual pain, while the tables are not literal wooden constructions, but metaphorical cakes). This sort of linear and cyclical movement is revealed as well by several incidents when non-Trojan characters key into the Trojans' memories. Turnus claims his loss of his fiancée is similar to Menelaus' loss of Helen (9.138–9), references the Trojans' viewing of Troy's destruction as he threatens their encampment with the same fate (9.144–5), and speaks of himself as "an Achilles, found even here" (*hic etiam inventum . . . Achillem*, 9.742). Numanus Remulus portrays the Italians' siege of the Trojans as a repetition of the Trojan War (9.598–9). Juno and Venus also depict history as repeating with significant changes. Juno casts Aeneas as "another Paris" (7.321–2) and terms the Trojans' new settlement "Troy" (10.74), while Venus speaks of how certain aspects of the Trojan War are occurring again (10.26–9, 55–62).

[73] See J. R. Gillis 1994, 3: "The core meaning of any individual or group identity, namely, a sense of sameness over time and space, is sustained by remembering; and what is remembered is defined by the assumed identity." See Freeman 2010, 68 for references to works that explore this reciprocal process from the perspective of psychology.

[74] P. Hardie 1986 claims that the Roman state is depicted as filling both the human and cosmic realms.

by its location and the narrator's comments, reveals how Evander sets his site's history in mnemonic terms, using the same perspective that governs his daily interactions. Memory is endowed with a similar importance in Anchises' orders to Aeneas about Rome in *Aeneid* 6 and in a cluster of episodes connected with the Trojans' search for their new home in *Aeneid* 3 and 7. Yet even as the Trojans strive to base their progress to Rome on recollection, the difficulties that attend this process raise questions about the likelihood of its success, particularly in the face of the oblivion and concomitant loss of identity associated with and perhaps demanded by Rome's origins.

Evander's interactions with Aeneas at Pallanteum vividly embody mortal efforts to operate by remembering. Pallanteum stands at the site where Rome will one day exist, and this location lends the city a sense of tremendous significance, setting its links with the past as a potential paradigm for the method and character of Rome's foundation. On the human scale of time, as Aeneas and Evander walk around Pallanteum, they build their alliance upon a memory of the past, and the episode provides another iteration of the typical pattern of progress via remembering. After hearing Aeneas' request for assistance, Evander tells Aeneas how Anchises visited his childhood home long ago. Out of all the Trojans who came to Arcadia, Aeneas' father impressed him the most: "How I remember the words of your parent, great Anchises, as well as his voice and face!" (*ut verba parentis* | *et vocem Anchisae magni vultumque recordor!* 8.155–6).[75] Evander yearned to interact with Anchises: "My mind was burning with youthful love to question the man and to join my right hand to his" (*mihi mens iuvenali ardebat amore* | *compellare virum et dextrae coniungere dextram*, 8.163–4). Now, when Evander announces to Aeneas that he will help him, he depicts his decision as a fulfillment of that remembered desire: "Therefore also my right hand, which you seek, is joined in treaty" (*ergo et quam petitis iuncta est mihi foedere dextra*, 8.169).[76] Even though the circumstances have changed (Evander is now old and in power, and the Trojan who comes to his city is asking for help), the king remembers a similar situation from his past and sets that recollection as a guide for his decisions.

At the same time as recollection plays a role in Evander's immediate decisions, the narrator's structuring of the scene explores the role memory plays in interactions that extend over a much longer time period. Evander speaks at length to Aeneas about the history of his city's location. The

[75] The theme of memory is also fronted in the following line, where Evander introduces his narrative of the episode with "I remember" (*memini*, 8.157).

[76] C. Lloyd 1995, 5 also notes Evander's emphasis on memory as a determinative factor in his decision.

site was first inhabited by Faunus and nymphs (8.314–8). From that time followed Saturn (8.319–27); a band of Ausonians (8.328–9); Thybris and other kings (8.330–2); and, lastly, Evander (8.333–6).[77] While Evander does not explicitly say this his city commemorates all of these earlier inhabitants, he does reveal that (8.355–8):

> haec duo praeterea disiectis oppida muris,
> reliquias veterumque vides monimenta virorum.
> hanc Ianus pater, hanc Saturnus condidit arcem;
> Ianiculum huic, illi fuerat Saturnia nomen.

> Furthermore, you see these two cities with their walls thrown down, the remains and monuments of ancient men. This citadel founded by Janus, that by Saturn; this one is called the Janiculum, that one was called Saturnia.

Evander and his people remember what came before,[78] even on a larger scale of time, and these memories of earlier civilizations raise the questions about what will be Rome's links with its predecessors.

This issue comes to the fore when the narrator complements Evander's description of the location's history with his own glance into the site's future. The narrator first expands his song's temporal breadth toward his present day when the Trojans sail into Pallanteum. Opening the episode, this temporal expansion signals the extraordinary links between Evander's city and Rome (8.98–100):[79]

> muros arcemque procul ac rara domorum
> tecta vident, quae nunc Romana potentia caelo
> aequavit, tum res inopes Evandrus habebat.

> Far off the Trojans see the walls and the citadel and the scattered homes, which now Roman power has made equal with the sky, but at that time were Evander's humble kingdom.

As Aeneas approaches Evander's town, the audience draws closer to their city's history. This temporal shift soon occurs again. As Evander proudly points out his city's landmarks to Aeneas, the narrator overlays Rome's

[77] Feeney 2007, 163–4 notes how these foundations, destructions, and refoundations project a "revolution of time... that keeps on revolving, not just back up to the Golden Age, but back down again." See also Rea 2007, 91 on the emphasis "on the cycle of the individual successes and failures of each founder." Novara 1986, 69–88 argues that there was steady progress in these foundations.

[78] The Arcadians' commitment to remembering the past is reinforced by their commemoration of Hercules on the day of the Trojans' arrival. As Papaioannou 2003, 687–8 remarks, Hercules' deeds at Pallanteum comprise both Pallanteum and Rome's past.

[79] Gransden 1976, ad 99–100 remarks that the "clash between 'epic time' and 'real time' is striking."

spatial markers and monuments onto Pallanteum (8.337–61): a simple gate is linked with its Roman name; a particular grove is marked out by Romulus' use of it as an asylum; the Capitoline's rustic houses are said now to be golden; and when Aeneas and Evander look upon a herd of mooing cows, the narrator reveals that these animals graze precisely where the Roman forum and an elegant neighborhood will one day exist.[80]

For the epic's audience, this civic tour offers a temporal map of their city, one where the past comes around again in a new manner. The same location will be inhabited once more, but the particulars of what exists there change. While the narrator does not specify that Rome will someday remember Pallanteum, the aetiology of the Carmental gate hints that certain aspects of Evander's civilization will not be forgotten. Right after Evander finishes telling Aeneas how the warnings of his mother Carmentis drove him to settle in this location, the narrator describes Aeneas and Evander's progress through the landscape (8.337–41):

> vix ea dicta, dehinc progressus monstrat et aram
> et Carmentalem Romani nomine portam
> quam memorant, nymphae priscum Carmentis honorem,
> vatis fatidicae, cecinit quae prima futuros
> Aeneadas magnos et nobile Pallanteum.

> Evander's words were scarcely complete, and then, moving on from there, he shows Aeneas both the altar and the gate which the Romans call Carmental, an ancient honor of the nymph Carmentis, the fate-speaking seer, who first sang that the sons of Aeneas would be great and Pallanteum would be noble.

Several factors indicate that Rome will still have a memory of Evander's time. Along with the gate's aetiological name, the narrator's vocabulary reinforces its power to commemorate Evander's mother: he selects *memorant* to describe the naming of the gate and *cecinit* to describe Carmentis' predictions, two words with mnemonic associations.[81] This aetiology stands as part of the episode's extraordinary juxtaposition of progress on the human scale (as seen in Evander and Aeneas' interaction) and the cosmic scale (as seen in the interlacing of Rome and Pallanteum's landmarks, along with Evander's description of earlier cities). The audience sees how one city after another arises, with a memory present of what came before in the monuments of Pallanteum as well as of Rome. While identity

80 Wiseman 1984, 123 points out how the audience could imagine seeing all these locations in an easy walk.

81 For *memorare* see pp. 11–13 and for *canere* see p. 126.

is not preserved intact through each foundation and refoundation (in the transition between Saturn and the Ausonians, the city changed its name, setting aside a marker of identity (8.39)), traces do remain. If Rome will be the culmination of this urban pattern, then it too might have some mnemonic connections with the Trojan past.

If the episode at Pallanteum draws a parallel between Evander's need to remember in his daily interactions and his conception of events on a larger scale, then one could expect the Trojans' behavior to be marked by similar characteristics. Yet the oblivion of rebirth in the underworld and Apollo's comments about Troy's limitations argue against any connection of memory between Rome and Troy, and two examples show how the Trojans' mnemonic engagement in regard to Rome's foundation is far from straightforward, and may even necessitate a type of oblivion. Both of these instances involve Anchises, who, after nearly refusing to leave Troy, becomes a pivotal figure in the Trojans' journey to a new city. One occurs as Anchises issues orders to his son that center on remembering; the other concerns the Trojans' struggle to figure out their destination.

A conflict between remembering and forgetting arises because of the orders Anchises gives to Aeneas in the underworld. While other races may excel in sculpture and oratory, Rome, says Anchises, will stand unsurpassed in the art of ruling (6.851–3):

> tu regere imperio populos, Romane, memento
> (hae tibi erunt artes), pacique imponere morem,
> parcere subiectis et debellare superbos.
>
> Remember, Roman, these will be your arts: to rule over nations rightly, and to impose a custom on peace, and to spare the subjected and subdue the proud.

The defining aspects of Roman rule are presented as important information that Aeneas ought to remember. Yet, as R. Alden Smith points out, the link between memory and Roman rule goes even deeper. Anchises' order "remember" (*memento*) implies that remembering will be a key aspect of Roman *imperium*, and the imperative "shows that ruling must be done by memory: one must have a clear picture of the past in order to regulate the present or future."[82]

Anchises' remarkable use of the epithet "Roman" (*Romane*, 6.851) to address Aeneas creates a tension surrounding Rome and memory. This is the only time *Romanus* is used in the vocative to modify a character in

[82] Smith 2005, 89.

the *Aeneid*,[83] and, due to its singularity, the adjective has a tremendous power. As Roland Austin observes, the effect of *Romane* is that "Anchises now speaks not to Aeneas alone but to each future Roman."[84] The word acts as a bridge from Aeneas' present to the future his actions guarantee, and it makes the epic's Roman audience as responsible for remembering Anchises' orders as Aeneas is. Yet Anchises speaks his injunction in a setting where forgetting is the prerequisite for progress: souls return to life only after drinking from the Lethe River. This pull between remembering and forgetting grows when Aeneas never explicitly remembers anything from the underworld.[85] Anchises tells his son (and future Romans) to remember, but Aeneas, at least, appears to forget.[86]

The Trojans' search for their destination offers one of the most vivid illustrations of the difficulty of remembering events from the distant past and applying them to the present. In an oracle from Apollo early on in their wanderings, they learn that they should settle in their ancestor's homeland. Identifying this location, though, is not an easy task: Troy's founders came from both Crete and Italy.[87] Anchises tells the Trojans they need to go to Crete, and he prefaces his advice with an important caveat: "If I rightly remember the things that I heard" (*si rite audita recordor*, 3.107).[88] He characterizes his answer as a memory, with the implication that stories of Troy's foundation have been passed down orally from one generation to the next. Remarkably, this theme has already been foregrounded by Aeneas' description of Anchises before he speaks: "My father, reflecting on the monuments of the ancient men" (*genitor veterum volvens monimenta virorum*, 3.102). Aeneas' specification that his father is concentrating on "the monuments of the ancient men" (*veterum . . . monimenta virorum*) reveals

83 Its only other appearance in this case comes when the narrator uses it to describe a present-day Roman whose ancestor competed in Anchises' funeral games: "And Cloanthus sailed on blue Scylla, from whom your family stems, Roman Cluentus" (*Scyllaque Cloanthus | caerulea, genus unde tibi, Romane Cluenti*, 5.122–3).

84 Austin 1977, ad 851.

85 Most 2001, 169–70 demonstrates that the audience never sees Aeneas remembering anything from the underworld.

86 In addition to *memento* (6.851), an explicit order to remember the theme of remembering also appears in the narrator's description of some of the last portions of Anchises' advice to Aeneas: "Then he was telling the hero what wars he must wage next" (*exim bella viro memorat quae deinde gerenda*, 6.890). *Memorat* hints that Anchises expects and desires Aeneas to remember what he tells him.

87 For the Trojans' origins and their relation to this oracle, see Herzog 1993, 100–1; Horsfall 2000, ad 195 and 206–11; and Horsfall 2006, ad 94, 96, 103, and 117. On Vergil's treatment of Dardanus and the Trojan heritage, see Buchheit 1963, 151–72.

88 Herzog 1993, 101 also notes that Anchises bases his interpretation on his memory. For a sympathetic reading of Anchises' mistake, along with bibliography on the passage, see Armstrong 2002, 322–4.

that some commemoration of these founders, whether in monuments, written records, or oral tradition must have existed at Troy.[89] Although he draws upon what he remembers seeing and hearing, Anchises is mistaken. When the Trojans follow his advice and sail to Crete, their settlement is besieged by disease.[90] Anchises' answer was wrong, and somewhere, whether the fault lies with Anchises, those old Trojans who passed down the story to him, or the monuments at Troy, social memory was corrupted.

With his settlement threatened, Aeneas learns the location where the Trojans must go. Appearing to him in a dream, the Penates specify that Apollo meant the Trojans' Italian origins, not their Cretan ones. While one of Troy's founders, Teucer, did come from Crete,[91] Apollo was thinking of Dardanus, who set out from Italy. Therefore Anchises' answer, which technically could have been correct, did not come from a memory that properly matched Apollo's oracle. Anchises' failure symbolizes the difficulty of remembering events from long ago, even culturally central information concerning a city's foundation. The Trojans' initial mistake and the troubles they suffer on account of it begin to reveal the challenges they face in founding a city that exists on the cosmic level of time but is the product of human actions.

Remarkably, as soon as Anchises learns of his error, he shares a new memory that coincides with his new understanding of Apollo's orders. He tells Aeneas: "Now I remember that Cassandra used to predict that these things were owed to us, and she often called Hesperia and Italy our kingdom" (*nunc repeto haec generi portendere debita nostro | et saepe Hesperiam, saepe Itala regna vocare*, 3.184–5). Once again, Anchises bases his interpretation of Apollo's prophecy on a memory, this time a memory of another prophecy which he doubtless did not believe at the time, but now deems worthy of citing as a source after it has been independently verified.[92] In doing so, Anchises leaves his earlier, mistaken recollection to be forgotten, replacing it with a memory that matches up with Apollo's oracle. No independent evidence exists to verify whether

[89] As Roller 2004, 5 points out, writing about Roman culture in general, the word *monimentum* may refer to a physical commemoration, the historical tradition, a ritual, or even people's names. See also Meadows and Williams 2001, 41 on how *monumentum* can describe the "ritual, rhetorical, [and] architectural" forms of reminding the Romans of important information.

[90] J. Miller 2009, 118–9 figures Apollo as the probable cause of the disease.

[91] See Horsfall 2006, ad 104.

[92] Accentuating the theme of memory even further, Aeneas introduces his father's speech with *memorat* ("he says," 3.182), a verb that itself introduces the idea of recollection (see pp. 11–13 for discussion of this). Highet 1974, 189 points out that Vergil varies the verbs that introduce and end speeches in the *Aeneid* and that the poet "often makes them indicate the emotional state of the speaker, together with his relation to his hearers."

Cassandra ever said this to Anchises, but, like Aeneas with the tables prophecy, Anchises persuades the Trojans to accept his purported memory as an actual event from the past.[93] Anchises' recollection of Cassandra demonstrates how important it is for him to build his present decisions on his memory of the past. By doing so, he may satisfy both his and the Trojans' desire to understand their new destination not as a break from the past, but rather as something grounded in it. Anchises can be satisfied with the effect of his replacement memory. The Trojans' story takes on a more cohesive tone and includes a smooth transition between their loss at Troy and their future reign.

A later interaction in Italy reveals that the entire Trojan community comes to possess a memory that mirrors Apollo's injunction and Anchises' newfound remembrance. After arriving in Italy, Aeneas sends out envoys to the area's rulers. Latinus, one of these kings, tells the Trojans about their race's origins (7.205–7):

> atque equidem memini (fama est obscurior annis)
> Auruncos ita ferre senes, his ortus ut agris
> Dardanus Idaeas Phrygiae penetrarit ad urbes.
>
> And indeed I remember (the story has become rather obscure over the years) that the old men of Aurunca used to say that Dardanus, raised in these lands, had reached the towns of Phrygian Ida.

Latinus states that his version of the Trojans' heritage is dependent upon recollection, just as Anchises did. But Latinus' memory, unlike Anchises' initial memory, is in accord with Apollo's oracle: it sets Troy's beginnings in Italy with Dardanus, not in Crete with Teucer. When Aeneas' envoy replies, his words show that the Trojans have modified their social memory to agree with the Penates' clarification of the oracle and Anchises' new memory. The envoy says: "Dardanus was born here, Apollo summons us back here and presses us on with great orders" (*hinc Dardanus ortus, | huc repetit iussisque ingentibus urget Apollo*, 7.240–1).[94] Anchises' interpretation of Apollo's words has become the Trojans' oikotype. As a result, they are now able to use their memories of the past to advance in the manner typical of the human scale of time. Their initial trouble in doing so, however, reveals the potential fallibility of remembering on a cosmic scale.

[93] Assuming that Cassandra did prophesize this to Anchises, it is only now, after he has experienced the Trojans' failure on Crete, that he recognizes the truth and significance in her words (for more on the process of past events gaining a different meaning from further experiences, see Freeman 2010, 59–60).

[94] For this interpretation of *repetit*, see Horsfall 2000, ad loc.

Anchises succeeds because he voices a recollection of an incident that agrees with information that he has learned in the present, and the Trojans now successfully interact with Latinus because they appropriate Anchises' new memory as their oikotype. Their old beliefs about the cultural origins are no longer remembered.

The tension in the Trojans' quest to discover their destination, although it is eventually resolved, raises serious questions about Rome's relation to memory, the past, and Trojan identity, just as Anchises' orders about remembering do. For Aeneas, Rome stands as the pinnacle of his short- and long-term future: the town he is soon to found in Italy will culminate in that famed city. Anchises' description of the cycle of souls places oblivion at the root of Rome, and Apollo's words to Ascanius affirm a break between Troy and Rome, characterizing the divide as beneficial. This sort of complete oblivion is different from the piecemeal forgetting that marks Aeneas and the Trojans' recollections, a forgetting that consists of the loss of certain details about the past (e.g., Celaeno's authorship of the tables prophecy) as new memories are constructed (a tables prophecy narrated by Anchises). Although the Trojans are willing to forget certain elements of their past that may appear vital to their culture (such as their city's Cretan origins), they replace that memory not with a blank past, but with a new recollection. The underworld's divinely enforced oblivion seems to indicate that Aeneas needs to jettison his past completely, yet he and the Trojans grapple with understanding their present and future through manipulating memory, trying (and sometimes failing and trying again) to create a past that will match their present and future.

Memory's end

If Rome's foundation is a difficult goal to achieve by remembering alone and the Trojans' enemies turn to their past as a means of intimidation, why do Aeneas and the Trojans move forward via recollection? Diomedes, of all people, offers insight into his erstwhile foes' behavior. One of the few characters in the *Aeneid* who mentions a desire not to remember, Diomedes does so in response to the Latins' request for help in their battle against the Trojans. When Latin envoys come to his city in Italy, Diomedes emphatically refuses to fight (11.278–80):

> ne vero, ne me ad talis impellite pugnas.
> nec mihi cum Teucris ullum post eruta bellum
> Pergama nec veterum memini laetorve malorum.

> No indeed, do not drive me to such battles. Neither is there any war for me with the Trojans after Pergamum's destruction nor do I take joy in remembering old sufferings.

In line 280 Diomedes literally says, "I neither remember nor rejoice in the old troubles" (*nec veterum memini laetorve malorum*), yet he has just spent the last twenty verses describing the tribulations he and his comrades endured after leaving Troy. And, what is more, he will spend the next twelve recollecting Aeneas' astounding fighting ability and exceptional piety.[95]

Since Diomedes' speech shows that he does in fact remember, it is more plausible to interpret the two verbs in line 280 as a hendiadys, producing the single meaning: "I find no joy in remembering."[96] Even though Diomedes would prefer not to remember the Trojan War, he is forced to do so since the Latins confront him with a situation that resembles it. No Lethean drink offers him oblivion, and, in spite of his wishes, he cannot forget the past. It has become a part of him which no amount of effort can excise,[97] and his memory stands as a way for him to understand his present state and frame his decisions for the future.

One explanation for Aeneas' behavior is that he, like Diomedes, is unable to forget the past simply by choosing to do so, especially when new situations remind him of it. This is likely true, but it still does not completely account for the way Aeneas interacts with memory. For while Diomedes, a member of the winning side at Troy, speaks of his desire to forget, Aeneas, who carries a much heavier parcel of memories, never expresses such a wish.[98] Rather, he makes a persistent effort to frame his present and future through remembrances. Two other factors more specific to Aeneas help to explain this tendency.

One of these relates to Aeneas' need to evaluate the unknown. Guided by shadowy and often deceptive prophecies, the Trojan leader must somehow make sense of his surroundings. His memories prove a useful tool for doing so. He approaches the process of recollection in the manner of one

[95] The memories surrounding 11.278–80 have little to do with the Greeks' victory and instead seem to be selectively chosen and refashioned in order to present a picture of Aeneas that will enable Diomedes to escape from another war. See Horsfall 2003, 171–2 on the way in which Diomedes has "rewritten" (171) his encounter with Aeneas and P. Hardie 2012, 139–40 on the differences between Diomedes' and the *Iliad*'s portrayal of the past.

[96] See Horsfall 2003, ad loc. and Fratantuono 2009, ad loc. on this hendiadys. Diomedes' sentiment validates Aeneas' doubting of his own statement that the Trojans would one day take pleasure in remembering their earlier troubles (see 1.203; 1.208–9; discussed on pp. 79–82).

[97] Eco 1988 persuasively argues that it is impossible to intentionally forget something; the most one can accomplish is to confuse particular memories "with other notions or other expressions" (259).

[98] While Aeneas certainly acknowledges that it can be painful for him to remember, he nowhere says he wants to forget. Diomedes' statement verifies Aeneas' claim that no Greek could hold back tears in telling of the Trojan War (2.6–8).

constructing a simile, searching for a likeness between past and present to make his future comprehensible. For instance, when Aeneas realizes that he is outnumbered by a group of foes, he turns to a set of spears that helped him slay his enemies in an earlier battle. The tables prophecy offers another illustration of this strategy. Here, Aeneas manipulates the past and constructs a memory for an event that never existed, but a memory that, all importantly, supplies him and his men with a palatable similarity between past and present. "This was that hunger" (*haec erat illa fames*, 7.128), Aeneas says after reciting his father's prophecy, and these words show his satisfaction in crafting a past that precisely maps onto the present. James Fernandez' argument about the significance of metaphors could be applied to Aeneas' behavior as well: "However men may analyze their experiences within any domain, they inevitably know and understand them best by referring them to other domains for elucidation. It is in that metaphoric cross-referencing of domains, perhaps, that culture is integrated, providing us with the sensation of wholeness. And perhaps the best index of cultural integration or disintegration . . . is the degree to which men can feel the aptness of each other's metaphors."[99] Aeneas analyzes his experiences within the domain of the past, and when the Trojans gladly accept his linking of Ascanius' joke to a memory of Anchises' prophecy, they set their own culture as one that looks to the past to understand the present.

It is not shocking that Rome, a city like no other, befuddles Aeneas' comparative efforts. Vergil's first poem, *Eclogue* 1, already marks Rome's singularity. Here one shepherd, Tityrus, tells another, Meliboeus, about the difficulty that plagued his attempts to imagine Rome (*Ecl.* 1.19–25):

> urbem quam dicunt Romam, Meliboee, putavi
> stultus ego huic nostrae similem, quo saepe solemus
> pastores ovium teneros depellere fetus.
> sic canibus catulos similes, sic matribus haedos
> noram, sic parvis componere magna solebam.
> verum haec tantum alias inter caput extulit urbes
> quantum lenta solent inter viburna cupressi.

> The city which they call Rome, Meliboeus, I foolishly thought similar to our city here, the one to which we shepherds are accustomed to drive sheep's tender lambs. In this way I knew that puppies were like dogs, in this way kids like their mothers, and so I was accustomed to compare big things with small. But indeed this city has lifted its head among others as high as cypresses are accustomed to do among pliant wayfaring-trees.

[99] Fernandez 1972, 58 (quoted in Short 2012, 109).

Tityrus begins by remarking in lines 19–21 how he naively thought Rome similar to his own city. He based this assumption on knowledge from his pastoral life, namely that young animals are smaller versions of the same species of adult animals, and that Rome therefore would be a larger version of their country town. Recognizing that Rome is unlike the towns he knows, he searches for a way to understand this dissimilarity through considering what he thinks are similar differences between large and small animals of the same species.[100]

Yet once Tityrus visited Rome, he realized his mistake: Rome is different from other cities in essence as well as in magnitude. To reflect this, Tityrus now compares two different species of trees, cypresses, and wayfaring-trees.[101] Tityrus' process of shifting his simile has some parallels with the Trojans' manipulation of their memories in their search for their homeland. When Anchises realizes his memory of a Cretan origin is incorrect, he voices another recollection, one that locates the Trojans' past in Italy and makes it fit with the future that Apollo specified. By substituting a memory that matches his present needs, Anchises shows that he, like Tityrus, is ready to change his field of comparison to reflect new knowledge.

Just as it did initially for Tityrus, Rome floats on the edge of Aeneas' ken. Tityrus' creative use of a pastoral simile to indicate differences of both quantity and quality shows that, for Tityrus at least, it is possible to understand Rome using one's typical field of comparison. The Trojans also appear capable of comprehending Rome, as evidenced by the change they make to their memories about their race's origins. Tityrus, though, has an advantage over Aeneas: he has actually visited the city. Doubts remain about whether Aeneas can understand enough about Rome's nature so that he can approach it via memory. Aeneas is afforded glimpses of Rome and her citizens, but he neither retains nor understands what he sees. He remembers nothing from the underworld's parade of Roman heroes, and, while he takes pleasure in his divinely made shield, he is pointedly ignorant of the Roman history engraved upon it: "Knowing nothing of the events, Aeneas rejoices in their pictures" (*rerum . . . ignarus imagine gaudet*, 8.730).

The question remains as to whether Aeneas can use his memories, his usual field of comparison for comprehending the future, to understand Rome and move toward assuring its existence. The poem sets Rome as a city hovering between human and cosmic time, a city that must therefore

[100] See Feeney 2007, 433–6 on the play between similarity and dissimilarity that governs similes in general.

[101] See Clausen 1994, ad loc. for the identity of the *viburna*.

be built upon the past even as its link with earlier times is severed. This dynamic portends that remembering, although it is a pliable and inventive process, will prove insufficient. Accordingly, it also implies that the Trojans' identity may not be passed down to the Romans. If Aeneas continues to frame his approach to Rome with his memories, then there will always be an aspect of it that lies beyond his reach. Memories generally make Aeneas' immediate surroundings comprehensible, but they cloud his progress toward his far-off goal.

A second factor, alongside its utility in the present moment, also attracts Aeneas to memory: his recollections allow him to reframe his past. So long as he avails himself of his memories, he may attempt to re-write the meaning of his disastrous history. Through the process of reconstruction, Aeneas creates a coherent identity for himself and the Trojans where their past leads to their present success and is accordingly worthy of preservation and praise.[102] Aeneas remembers certain parts of his past in a new way and fits them into his present purposes.[103] By integrating these events into his larger life story, he reorients them and thereby lessens their traumatic impact.[104] For instance, when he remembers the earlier efficacy of his spears at Troy, these weapons' previous use is no longer part of a losing effort but rather a meaningful precursor of success. Anchises' recollection of Cassandra's prophecy may be interpreted in this same way. Instead of standing as the confused and unbelievable ravings of a madwoman, Cassandra's predication may now be viewed as a prescient prediction, one whose full importance Anchises now understands and validates.

In a sense, Aeneas has figured out how to accomplish the wish he desperately expressed to the Sibyl: "May Troy's ill-fortune have followed us only this far; it is lawful also for you [gods and goddesses] to justly

[102] As Casey 1987, 292 notes "Each successive self can re-orient itself by altering its hold on old memories and weaving in new ones; it can reinterpret its history in a different manner; it can even represent itself to itself in a variant manner. Everywhere there is the production of personal identity, a production proceeding by the free remembering of the self by itself." (This is a useful description of the relationship between identity and memory that can apply to both individual and groups, but Casey may overstate the individual's power over this process with the adjective "free.")

[103] For more on the relation between present needs and the construction of memory, see Knapp 1989, 130, who argues that "our present sense of what matters" determines what is useful from the past and what is irrelevant.

[104] Olick 1999, 344 comments upon the challenge that traumas can pose: "Focusing on the mind's need to tell a coherent narrative, psychoanalysts have understood trauma as a stumbling block . . . If genuine communities are communities of memory that constantly tell and retell their constitutive narratives . . . there can be genuinely collective traumas insofar as historical events cannot easily be integrated into coherent and constructive narratives."

spare Pergama's race already" (*hac Troiana tenus fuerit fortuna secuta;* | *vos quoque Pergameae iam fas est parcere genti*, 6.62–3). Aeneas can still identify himself as a Trojan, but now he is a Trojan whose past is not a final, limiting, doom, but a productive part of his life.[105] Aeneas' behavior illustrates a characteristic of the *Aeneid* which David Ross perceptively captures: "Virgil has written a poem not so much about Rome's origins and its imperial present, but about the deceptive images that we continually make and remake to restore our past and imagine our future. There is no other way we can live, as a people or as individuals."[106] Ross' comment evokes something essential about the *Aeneid*: after all, it is not just Aeneas, but also the rest of the Trojans, along with their current and former foes, who take up the past with an active hand in an effort to grasp the future. In the process, they write a new narrative.

Yet the Trojans' predicament challenges Aeneas' mnemonic engagement with the past. Ross writes that "There is no other way to live, as a people or as individuals." This may be so, but Aeneas cannot live as a typical individual. He represents something greater than himself, and he comes to learn it and even accept it over the course of the epic. So far as Rome is concerned, memory may be limiting. As Anchises explains in *Aeneid* 6, the souls in the underworld must forget their pasts in order to become the great Romans of tomorrow, and the greatness of Rome may be such that it cannot be comprehended through recollections, even strongly manipulated ones. Moreover, the act of remembering is certainly not a process Aeneas completely controls. There are moments in the epic (its final scene not least among them) when recollections overpower him. Yet when Aeneas arrives in Italy, he starts this new phase of existence with his old memories and, hence, his old identity. Paradoxically, even though Aeneas learns that the souls in the underworld can only begin a new life by forgetting the past, he commits himself to using the past. For Aeneas, there is an abiding cultural and moral value in his history, without which it is not worth surviving.

[105] This is similar to Quint's argument, but with one significant difference. Quint 1989, 31 claims that the past must be "successfully repressed" in order for it to "be repeated *with a difference*" (emphasis original). It is undeniable that certain aspects of the Trojans' past are forgotten because of Aeneas' mnemonic manipulations: such as Celaeno's role as dread prophetess or the larger, negative context for Aeneas' earlier use of his spears. Yet this forgetting generally takes place under the sign of memory, as Aeneas consistently uses the language of recollection. Aeneas' reinvention of the past comes about because he uses his memories in a new situation, not because he buries his history wholesale.

[106] Ross 2007, 10.

In these transitional moments, Aeneas puts his memories of Troy to a productive use and, in doing so, remembers a way to a new past, one that allows him to retain his Trojan identity even while shedding its more debilitating associations. The narrator, though, reveals the potential problems of living in this manner. A struggle grows between the oblivion that Rome demands and the engagement with memory Aeneas seeks. It is a problem the *Aeneid* is intensely interested in exploring, one that draws in issues related to time, identity, and change. To fully investigate it we must understand better how Aeneas comes to possess this devotion to remembering and commemorating his Trojan past, along with what role he envisages memory playing in his interpersonal interactions. In order to begin this project, Chapter 2 turns back to the first books of Vergil's epic, where Aeneas confronts Troy's destruction and the pressing questions of remembrance that arise almost immediately after its fall.

CHAPTER TWO

The challenge of Troy

The *Aeneid*'s action begins several years after Troy's destruction, but the passage of time does not erase that city's presence. If anything, Troy's devastating loss, coupled with the Trojans' inability to find a new home, sets Troy firmly in the center of their consciousness, perhaps even more so than when its existence was a given. Driven from their homeland and deprived of a presumably permanent marker of their identity, the Trojans must figure out who they are and what their past means to them in the midst of new and challenging situations. Scholars generally portray the Trojans' relationship with their city as a dangerous distraction, one that could leave them hamstrung by a stultifying devotion to a dead society and unable to move toward Rome's foundation.[1] Such a view grows out a perspective that looks back from the finished product of Rome, a vantage point that figures Troy's disappearance as a tidy and foreordained result toward which the epic ought to hasten.

This approach overlooks the tenacity and complexity that characterize the idea of Troy in the epic's opening books, properties that prove vital for understanding the actions of both those who strive to commemorate it and those who prefer to cast it into oblivion. Instead of approaching Troy and its memory from a point of view that assumes, even welcomes, its disappearance, this chapter concentrates on several of the epic's earliest episodes where the city's meaning is still very much in flux. Here, this chapter argues, Aeneas struggles to figure out how to create a new remembering community that will honor the Trojans' memories of Troy and carry them into the future. In doing so, he orients himself toward

[1] In general, readers of the *Aeneid* claim that the abandonment of the idea of Troy is ultimately a positive for the Trojans and Romans. Vance 1973, 125, in a chart of oppositions in the *Aeneid*, sets Troy in the "evil" column, opposed to Rome; Cairns 1989, 128 writes of the "taint of Asia"; Feeney 1984, 182 argues that in Vergil "Troy represents, at the least, degeneracy and moral shabbiness"; and Jenkyns 1998, 441 warns that Aeneas' attachment to Troy "must change and develop if it is not to collapse into a pusillanimous nostalgia."

the task of ensuring Troy's remembrance and honoring that city with an evolving and creative mode of commemoration.

Four passages from *Aeneid* 1 and one from *Aeneid* 3 focus squarely on why and how Troy should be remembered: the narrator's opening characterization of Juno, Aeneas' first two speeches, his reaction to Juno's temple, and his account of the Trojans' visit to Buthrotum. The epic's exploration of Troy's mnemonic potential begins with the narrator's description of Juno's memories of the Trojans. The goddess offers a stark example of a vengeful engagement with the past, an engagement that initiates the *Aeneid*'s action and sets the relationship between memory and trauma as central to the epic. Aeneas' initial speeches to his men, along with his response to paintings depicting the Trojan War, all play on the Trojans' desire to remember the past and, perhaps even more importantly, be remembered themselves. These scenes showcase a conflict between Juno's and Aeneas' goals: the goddess aims to destroy the Trojans and any chance for them to be enshrined in memory, while Aeneas works to ensure that he and his men, along with their destroyed city, are appropriately remembered. Lastly, Aeneas' rendition of the Trojans' visit to Buthrotum adds new details to this portrait: an episode that took place several years earlier, its telling shows that Aeneas has now begun to understand and evaluate the variety of ways in which he might commemorate Troy.

Beginning in the past

Vergil's *Aeneid* is only a few lines old and the narrator has just begun to elaborate on the subject of his song when there is the first mention of memory (1.1–7):

> Arma virumque cano, Troiae qui primus ab oris
> Italiam fato profugus Laviniaque venit
> litora, multum ille et terris iactatus et alto
> vi superum, saevae memorem Iunonis ob iram
> multa quoque et bello passus, dum conderet urbem
> inferretque deos Latio, genus unde Latinum
> Albanique patres atque altae moenia Romae.

> Arms and the man I sing, who was the first to come from the coast of Troy to Italy and the Lavinian shores, a refugee by fate, much-tossed both on land and sea by the force of the gods, on account of the unforgetting anger of savage Juno, and who suffered much also in war, until he could found his city and bring the gods to Latium,

> from whence sprang the Latin race and the Alban fathers and the walls of high Rome.

Nestled amongst those typical building blocks of epic, an opening declaration of the poem's subject and a teleological outline of its narrative, the fourth line of the *Aeneid* is simultaneously superfluous and essential. Strictly speaking, it is unnecessary to the sentence's syntax (which would still be flawless if line 3 led directly into line 5) and to its action (which could flow smoothly from one type of suffering to another). Yet, at the same time, the verse is absolutely indispensable: coming between descriptions of two aspects of Aeneas' toils, it offers an explanation for his pains. The hero suffers because of the force of the gods; more specifically, he suffers on account of Juno's unforgetting anger.

Memory's intrusion into the epic's first lines evokes one of its defining qualities. Just as this verse is unattached from its poetic surroundings yet necessary for understanding them, memory stands apart from the present in its focus on the past even as it influences a character in the here and now. In regard to *Aen.* 1.4, the events Juno remembers are far removed from the present time, yet they impact her current behavior to the greatest extent. Juno, as the narrator will soon reveal (1.25–8), regards these past deeds as injustices suffered at the Trojans' hands, and the arc of her memory brings them to bear upon Aeneas.

The epic's course is barely sketched out when the narrator delves into the reason for his hero's toils in line 4. Its first words, "by the force of the gods" (*vi superum*), pin Aeneas' sufferings on anonymous immortal agents, but the rest of the line reveals a more particular reason.[2] The shifts from anonymous gods (*superum*) to a specific goddess (*Iunonis*) and from a vague force (*vi*) to a precise type of passion (*memorem . . . iram*) suggest that the narrator pinpoints the cause that drives Juno. An etymological wordplay in this line makes that cause seem all but preordained. The proximity of the words "Juno" (*Iunonis*) and "unforgetting" (*memorem*) calls to mind the goddess' epithet *Moneta*. *Moneta*, derived by the Romans from "to remind" (*monere*),[3] may be loosely taken to mean "the reminder," and Juno earned the title when she reminded the Romans to guard the Capitoline.[4]

[2] Austin 1971, ad loc. notes that the "implication in *superum* is made more precise by *Iunonis ob iram*."

[3] *Monere* was in turn derived from *memoria* ("memory"). See Maltby 1991, *memoria*; and Varro *L.* 6.49.

[4] A scholiast to Lucan 1.380 supplies the story: "Juno is called Moneta. For since she moved the Senones back from the Capitoline, she is called Moneta, because she reminded [the Romans] to guard the Capitoline" (*Moneta Juno dicta est. cum enim Senones a Capitolio removisset, Moneta dicta est, quod monuisset ut Capitolium tuerentur*). See Ernout and Meillet 1932, *Moneta*; *OLD Moneta*; and Maltby

Although it is Juno's anger that the narrator describes as "unforgetting" (*memorem*), the word's appearance alongside the goddess' name recalls her epithet. It reaffirms that remembering is an essential aspect of Juno's being and foreshadows that her long memory will yield an epic of suffering for Aeneas.[5] At the same time, the allusion to Juno Moneta brings out the range of effects Juno's memory can have on the Romans: the same divinity whose mindfulness once saved (or, will save)[6] the Romans now persecutes their forebears with particular intensity due to her recollections.

The uniqueness of Juno's memory is further foregrounded by the phrase's construction: *saevae memorem Iunonis ob iram* ("on account of the unforgetting anger of cruel Juno," 1.4). The quintessentially Vergilian interlacing of two nouns and their adjectives knits the words together into a unit, simultaneously completing the line's sense and meter.[7] Within that unit, the combination of *memorem* ("unforgetting") and *iram* ("anger") is startling. *Memor* is typically applied to a person or god, and this is the earliest extant use of the adjective to modify a feeling.[8] By modifying "anger" and not "Juno" with "unforgetting," the narrator calls special attention to the consequential relationship between Juno's memory and anger. As one recent critic observes, rage over any harmful incident typically peaks "right away" and then fades "over time."[9] Yet this does not at all

1991, *Moneta*. See also A. Hardie 2007, 556–60 and Meadows and Williams 2001, 33 on the possible significations of the name *Juno Moneta*.

5 Such wordplay involving a character's name often hints at his or her function in the epic (O'Hara 1996, 66–73).

6 For the epic's audience, Juno Moneta is in the past, while she is far in the future vis-à-vis the narrative present.

7 This sort of innovative conjunction is typical of Vergil's style (Lyne 1989, 13).

8 See *TLL memor* 660.64–6; *OLD memor* 5; Austin 1971, ad 1.5; and A. Hardie 2007, 572. A strikingly similar phrase is found at Aesch. *Ag.* 155: "unforgetting Anger" (μνάμων Μῆνις), which is discussed further below. Two other examples of this phrase in Greek tragedy include Aesch. *Prom.* 516 and Soph. *Aj.* 1390. Livy also modifies *ira* with *memor*: "It is said . . . that not only did the name of the Potitii die out, but even the Censor Appius became blind some years later because of the unforgetting anger of the gods" (*traditur . . . nec nomen tantum Potitiorum interisse sed censorem etiam Appium memori deum ira post aliquot annos luminibus captum*, 9.29.11). Oakley 2005, ad loc. notes that "Aesch. *Ag.* 155 μνάμων Μῆνις may have influenced the Latin writers, but there the collocation is less striking, since in Greek Μῆνις ["Anger"] is personified quite often." Because of the uncertainty about the publication date of Livy's history, it is unknown whether Vergil or Livy is using the other's phrase, whether each arrives at the phrase independently, or whether they derive it from a no longer extant source.

9 Fisher 2002, 72. Fisher 2002, 164 writes that anger occurs when "the will has been outraged . . . by events . . . contrary to what the will knows itself to want," a view close to that of Fantuzzi and Hunter 2004, 117. Fisher's characterization of anger as a rational response to an unjust act is representative of one ancient philosophical approach that treats anger as something that arises in response to an initial offence and is focused upon an "identifiable, present, responsible, rational agent," who is "of comparable social status" (Wright 1997, 172–3). This pattern of rage that crests and then falls is similar to the Stoic belief that emotion

describe Juno's wrath, which still burns hot even though its causes are long past.

The narrator's choice of adjective to modify the goddess' anger reveals why it persists. From one perspective, Juno's rage is built upon her memory of past incidents, and this memory remains with her through time. While mortals' recollections are threatened by forgetting, or, in the end, extinguished by the process of rebirth after their deaths,[10] the immortal Juno is free from any such oblivion. From another perspective, her anger serves to reinforce her memory.[11] *Memorem* also shows that her anger reminds her of the past wrongs that cause it.[12] Her "unforgetting anger" is thus self-perpetuating: inspired by memories of past wrongs, it stands as a metaphorical monument to those injustices, preserving their memory and its own force. This circle embodies the reciprocal influence between memory and identity. Juno's memories of wrongs sustain her identity as a bitter enemy of the Trojans, and she remembers these specific injuries because she identifies herself as the Trojans' foe. Unlike mortals, whose memories are expunged before their rebirth and who strain to pass down their recollections to future generations, Juno can carry her memories and her rage forward for an indefinite time, if she dedicates herself to doing so.

Shortly hereafter, the narrator wonders about the effects of her rage. Near the proem's end, he pointedly states that Juno attacks "a man remarkable for his piety" (*insignem pietate virum*, 1.10) and then asks: "Can there be a wrath so great in the hearts of the gods on high?" (*tantaene animis caelestibus irae?*, 1.11). Following hard upon his declaration that Juno makes a pious man suffer, the narrator's anguished question hints that there is something

dissipates over time. See also Nussbaum 1994, 381–2, who argues that a like concept is found in Chrysippus' writings. Nussbaum writes that judgments that are the equivalent of passions must be *prosphaton* ("fresh") and this quality is what gives them a "tearing and wrenching" impact. It is only as time passes that the "proposition" loses "its extreme sharpness, its intrusive cutting edge" (382). The propositions that influence Juno (namely, these earlier incidents) never lose their edge. For an overview of ancient conceptions of anger, especially in relation to the *Aeneid*, see Gill 1997a; Galinsky 1988, 328–40; Putnam 1990, 10–16; and Fowler 1997a.

10 See pp. 34–6.

11 *Memor* is most frequently used to indicate a person who remembers (*TLL* 656.33–661.47). Since the narrator soon describes Juno engaging in that very activity, the meaning of the adjective can be transferred to the goddess.

12 See *TLL* 661.48–63 for the meaning of "reminding." It is much less common than the adjective's other meaning, "remembering," but parallels may be found in Vergil's contemporaries, such as Hor. *C.* 1.13.12: "The passionate boy pressed a reminding mark upon her lips with his teeth" (*puer furens | impressit memorem dente labris notam*). Just as this amorous marker brings to mind its origins, so too does Juno's anger. Also see Servius ad 1.4, who notes that the adjective can have both passive ("remembering") and active ("reminding") meanings.

wrong with the goddess' behavior.[13] Juno's memory is pinpointed as the core of this problem by an allusion to Aeschylus' *Agamemnon* in the earlier phrase "unforgetting anger" (*memorem . . . iram*, 1.4). These two words recall Aeschylus' description of the wrath of the Furies as "unforgetting Anger" (μνάμων Μῆνις, *Ag.* 155). As Eduard Fraenkel notes, μνάμων ("unforgetting") is a "natural enough" quality to emphasize in the Furies, since Zeus' vengeance never forgets "to punish the guilty."[14] In contrast with this situation in *Agamemnon*, the *Aeneid*'s narrator pointedly shows that Juno is punishing a man famed for his piety, not marked by guilt. The narrator's question, then, about the goddess' wrath points back to Juno's memory and indicts the role it plays in her persecution of Aeneas. If the Furies' anger is unforgetting since those goddesses need to remember the deeds of the guilty, then it is problematic that Juno's wrath possesses that same quality, for it centers on a man who himself has done her no harm.

The narrator soon reveals further details about this interaction. After describing the goddess' concern that the Trojans' descendants will one day destroy her beloved Carthage, he places Juno's fears about that city's future parallel to her memories of the past (1.23–8):

> id metuens veterisque memor Saturnia belli,
> prima quod ad Troiam pro caris gesserat Argis –
> necdum etiam causae irarum saevique dolores
> exciderant animo; manet alta mente repostum
> iudicium Paridis spretaeque iniuria formae
> et genus invisum et rapti Ganymedis honores.

> Saturnia, fearing this [Carthage's destruction] and remembering the ancient war, which she had first[15] waged against Troy on behalf of her dear Greeks – and still the causes of her wrath and violent resentment had not yet fallen out of her thoughts; stored away in the depths of her mind, the judgment of Paris remains and the injury done to her spurned form and the hated race and the honor given to stolen Ganymede.

The content, syntax, and pacing of these lines offers a portrait of the working of Juno's memory. While the syntax of line 23 implies that her apprehension about the future and her memories of the past are equal

[13] Segal 1981, 70 notes how the question "cuts to the heart of the meaning of the world order." Perkell 1999, 31 writes that it implies that in a "moral universe the pious man would be rewarded by the gods."

[14] Fraenkel 1950, ad loc.

[15] See Conington 1884, ad loc. and V. *Geo.* 1.12 for this adverbial interpretation of *prima*.

causes for her action, it soon becomes apparent that this is not at all the case.

Juno's worries about Carthage are relayed with relative detachment,[16] but her recollection of past incidents is suffused with rancor. Juno's memory of the Trojan War, first described innocuously enough in line 23 and then elaborated upon in line 24, stands as a trigger for her recollection of earlier wrongs.[17] The thought begun in line 23 never finds its syntactical completion, as the narrator instead describes not what Juno remembers but rather what emotions those memories prompt. The aposiopesis at the end of line 24 leads into a hasty movement from the "causes of her wrath" (*causae irarum*) to the "violent resentment" (*saevi . . . dolores*) they breed, with two elisions (*necdum etiam . . . causae irarum*) revealing the headlong rush of Juno's memory and emotions. The two are knit together, and the perseverance that marks Juno's recollections is brought out by line 26, which states twice over that the causes of the goddess' anger do not slip from her mind.[18] The structure of these verses underscores how Juno grimly cherishes each incident and the emotion it creates.

The earlier incidents Juno remembers no doubt dictated her opposition to the Trojans at Troy and still gall her now. There are three older injustices at the root of these memories, none of which directly involve Aeneas: Paris' selection of Venus as the most beautiful goddess over Juno and Athena; Jupiter's dalliance with Electra, which produced Dardanus, the founder of the Trojan race; and the honor Jupiter gave to Ganymede, a Trojan youth snatched up to serve as the gods' wine steward. Three times

[16] Juno's knowledge about Carthage is heard and not experienced (as indicated by "she had heard" (*audierat*, 1.20)). The very act of hearing distances the threatened actions by subordinating them in indirect discourse. E. L. Harrison 1984, 106 argues that the significance of *audierat* is that it permits Juno to resist fate, since she only hears about its path.

[17] Feeney 1984, 183 and 1991, 131–2; Perkell 1999, 34; Fantuzzi and Hunter 2004, 118; and Syed 2005, 147 do not distinguish between the power of these two motivations. E. Harrison 1984, 107 implies that Juno's worries about Carthage are more significant than "old grudges," since the former are described in eleven lines and the latter in six. This discrepancy in length, though, is overshadowed by the emotional markers attached to her memory and by the fact that it is identified twice over as a cause of Aeneas' suffering (1.4 and 1.29). On Juno's anger, see also Dyson 2001, who argues that the emotion arises because of Aeneas' improper sacrifices to the goddess.

[18] There may be an etymological wordplay in this line involving "to remember" (*meminisse*). Varro derives "to remember" (*meminisse*) from "memory" (*memoria*), since "there is a motion again toward that which remained in the mind" (*id quod remansit in mente rursus movetur, L.* 6.49). The phrase "it remains in her mind" (*manet . . . mente*, 1.28) almost exactly corresponds with Varro's phrase "it remained in the mind" (*remansit in mente*, Var. *L.* 6.49). This near repetition may characterize Juno as the textbook definition of one who willfully remembers. A. Hardie 2007, 572 also notes the possibility of this etymological relationship. See White 1993, 319–20 on another instance of Vergil's use of Varronian etymologies and 185 on the general relationship between Varro and the Augustan poets.

someone is preferred to Juno, and three times her will is frustrated. The narrator's description of each incident, focalized from Juno's perspective, offers further insight into her process of recollection. After first blandly describing the event as "Paris' judgment" (*iudicium Paridis*), the rest of line 27 captures the acidic disrespect Juno felt then and still feels now over not being chosen most beautiful. *Genus invisum* may be read as a reference to the role of Jupiter's philandering in beginning the Trojan race,[19] a reflection of Juno's present hatred ("the hateful race"),[20] or a phrase that contains both of these ideas, thus further knitting together memory and anger.[21] The final phrase, *rapti Ganymedis honores*, is equally suggestive. *Rapti* surely stands in the genitive singular and modifies *Ganymedis*, but its juxtaposition with *honores* hints at an alternative construction, where *rapti* modifies *honores*, designating "the stolen honors of Ganymede." This reading reveals Juno's belief that the attention and honors lavished upon Ganymede were rightly hers.

Juno's memories and the emotions associated with them occasion her persecution of the Trojans (1.29–33):

> his accensa super iactatos aequore toto
> Troas, reliquias Danaum atque immitis Achilli,
> arcebat longe Latio, multosque per annos
> errabant acti fatis maria omnia circum.
> tantae molis erat Romanam condere gentem!
>
> Since she was burning up over these things, Juno kept driving the Trojans to and fro over the whole sea, the remnants left by the Greeks and harsh Achilles, and she was keeping them far off from Latium, and for many years they were wandering around all the oceans, driven by the fates. So great a labor was it to found the Roman race!

The beginning of line 29 reaffirms the causal relationship between Juno's memories and her present hostility toward the Trojans.[22] In contrast, Juno's fear of future events, set down as a motivation for her actions in line 23, is not

[19] Austin 1971, ad loc. advances this reading, noting how Dardanus was a product of Jupiter's affair with Electra.

[20] J. Henry 1873, ad 1.32 argues that the phrase reflects not a specific reason for Juno's hatred but rather the general idea that they are "an abomination to her."

[21] Building on the suggestion by J. Henry 1873, 217–8, Fowler 2000, 48–9 finds both of these ideas present, with the phrase alluding to Dardanus as well as representing how Juno herself thinks about the Trojans.

[22] As Putnam 1995, 32 notes, the description of Juno as "burning up over these things [i.e., her memories]" (*his accensa*, 1.29) marks the completion of her emotional evolution from being "merely anxious and mindful" at the beginning of the proem to being "set aflame by the end."

mentioned again. A remarkable persistence characterizes Juno's memory-based hostility: it began before the Trojan War and continues after it. A similar constancy marks the actions her memory inspires now. The narrator describes them in the imperfect ("she was keeping them off" [*arcebat*]), a tense in the *Aeneid* that "provides more general background information."[23] Here that background is filled with a vindictive and obsessive pursuit, a revenge inspired by memory.

The narrator soon confirms that Juno manipulates her memories. He sets her inner pain as the catalyst for the epic's first actions (1.34–7):

> vix e conspectu Siculae telluris in altum
> vela dabant laeti et spumas salis aere ruebant,
> cum Iuno aeternum servans sub pectore vulnus,
> haec secum . . .
>
> Scarcely out of sight of Sicily, the Trojans were happily sailing into the deep sea and churning up salty froth with their bronze bows, when Juno, nursing an eternal wound under her breast, spoke these things to herself . . .

The Trojans' behavior – joyful, energetic, and communal – offers a strong counterpoint to Juno's: the goddess, alone, nurses her grief and anger. Entangled with such emotions are Juno's painful memories. These lines hint that Juno chooses to sustain them as well, as the narrator shows that the goddess keeps the pain caused by earlier events, and, implicitly, her recollection of them, fresh in her mind.[24] She willfully lingers over past injuries.[25]

What do such memories inspire the goddess to do? Juno immediately launches into a monologue full of indignation over her ineffective battle against the Trojans. As opposed to Homeric type scenes, where gods engage in dialogue with one another, Juno communicates with no one.[26]

[23] Mack 1978, 48.

[24] Herzog 1993, 81 argues that the prologue portrays Juno as a captive of her memory. The situation is more complex. Juno's memories inspire her to act, but they are memories that she actively holds onto. If we continue with Herzog's metaphor, she is both captive and jailer.

[25] For similar acts of memory manipulation in Livy, see Jaeger 1997, 104–5, 107–8, 120, 166–8; in Aeschylus' *Agamemnon*, see Scodel 2008, 118.

[26] The construction "these things with herself" (*haec secum*) implies that Juno's words are heard by no other (Conington 1884, ad 1.37; and Austin 1971, ad 37). This is confirmed by the way the narrator signals Juno is finished speaking: "the goddess, thinking over such things with herself in her inflamed mind" (*talia flammato secum dea corde volutans*, 1.50). Highet 1974, 193 points out how Juno's inner turmoil is reflected in the fact that the beginning of her speech, unlike most speeches in the Aeneid, does not coincide with the beginning of a line. Feeney 1983 argues that speech in the *Aeneid* generally does not exhibit the cooperative and healing aspects it displays in Homeric epic, and this first example certainly fits that pattern.

Her interactions with memory lead to and spring from a solitary rage, establishing the relationship between memory and trauma as a central and challenging theme in the epic.[27] Remembering past traumas herself, Juno draws upon them now to foist yet another trauma onto Aeneas and the Trojans, thus initiating a series of attempts to harness the recollection and commemoration of past suffering.

Troy's presence

Just as the narrator's initial description of Juno centers on her memory and her wish to destroy the Trojans, Aeneas' first words in the epic also relate to Troy and recollection. Yet Aeneas' speech is not one of rage or vengeance. Instead, he laments his inability to enjoy the sort of social memory that Troy's existence made possible. In the midst of Juno's sea storm, Aeneas cries out to the heavens (1.94–101):

> o terque quaterque beati,
> quis ante ora patrum Troiae sub moenibus altis
> contigit oppetere! o Danaum fortissime gentis
> Tydide! mene Iliacis occumbere campis
> non potuisse tuaque animam hanc effundere dextra,
> saevus ubi Aeacidae telo iacet Hector, ubi ingens
> Sarpedon, ubi tot Simois correpta sub undis
> scuta virum galeasque et fortia corpora volvit!

> O three and four times blessed those were, whose lot it was to die before their fathers' faces under Troy's high walls! O Diomedes, strongest of the race of Greeks! That I was not able to meet my death and pour out this spirit of mine by your right hand on the fields of Troy, where fierce Hector lies killed by Achilles' spear, where great Sarpedon lies, where the Simois river carries so many shields of men snatched up under its waves along with their helmets and strong bodies!

With destruction all around him, Aeneas wishes that he had died long ago. Like all heroes who face death at sea, Aeneas finds his glory imperiled. Unable to battle with nature in the way that he would with a mortal opponent, he is robbed of any opportunity to display his singular excellence.[28]

[27] Memory holds an "importance" for epic narrative in general, as Fantuzzi and Hunter 2004, 118 remark; its role in the *Aeneid* is given even greater prominence than usual, as it sparks the epic's action and continues to exert an extraordinary influence on the characters. Many scholars interpret *Aeneid* 1 and, in particular, its proem as programmatic; see, for instance, Pöschl 1970, 14; Conte 1986, 71; Cairns 1989, 3; Feeney 1991, 130, 136; and Perkell 1999, 29.

[28] Fisher 2002, 118–22.

Furthermore, a death at sea would not even allow Aeneas' suffering to be remembered: if he does perish on the deep, he will secure no grave.[29]

A comparison with this speech's two Homeric models points to the likelihood that Aeneas also fears the loss of a more specific benefit to which he only alludes here. *Iliad* 21.272–84, where the Simois River nearly overwhelms Achilles, and *Odyssey* 5.299–312, where Odysseus fears for his life on the ocean, share several elements with this Vergilian passage: in each, a hero, about to suffer a watery death, wishes that he could have died at Troy.[30] Upon comparison with Achilles' and Odysseus' words, one element is missing from Aeneas': a statement of what he would have gained from a death at Troy. If Hector had killed him, Achilles says, "Then a good man would have killed me, and he would have slain a good man" (τώ κ'ἀγαθὸς μὲν ἔπεφν', ἀγαθὸν δέ κεν ἐξενάριξε, *Il.* 21.280); and Odysseus claims that, if he had died at Troy, "Then I would have received funeral rites, and the Achaeans would have carried on my glory" (τῶ κ'ἔλαχον κτερέων, καί μευ κλέος ἦγον Ἀχαιοί, *Od.* 5.311). Unlike these two Homeric heroes, Aeneas nowhere explicitly reveals the benefits a death at Troy would have conferred.

This dissimilarity prompts a search in Aeneas' speech for any suggestions of a more specific benefit of which he is deprived, and suggestions of just this sort appear in his two bitter apostrophes in lines 94–7. When Aeneas addresses the fortunate ones who died at Troy, he places their final moments within the family, the most intimate of human communities.[31] Saying that he envies those who fell "before their fathers' faces under Troy's high walls" (*ante ora patrum Troiae sub moenibus altis*, 1.95), Aeneas

[29] Dyson 2001, 74: "Death without burial, especially in the oblivion of waves . . . [was an] epic hero's nightmare." At *Od.* 4.710 Penelope expresses the worry that a death at sea will wipe Telemachus' name off the earth.

[30] There are no precise verbal echoes connecting Aeneas' speech with the Achillean passage, but the two scenes are linked by clear thematic similarities. An obvious repetition connects this passage with *Od.* 5.299–312. 1.94–5 is a close adaptation of *Od.* 5.306–7: "Three and four times blessed are the Greeks who died then at wide Troy while bearing service to the sons of Atreus" (τρὶς μάκαρες Δαναοὶ καὶ τετράκις, οἳ τότ' ὄλοντο | Τροίῃ ἐν εὐρείῃ, χάριν Ἀτρεΐδῃσι φέροντες). (For the manner in which this allusion to Odysseus' speech invites the consideration of larger parallels between Aeneas and Odysseus' situations, see Farrell 1991, p. 268 n. 127.) Beye 2006, 253–4 compares Aeneas' speech with these same two passages. He concludes that Aeneas wants "the public recognition" due to a hero and to be in the company of Homer's "great men" rather than to be trapped in his current situation and poem. O'Sullivan 2009, 457 reads this scene from a metapoetic perspective, arguing that Aeneas takes on "the poet's anxieties" about his relationship with Homer and his ability to complete his story.

[31] Contra Quint 1993, 29, who argues that Aeneas shows a desire for "an anonymous immersion into the waves of his native Simois." This ignores Aeneas' status. The mass of men rolled about by the Simois stands as a backdrop to the deaths of the much more famous Trojan fighters, among whose ranks Aeneas was surely counted. In fact, Aeneas imagines a death at the hands of Diomedes.

sets the death of these men within the temporal fabric of their lineage.[32] While Aeneas centers this image on fathers, he still includes the larger Trojan community as witnesses, for a location before the city's walls would be highly visible to all.[33] He expands this community even further to include all the city's warriors when he bemoans the fact that he did not fall on "the fields of Troy" (*Iliacis . . . campis*, 1.97). The gesture of centering the death that eluded him within a series of Trojan communities hints at Aeneas' impossible hope that his death could become a social memory, one that would ordain his status as a hero and offer a presently unattainable comfort.

The sea storm sets any such commemoration beyond Aeneas' reach. His father is dead, and the winds and waves threaten not just him alone but all who sail with him. Aeneas' opening speech encapsulates the weight he carries with him on his voyage from Troy. He leaves that ruined civilization conscious of the fact that, unless he succeeds in founding a new city, no society will remember him and his followers. He ventures forth on the verge of oblivion, knowing that his only hope for being remembered lies in securing a new beginning. Yet Aeneas' burden is even greater than this, since the continued existence of any Trojan memories of Troy also hinges upon his mission. If every Trojan dies out, Troy will exist only in the jaundiced recollections and jingoistic monuments of its conquerors, a characterization of the city that would sting the Trojans' hearts. In order to guarantee the survival of their recollections of Troy and, indeed, even a memory of themselves, Aeneas and the Trojans must ensure their own survival.

Aeneas' desire for an impossible communal commemoration reveals that he is capable of looking toward the future and is genuinely concerned with how he will be remembered by generations to come. An earlier generation of scholars, though, viewed this speech as focused exclusively on the past, a conception of Aeneas' priorities that has a significant impact on the

[32] Aeneas' reference to fathers, which has no model in Achilles or Odysseus' speech (Galinsky 1996, 123 and O'Sullivan 2009, 455 note this as well), makes his words more personal and poignant than their Homeric counterparts. The reference cannot but help to call attention to the recent death of Anchises, who can now neither witness nor commemorate his son's end. Stahl 1981, 161 incisively remarks that this speech reveals Aeneas' desire to "achieve paternal recognition of his heroism – as opposed to the present threat of drowning in inglorious anonymity."

[33] As Perkell 1999, 40 notes, these lines depict Troy as a place "where people see their sacrifice, where they are known and loved." At *Il.* 22.108–10 Hector stresses the glory that attends a death before the city walls, and when Aeneas describes Hector's appearance in a dream, he too notes the communal location where that death occurred: "around the fathers' walls" (*circum . . . . muros* | *. . . patrios*, 2.278–9).

evaluations of his words and deeds. To claim, for instance, that Aeneas "thinks only of the past,"[34] overlooks the yearning in the hero's words for a community that will remember him in the future. Such an interpretation denies him the ability or desire to think of how the future will remember the present, and he becomes a person who can only look to earlier times, with no motivation to gain glory by acting for himself in the here and now.[35]

Yet Aeneas shows the strongest desire to be remembered in the future. With regard to epic convention[36] and Roman society[37] this mnemonic outlook is not at all radical. Achilles' behavior in the *Iliad* offers a prime example from the epic sphere, as the idea of how he will be remembered is never far from his mind, and for Romans the "production of memory was the aim and reward for effort and achievement."[38] What is more, the most powerful evidence for this idea's relevance to Aeneas comes from Anchises' conception of Roman values in *Aeneid* 6. Speaking with his son in the underworld, Anchises details the categories of people who merit admission to Elysium upon their death. He includes amongst them those who "won the memory of men by their merits" (*sui memores aliquos fecere merendo*, 6.664).[39] In this formulation, being remembered serves as a reward for valorous actions and stands as the marker of a man who has earned a place in Elysium. Such a belief can drive men to act in the present with the goal of being remembered. Although Aeneas' speech surely reflects his devastating memories of the past and, in the midst of a terrifying storm, future commemoration appears unattainable, he nonetheless alludes to the hope that, if he is able to survive, future men may remember his actions. With this perspective, commemoration can offer solace even for death, so long as a remembering community survives.

[34] Clausen 1964, 140. Pöschl 1970, 35 notes the focus on memory in this speech, but he, like Clausen, does not remark upon the future commemoration Aeneas desires.

[35] This view fits with influential early characterizations of Aeneas as one whose "personal voice" is linked to his capacity to suffer (Parry 1963, 79) and who makes "sacrifices [for Rome] not merely of life but of happiness and personal ambitions" (Bowra 1945, 13). Even a more recent work like Conte 1986 envisions memory as something that solely offers a regretful look to the past: Aeneas' "memory of the past – a private, backward-looking glance – contrasts with the direction of fate. Confined to the pauses in the epic action, never obliterated but never given its own place in the blueprint of the poem, memory persists as regret" (181). This view overlooks Aeneas' use of memory to guide the Trojans' progress and his concerted effort to make sure that he himself is remembered.

[36] The words of Vernant 1991, 68 on glory in Greek epic are applicable here: "For the hero to attain *kleos apthiton* [immortal glory], it is essential that his name and exploits be known by men to come, that they persist in memory."

[37] See pp. 16–20 for further discussion of this.

[38] Flower 2006, 3.

[39] Rodgers 1992 argues that this phrase specifically points to those who performed a service for Rome.

Aeneas elaborates on this idea a bit later, after he and his men find safety on unknown shores. With everyone gathered for a meal, he addresses his followers. In a speech that foreshadows his interaction with Dido, Aeneas tries to use memory to change how his men feel about their present situation (1.198–207):

> o socii (neque enim ignari sumus ante malorum),
> o passi graviora, dabit deus his quoque finem.
> vos et Scyllaeam rabiem penitusque sonantis
> accestis scopulos, vos et Cyclopi saxa
> experti: revocate animos maestumque timorem
> mittite; forsan et haec olim meminisse iuvabit.
> per varios casus, per tot discrimina rerum
> tendimus in Latium, sedes ubi fata quietas
> ostendunt; illic fas regna resurgere Troiae.
> durate, et vosmet rebus servate secundis.

> O companions (for we are not ignorant of earlier disasters), you who have suffered worse things, a god will give an end also to these hardships. You have approached ferocious Scylla and the deeply sounding cliffs, and you have known the Cyclopses' rocks: call back your courage and dismiss gloomy fear; perhaps one day it will be pleasing to remember even these things. Through various misfortunes, through so many critical turns of events, we are directing our course to Latium, where the fates offer a peaceful home; there it is the will of heaven for Troy's reign to rise again. Hold out, and save yourselves for better times.

The first two lines of Aeneas' speech encapsulate his goal of rallying the Trojans through an appeal to their shared experiences and hopes. His opening address, "O companions" (*o socii*, 1.198), forms his audience into a cohesive unit; and the parenthesis that completes the verse and the second address that opens line 199 define that unit through common remembrance of earlier difficulties. Aeneas' promise of a conclusion to their current devastation, meanwhile, holds out the idea of a better future, with the idea implied by "also" (*quoque*) that since other hardships have come to an end, these will too.[40]

The remainder of Aeneas' speech expands on the details of this temporal movement from past to future, elaborating further on the role recollection might play therein. Recalling the phrase "for we are not ignorant of earlier disasters" (*neque enim ignari sumus ante malorum*, 1.198), Aeneas specifies

[40] In addition to having an additive force (*OLD* 2), *quoque* also likely marks out the extreme difficulty of the Trojans' current trouble (*OLD* 3 "Even, indeed, actually, etc.").

in lines 200–2 the particular experiences that the Trojans share, experiences they somehow survived. Now, Aeneas shifts his temporal perspective, and memory stands as the pivot on which he rotates his speech. He imagines a future when his men may reminisce about their current losses from the sea storm: "Perhaps it will be pleasing one day to remember even these things" (*forsan et haec olim meminisse iuvabit*, 1.203).[41] Somehow, Aeneas hopes, the future will be better,[42] and from that vantage point the Trojans might take pleasure in remembering their present troubles. Aeneas asks the Trojans to imagine a future recollection of the present, just as line 198 shows that they have memories of their earlier experiences. By framing the current time with present memories of the past and prospective future memories of the present, Aeneas provides continuity for the Trojans. He expands their temporal frame beyond the recent sea storm that came near to being a "cosmic catastrophe."[43] This reassures the Trojans that their trials are fleeting (since they will come to an end and be only a memory), yet worthwhile (since their community will still exist to remember them).

Aeneas' commitment to remembering the past becomes even more noteworthy in comparison with a scene from *Odyssey* 4. Here, Telemachus visits Menelaus and Helen in search of news of his father. As Menelaus tells the young man about Odysseus, everyone begins to weep, and Helen decides to doctor their wine with a drug "banishing pain and anger, bringing forgetfulness of all bad things" (νηπενθές τ' ἄχολόν τε, κακῶν ἐπίληθον ἁπάντων, *Od.* 4.221).[44] In Homer's description, painful memories and emotions are closely linked together. Having enjoyed the wine, Menelaus and Helen are able to tell Telemachus stories of Odysseus without sadness. Sheila Murnaghan remarks that this drug offers consolation by creating "instantaneously the detachment from loss that ordinarily comes with time."[45] Helen recognizes that the passage of time has not yet graced them with feelings of detachment, and her actions, in fact, may even signal a doubt that this detachment may ever arrive.

This Homeric passage depicts a situation not terribly different from the future time Aeneas imagines in his speech: a gathering of people who

[41] The deictic *haec* indicates that Aeneas refers to the Trojans' current suffering, picking up on *his* from line 199. For parallels to this belief about memory, see Austin 1971, ad 203.

[42] MacDonald 1987, 41 writes that although 1.203 means on the surface "that better times are coming," it nonetheless implies "that perhaps so much worse is on the way that even this, bad as it is, will seem preferable." This implication, though, is ruled out by the following lines, which imagine the Trojans' success in Italy.

[43] P. Hardie 1986, 93 cites several passages representing the storm as threatening the entire world.

[44] For more on Helen's drug, see Heubeck, West, and Hainsworth 1990, 220–1.

[45] Murnaghan 1987, 161 n. 23.

remember past troubles. In comparison with this scene, Aeneas' actions appear in a new light. Like Helen, Aeneas recognizes the natural link between emotion and memory. Yet, unlike Helen, whose actions show her doubt that pain can be divorced from the memory of traumatic events, Aeneas voices a belief that horrific events can be pleasantly remembered once they have receded into the past. While Helen anaesthetizes memory, Aeneas characterizes shared recollections as a possession that can bind the Trojans together and make their losses bearable.[46]

Right after Aeneas finishes speaking, though, the narrator describes his true feelings: "Aeneas says such things in speech and yet troubled with great worries he makes a pretense of hope on his face and presses his pain deep into his heart" (*talia voce refert curisque ingentibus aeger | spem vultu simulat, premit altum corde dolorem*, 1.208–9).[47] The narrator's description of these hidden emotions reveals that Aeneas does not believe what he tells his men,[48] and the narrator's subsequent depiction of the Trojans' continued weeping (1.216–22) makes clear that Aeneas' words do not calm them. While the narrator's revelation does not specify precisely what part of his speech Aeneas doubts, his mnemonic claim is a likely candidate. Aeneas already couches this promise in terms so reticent that they almost invite doubt: "Perhaps one day it will be pleasing to remember even these things" (*forsan et haec olim meminisse iuvabit*, 1.203).[49] Moreover, in comparison with the scene from *Odyssey* 4, Aeneas' outward reliance on the distancing effect of time appears naïve, a promise that he cannot bring himself to

[46] This characteristic of memory is not found in the *Iliad*. There, characters do "not remember anything simply for the pleasure of memory" (Martin 1989, 80).

[47] There is a striking connection between the last phrase here describing Aeneas' feelings and the narrator's earlier declaration that Juno's memories "remain, stored away in the depths of her mind" (*manet alta mente repostum*, 1.26). While the goddess' memories stay in her mind and goad her on to rage, Aeneas suppresses his painful emotions and strives to convince his men that memory may offer solace.

[48] This revelation is all the more powerful since nothing similar appears in another Homeric model for this Vergilian passage in *Odyssey* 12. Here, as the Greeks approach Scylla and Charybdis, Odysseus promises his men that they will one day remember these dangers. When Odysseus finishes speaking, the narrator reveals not that Odysseus doubts what he said, but rather that he has simply not told his men about the dangerous Scylla (*Od.* 12.223–5). Vergil adds emotion to his scene in the *Aeneid*, both in what Aeneas says to his men (Odysseus makes no mention of pleasure in these prospective recollections) and also in the revelation of the burden that Aeneas bears alone.

[49] For further evidence that Aeneas doubts that such terrible events can ever be happily remembered, see Diomedes' statement at 11.280: "And I do not take joy in remembering old sufferings" (*nec veterum memini laetorve malorum*). The same can be said of 6.514, where Deiphobus, a dead Trojan, indicates to Aeneas the pain involved in remembering Troy's fall: "It's necessary to remember it all too well" (*nimium meminisse necesse est*). Segal 1981, 70 and Herzog 1993, 90 both claim that in this speech Aeneas emotionally distances himself from the past; this, though, ignores the impact of line 209, which shows that Aeneas feels strongly about the past indeed, but just does not express it to his men.

believe.[50] At least at this point, Aeneas doubts that the Trojans' past can be integrated into a successful future. He is different from Juno in that he fastens onto these traumatic memories not as incitement for anger but rather as a tool to calm his followers.[51] Nonetheless, Aeneas has not entirely figured out what role his recollections will play in the future.

A bit later, memory's pleasure and comfort become tangible, as Aeneas finds himself before the very sort of commemorative monument he believed was out of reach during the sea storm. What makes this representation of the past so remarkable is that, despite its location in a foreign city, Aeneas views it as a testament to Troy's enduring worth. As Aeneas waits for Dido in the center of her rapidly growing city, the narrator calls attention to this moment as an emotional turning point (1.450–8):

> hoc primum in luco nova res oblata timorem
> leniit, hic primum Aeneas sperare salutem
> ausus et adflictis melius confidere rebus.
> namque sub ingenti lustrat dum singula templo
> reginam opperiens, dum quae fortuna sit urbi
> artificumque manus inter se operumque laborem
> miratur, videt Iliacas ex ordine pugnas
> bellaque iam fama totum vulgata per orbem,
> Atridas Priamumque et saevum ambobus Achillem.

> In this grove for the first time the arrival of a new matter softened his fear; here for the first time Aeneas dared to hope for safety and to trust more confidently in his affairs, ruined though they may be. For while he looks over each thing under the great temple as he waits for the queen, while he marvels at the city's good fortune and the workmanship and toil of the craftsmen laboring in concert with one another, he sees the battles of Troy in order and the wars already widely known throughout the whole world, the sons of Atreus and Priam and Achilles harsh toward both.

Lines 450–2 produce a sense of intrigue and expectation. "First" (*primum*), repeated in 450 and 451, emphasizes a consequential shift in Aeneas' feelings,

[50] His preliminary remarks to his narrative of Troy's downfall show that he remembers these events with great pain and that he imagines the same is true even for the victorious Greeks (2.3–13). See pp. 101–2.

[51] The narrator's description of Aeneas directly before he speaks confirms this opposition with Juno: "He soothes their mournful hearts with words" (*dictis maerentia pectora mulcet*, 1.197). Just a bit earlier, the narrator tells how Neptune calms the storm raised by Juno, comparing the god to a man who settles a seditious mob: "He guides their spirits with words and soothes their hearts" (*ille regit dictis animos et pectora mulcet*, 1.153). The use of *mulcet* at 1.153, linked with an action directly opposed to Juno, associates Aeneas with that same opposition in 1.197.

a change underscored by the verb "dared" (*ausus*, 1.452). It hints at the depth and plenitude of Aeneas' earlier disappointments as well as the potential pain he risks merely by hoping and trusting once more.[52] It is not until lines 456–8 that an explanation for this hope appears: painted on Juno's temple are scenes from the Trojan War.[53]

Aeneas' remarks to his fellow Trojan Achates provide a clue as to what significance he finds in these paintings (1.459–63):

> constitit et lacrimans, "quis iam locus," inquit, "Achate,
> quae regio in terris nostri non plena laboris?
> en Priamus. sunt hic etiam sua praemia laudi,
> sunt lacrimae rerum[54] et mentem mortalia tangunt.
> solve metus; feret haec aliquam tibi fama salutem."

> He stood still and weeping says, "What place, Achates, what region in the world is not already full of our toil? Look – it's Priam. Even here there are prizes for valor all its own, and there are tears for men's lot, and mortality touches the mind. Get rid of your fears; this fame will bring some safety to you."

These representations key into Aeneas' memory in a powerful way. On one level, Aeneas is simply pleased at the fact that his and others' past actions have been commemorated.[55] This is brought out by the phrase "the wars already widely known throughout the whole world" (*bellaque iam fama totum vulgata per orbem*, 1.457), and confirmed by the adverbs "already" (*iam*, 1.459) and "here" (*hic*, 1.461). Consignment to oblivion, which was a distinct possibility in the sea storm, has been averted. Although the visual reminders of these destructive events certainly bring Aeneas pain, the mere fact that the Trojans are remembered offers a measure of hope as well.[56]

[52] E. Harrison 1972–3, 21 points out how Aeneas' "emotional isolation" has been brought to its peak just a bit earlier by Venus' sudden departure from her son (see his reaction to that departure at 1.407–9).

[53] This is the first of several examples in the *Aeneid* of a material object that activates the memory of the viewer. E. Henry 1989, 18–42 surveys such objects.

[54] The possible translations of *sunt lacrimae rerum* are vast. Wharton 2008, 274 argues that the multitude of inferences that may be drawn from the utterance all lead toward the idea that "Aeneas is communicating that the people who made these artworks are likely to have sympathy for" the Trojans. This is the general import I take from the phrase as well.

[55] Aeneas sees a representation of himself at 1.488.

[56] Pöschl 1970, 63 writes that Aeneas is engrossed in "melancholy contemplation" and "mournful quietude." (Rutledge 1971–72, 112; Paschalis 1997, 67–8; and Casali 2008, 188 also point out the grief in these lines.) There is surely sadness for Aeneas in the representations of his now dead compatriots, but just as important is the pleasure and possibility of safety that he takes from their commemoration.

Above and beyond a basic pleasure in the commemoration of his people's deeds, Aeneas also seizes upon the paintings as a marker of the character of the community that created them. The arrangement of line 461 illustrates his surprise that a commemoration of the Trojans' deeds exists in a Carthaginian temple to a goddess whom he suspects to be opposed to the Trojans:[57] the phrase "even here there are" (*sunt hic etiam*), following Aeneas' exclamation over Priam, isolates the importance of the temple's location in a foreign city. Aeneas finds evidence for the Carthaginians' "humanity" in these murals,[58] deducing from their commemorative decisions that they are sympathetic to the Trojans' plight. More specifically, Aeneas probably comes to believe that Dido, as the Carthaginians' ruler and the work's likely commissioner, shares his perspective on the past.[59]

The narrator, though, takes care to point out that Aeneas is deluding himself. As Aeneas draws reassurance from these scenes, the narrator questions the grounds of his reaction: "Aeneas feeds his soul on an empty picture as he groans aloud, and he wets his face with a coursing flood of water" (*animum pictura pascit inani | multa gemens, largoque umectat flumine vultum*, 1.464–5).[60] The possible implications of *inani* are many, but one likely interpretation, especially considering the contrast between the insubstantiality of the picture and the excess of Aeneas' reaction, is that the

57 While Aeneas is nowhere directly informed of Juno's enmity, Helenus' prophecy to him at Buthrotum implies that she is an enemy of the Trojans. The seer says that Juno forbids him from telling Aeneas certain things (3.380), and he also warns Aeneas that his only route to success is to propitiate the goddess (3.433–40). Although Aeneas could of course be embroidering the memories he shares with Dido in *Aeneid* 3, it seems unlikely that he would falsely portray the Carthaginians' tutelary goddess as opposed to the Trojans. (Aeneas does claim (2.612–4) that he sees Juno participating in Troy's destruction, but here she is just one of a host of immortals he witnesses wreaking havoc in the city.)

58 Clay 1988, 197. Barchiesi 1999, 335 makes a similar point, noting that Aeneas realizes that he has come to a land of people "who are capable of compassion." Segal 1981, 78 notes that Aeneas, as he views the paintings in Juno's temple, "casts Dido into the role of sympathetic spectator-reader of his past."

59 The anonymity of the artisans, Putnam 1998, 216 argues, points to Dido's role as the composition's "guiding spirit." For this same view, see Clay 1988, 198, 200. See Barchiesi 1997, 277 on the "contextual pointers" that reinforce Aeneas' reading of the ekphrasis. Also, as Clay 1988, 200 notes, Dido's assurance to Ilioneus ("Free your heart from fear, Trojans, put away your worries" (*solvite corde metum, Teucri, secludite curas*, 1.562)) is quite close to the conclusion Aeneas draws from the paintings: "Release your fear" (*solve metus*, 1.463).

60 Could the narrator's statement be a focalization from Aeneas' perspective and reflect the hero's awareness that the comfort these scenes provide is empty? On this interpretation, Aeneas' tears would arise from a mixture of his sadness at seeing representations of his lost comrades as well as from a feeling that those representations are somehow unsatisfying. This is unlikely, since just a few verses earlier (1.451–3), the narrator declares that Aeneas first began to hope and trust when he looked at this temple.

comfort Aeneas draws from the pictures is unfounded.[61] Aeneas' emotional response is as fulsome as the images he looks upon are empty, and the narrator points out to the audience that there is simply nothing that justifies Aeneas' reaction.[62] The pictures doubtlessly celebrate the Greeks' victory, set as they are in a shrine to Aeneas' fiercest and most determined immortal enemy and in a city that will wage war against Rome three times over.[63]

Aeneas' reaction reveals his need to believe that Troy is commemorated in a favorable way. If his first speech demonstrates his yearning to be remembered, then it is easy to understand how he would greet this memorial with happiness. After all, it records his own actions along with those of his dead comrades. In his second speech, delivered on Carthage's shores, Aeneas misleads his men with the claim that they would one day remember their present sufferings with pleasure. Now, he seems to mislead himself. Dido must have commissioned these scenes to celebrate Juno's victory over Troy, yet she cannot control how each viewer interprets and responds to them.[64] Her intentions, though, are immaterial to Aeneas. It would be excruciating for him to acknowledge that this monument memorializes Trojan defeat.

[61] On the potential connotations of *inani*, see Putnam 1998, 25 (who argues that *inani* reflects the difference between the value the reader places in art as opposed to the characters' view of art as a stand-in for reality); Barchiesi 1999, 336 (who posits that the word may allude to the gap between art and the reality it portrays and/or it may indicate that the reassurance Aeneas draws from the picture is "without basis [and] insubstantial"); and Syed 2005, 68 (who states that *inani* distinguishes between the "lifeless and empty images" and the "comfort, change, and hope" Aeneas laboriously draws from them). For an interpretation of this passage from a different perspective, see Bartsch 1998, 338, who argues that Aeneas' reaction "sets up a model for viewing that invites the participation of the viewer in making his own, positive meaning out of art."

[62] As Putnam 1998, 23 notes, Aeneas "add[s] his interpretive prejudice to what he views," and Dubois 1982, 33 remarks on how Aeneas ought not to be confident in any solace he draws from these scenes as "a version of the story of Troy which would be pleasing to Juno cannot be one that Aeneas would recognize as true." Lowrie 2009, 161 remarks how Aeneas' "assumptions reveal Roman expectations: monumental representation entails sympathetic praise." See Bergmann 1994, 248 on how the *Aeneid*'s audience would be ready to receive these images "in a particularly relevant and immediate way." For an analysis of how Romans looked at and responded to art, see Elsner 1995.

[63] See Johnson 1976, 103–5; Lyne 1987, 210; Lowenstam 1993; and Barchiesi 1997, 277 on the various ironies in this scene (in addition to *inani*) that raise the possibility that Aeneas may be deluding himself with hope.

[64] As Küchler and Melion 1991, 7, note, "images engender modes of recollection," but that does not mean that they dictate the meaning a viewer draws from them. (For an overview of the relationship between images and memory, see ibid. 1–46.) Tatum 1995, 169 remarks that "Unless a specific effort is made to work toward a common understanding of such signs, the significance that one intends to be 'remembered' can vary from one person to the next." With reference to the open-ended meaning of the statues and monuments of ancient Rome, see Favro 1996, 82; Barchiesi 2002, 3–4 and 6; and Gowing 2005, 143. Fowler, 2000, 193–217 and especially 206, advances the belief that "Nothing is more changeable than the meaning of a monument"; and Alcock 2002, 64–74 makes a similar point about how Athenian monuments could prompt variable memories depending upon one's personal history.

Instead, he succumbs to the temptation to find comfort in them. Beginning with Aeneas' initial spoken reaction, the emphasis is on his perspective throughout the narrator's description of the paintings.[65] Having wished for the unattainable in his first speech and having falsely promised his men a comforting memory in his second, Aeneas now gains an opportunity to secure precisely the kind of commemoration he thought impossible. It is an opportunity that he takes: looking over these scenes from his past and interpreting them based on his memories, he makes them into the compassionate commemoration of Troy that he so desperately needs them to be.

Troy made small

We learn more about Aeneas' need to commemorate Troy from his description of his visit to Buthrotum in *Aeneid* 3. Aeneas narrates this experience to Dido as part of his tale of Troy's downfall and the Trojans' subsequent wanderings, and, thus, even though it follows the scenes from *Aeneid* 1 in the epic's narrative, it precedes them chronologically. It is difficult to judge how much, if at all, Aeneas' representation of his visit differs from what actually occurred during his time at Buthrotum; we possess no record other than his.[66] What is far more significant than the "facts" of that visit, though, is how Aeneas, currently in the midst of searching for a way to ensure that he and Troy do not disappear from memory, constructs an autobiographical tale that depicts his experience at Buthrotum as a crucial

65 There are multiple indications that Aeneas is watching and reacting: "he was watching" (*videbat*, 1.466); "crying he recognizes" (*agnoscit lacrimans*, 1.470); "then he gives forth a great sigh from the depths of his heart" (*tum vero ingentem gemitum dat ab imo*, 1.485); "he caught sight of" (*conspexit*, *Aen.*1.487); "he recognized" (*agnovit*, 1.488); and "while Trojan Aeneas looked at these scenes in wonder" (*haec dum Dardanio Aeneae miranda videntur*, 1.494). R. D. Williams 1960, 150, Barchiesi 1997, 275, and Bartsch 1998, 337 draw attention to the passage's focus on the effect of these images on Aeneas. Hexter 1990b advances the opposite view. He argues that the reader chooses how to focus on and interpret the scenes on the temples. This understates the impact of the text's cues. While the reader may have a choice, he nevertheless bases his decision on what he reads, and, simply put, the narrator presents the scenes from Aeneas' perspective. The narrator's framing of this ekphrasis through Aeneas' perception is a Vergilian innovation (DuBois 1982, 35) and, as such, deserves due consideration.

66 Biow 1994, for instance, also acknowledges the possibility that Aeneas could mold his representation of the past to his present context. Through considering Aeneas' story in light of the information the Trojan learned about Dido in *Aeneid* 1, Biow 1994, 233 finds that Aeneas fashions similarities between himself and the Carthaginian queen by "sensitively tailoring his memory to acknowledge mutual bonds as he selectively incorporates her past into his." One example comes in Aeneas' inclusion of a dream-visit by Hector in his narrative, an episode similar to Dido's dream of her murdered husband, Sychaeus. See also, more generally, Fentress and Wickham 1992, 85 on possible motivations for changes in a story: "Every time a tradition is articulated, it must be given a meaning appropriate to the context . . . in which it is articulated. This necessity to reinterpret often lies behind changes within the tradition itself."

development in his understanding of how he should relate to his Trojan past.[67] As Aeneas tells it, the episode represents a pivotal moment in his search for a new homeland as he at last begins to understand how he may productively commemorate Troy.

After several failed attempts to found a city, Aeneas arrives at Buthrotum and finds himself in a location where Troy seems to have been literally recreated. The settlement was founded by two other Trojan refugees: Andromache, Hector's widow, and Helenus, a son of Priam. This unique city compels Aeneas to consider the relationship between past and future. Buthrotum is patterned after Troy in its architecture and geography, and its inhabitants, Andromache foremost among them, behave as if they were still living in that destroyed city. Most scholars claim that Buthrotum is "trapped in a sterile obsession with a dead past"[68] and that, as such, it demonstrates to Aeneas that the past must be left behind in order to succeed in the present.[69]

There are aspects of Aeneas' representation of his visit that can lead to this conclusion, yet his negative observations do not constitute the sum of his portrayal of that city.[70] Attention to the entirety of Aeneas' narrative uncovers the complexity of his reaction to Buthrotum; he does not leave the past behind here, just a certain mode of interacting with it.[71] Helenus and Andromache, together with Aeneas, are all grappling with the same question: how should they commemorate the city they have lost? Aeneas realizes over the course of his visit that the couple memorialize Troy in a manner that is largely static and concrete. While he sees flaws in this practice, he nonetheless marks the comfort they draw from their city,

[67] Brockmeier 2001, 270–1 notes the constructed nature of autobiographical narratives: "Autobiographically important episodes of a life are selected and turned into 'autobiographems' – a selection that cannot but pick a few episodes out hundreds and thousands of candidates . . . Most autobiographical narratives . . . are not primarily told to provide a fabula, the linear story of a life's events, but a *sjuzet*, a particular narrative composition of the fabula." For an extensive consideration of the relation of forms of autobiography to "truth" and "reality," see Freeman 2010, 154–83, esp. 158–9.

[68] P. Hardie 1998, 67. For similar statements, see P. Hardie 1993, 16 7.

[69] A majority of scholars regard Buthrotum as a stale and dead place, one which convinces Aeneas to turn away from his past. See Grimm 1967; Saylor 1970, 27; G. West 1983, 258; E. Henry 1989, 53; Bettini 1997; Reed 2007, 119; and O'Sullivan 2009, 466. A certain number also argue that Aeneas' visit to Buthrotum is almost like a trip to the underworld (Bright 1981, 42; Quint 1982 and 1999; and Hershkowitz 1991).

[70] The tendency to focus only on Aeneas' criticisms may have arisen out of arguments about the *Aeneid*'s compositional order that characterized *Aeneid* 3 "as a blot upon the perfection of the epic" (R. B. Lloyd 1957, 134).

[71] This argument builds upon some recent readings of this episode that acknowledge its nuanced character and point out that Aeneas at least partly empathizes with Helenus and Andromache's commemorative practices (Otis 1964, 260–1; Galinsky 1996, 124; Smith 2005, 74; Horsfall 2006, 235).

understands their impulse to preserve the past, and respects their choice of commemoration. Yet as Aeneas' time in Buthrotum progresses, his own and Helenus' comments make clear that Aeneas will respond to Troy's loss in a fundamentally different way, namely by honoring his destroyed home with a more evolved and less literal type of commemoration.

Aeneas begins to notice Andromache and Helenus' attitude toward the past soon after he arrives on Buthrotum's shores. He is greeted by Andromache, who happens to be performing sacrifices in front of Hector's empty tomb.[72] Shocked at seeing Aeneas, she asks him: "Are you alive? Or, if the kindly light has withdrawn, where is Hector?" (*vivisne? aut, si lux alma recessit, | Hector ubi est?*, 3.311–2). Andromache's mind moves toward recapturing her earlier experiences. Interrupted in the midst of mourning her dead husband, she imagines that she is in the underworld, set to be reunited with Hector. The end of her conversation with Aeneas mirrors this movement toward the past. Noting that Ascanius accompanies him, she asks Aeneas: "Do both his father Aeneas and his uncle Hector at all rouse Ascanius to ancient valor and manly courage?" (*ecquid in antiquam virtutem animosque virilis | et pater Aeneas et avunculus excitat Hector?*, 3.342–3). Andromache's question reveals a belief that past memories can encourage future generations to perform virtuous actions. Yet her subsequent behavior shows that she struggles to productively incorporate the past into her present life. She cries when she is done speaking, a weeping Aeneas describes as "purposeless" (*incassum*, 3.345). These tears echo the ones Aeneas earlier saw her shed before Hector's tomb (3.305), thus encapsulating her initial appearance within a mournful yearning for the past.[73]

Andromache's behavior at the end of Aeneas' visit confirms her desire to re-inhabit old relationships and relive past memories. She again focuses on Aeneas' son and here, even more forthrightly than before, sets Ascanius in the past. The gifts she offers him, consisting of a cloak from Troy and embroidered clothes, communicate her desire for Ascanius to keep a memory of her as a Trojan and retain a Trojan identity himself. She describes the clothes as "monuments of my hands" (*manuum . . . monimenta mearum*, 3.486)[74] and refers to herself as "Hector's wife" (*coniugis Hectoreae*, 3.488). Her last words emphasize this idea (3.488–91):

[72] Quint 1989, 22 draws a parallel between this tomb, "false and empty," and the city of Buthrotum, itself a "factitious copy."

[73] Quint 1989, 23 writes that this "initial meeting establishes the thematic argument of the Buthrotum episode: the dead Trojan past of Hector cannot be brought to life; the Roman future of Aeneas has taken its place."

[74] The giving of gifts as a reminder of oneself is not an odd thing to do in the *Aeneid* (see, e.g., 5.538 and 5.572); the purpose of Andromache's gifts, though, distinguishes her actions, as she is completely focused on recapturing the past.

> cape dona extrema tuorum,
> o mihi sola mei super Astyanactis imago.
> sic oculos, sic ille manus, sic ora ferebat;
> et nunc aequali tecum pubesceret aevo.

> Take the final gifts of your people, o you, lone surviving image to me of my Astyanax. Such were his eyes, his hands, his face. And now he would be becoming a man along with you, at the same age.

Andromache's gifts are just as much a connection for her to the past as they are a commemoration to remember her by in the future. In her eyes, the clothes she presents to Ascanius re-animate her memories of Astyanax, transforming Ascanius into the "image" (*imago*, 3.489) that her son would be if he were alive now. Ascanius exists not as a promise of future Trojan vitality, but rather as a stand-in for its denied present.

If Andromache wants to live in the past by bringing it back to life, then Buthrotum's layout offers her an excellent opportunity to do so. The city and its environs replicate Troy and the Troad in every possible detail.[75] This mimicry first becomes apparent when Aeneas sees Andromache "in a grove by the water of the false Simois river" (*in luco falsi Simoentis ad undam*, 3.302). Then, not much later, he learns how Helenus named the city's land Chaonia from Chaonian Troy. On his tour of the city, Aeneas sees more Trojan details (3.349–51):

> procedo et parvam Troiam simulataque magnis
> Pergama et arentem Xanthi cognomine rivum
> agnosco.

> I go forward, and I recognize little Troy and Pergama made similar to the great citadel, and a dry river named Xanthus.

Aeneas' observations seem to indicate a realization that this static and concrete attempt at commemoration is futile.[76] He calls Buthrotum's Simois "false," notes the disparity in size between Buthrotum and Troy, and remarks that the Xanthus, named after the Trojan River, runs dry. This follows on the heels of his characterization of Andromache's weeping as "purposeless" (*incassum*, 3.345).

Yet this does not constitute the entirety of Aeneas' reaction to the city. There are indications that he understands and even draws strength from

[75] Although it was "common practice for nomenclature to evoke – just as in the manner of the various Troys and Pergamas that we find attested – memories of the homeland" (Horsfall 1989, 18), Buthrotum goes far beyond this.

[76] See Bettini 1997, 11, who argues that Buthrotum copies the past "in a reduced and degraded form."

Helenus and Andromache's commemorative decisions. When recounting his tour to Dido, Aeneas tells her how "I embrace the threshold of the Scaean gate; the Trojans, too, enjoy the friendly city no less" (*Scaeae... amplector limina portae; | nec non et Teucri socia simul urbe fruuntur*, 3.351–2). He also chooses to remain at Buthrotum for a good number of days, partaking in Helenus' hospitality (3.356). At the same time that Aeneas recognizes that Buthrotum can never be Troy, he and his men find a measure of happiness in its familiarity.

Aeneas further expresses these feelings as he prepares to leave. In his farewell speech, he sets out his respect for Helenus and Andromache's way of life (3.493–5):

> vivite felices, quibus est fortuna peracta
> iam sua: nos alia ex aliis in fata[77] vocamur.
> vobis parta quies.
>
> Live happily, you whose fortune has already completed its course. We are called from one fate to another. There is rest for you.

There is a note of admiration, even envy, in Aeneas' departing words.[78] Helenus and Andromache's commemoration of Troy may be nostalgic, but that does not necessarily render it perverse or debilitating.[79] Aeneas recognizes Helenus and Andromache's satisfaction in inhabiting a reconstruction of the past, as the couple has constructed a monument of Troy that fulfills a particular need by offering a specific existence.[80] Aeneas, though, must still puzzle out his future and his approach to commemorating Troy.

In doing so, he will embark on a different tack than Helenus and Andromache. The mode in which Aeneas will commemorate Troy becomes apparent near the end of his visit. Helenus hints at it in his prophecy to the Trojans. He tells Aeneas at the end of his speech "Go on now and raise Troy to the heavens and make it great by your deeds" (*vade age et ingentem*

77 See Horsfall 2006, ad loc. for the possible meanings of *fata*.

78 E. Henry 1989, 53 notes this also. Further evidence for Aeneas' sympathy toward Andromache comes in his near-exact repetition of her words in 3.343 at 12.440 during the course of an order to his son. See pp. 163–4 for discussion of this.

79 Bal 1999, xi makes a similar point about nostalgia in general, and Alcock 2002, 41 remarks that current scholarship is more likely not to automatically treat such attitudes as "negative or . . . neutral developments," but instead to analyze them as an "active strategies of self assertion" (as she herself does at 51 and 96).

80 It is a mistake to separate Helenus' way of commemorating Troy from Andromache's, as Hardy 1991, 163 does. Both characters memorialize Troy in a static way, and the forward-looking aspect of memory that Hardy attributes to Helenus occurs not when he is talking about how he will commemorate Troy, but about how Aeneas will.

factis fer ad aethera Troiam, 3.462).[81] According to Helenus, Aeneas can commemorate Troy by creating an original achievement for that city by his actions. The past and the future are linked, but, in Helenus' formulation, Aeneas does not have to mimic the past in order to honor it.

Helenus' words open up a telling play on size. Earlier on, Aeneas notes that Buthrotum is but a small Troy, especially when its citadel is compared to the Trojan original (3.349–50). By emphasizing the difference in size between the two cities, Aeneas indicates that Helenus' and Andromache's reconstruction falls short of its goal of becoming Troy. More significantly, it hints that a literal commemoration can never replace the original. The original, after all, was more than just a place; it was also the people that populated it and the history that trailed behind it. Now, when Helenus tells Aeneas that he can make Troy "great" (*ingentem*), this designation contrasts with Aeneas' perception of Buthrotum's Troy as "little" (*parvam*, 3.349). By honoring the city metaphorically, Aeneas escapes from a mode of commemoration that aims to replace the original but always, inevitably, falls short. This sort of replicative commemoration is likely what Aeneas intended in his earlier settlement on Crete. When he addressed Apollo's oracle on Delos, he asked the god to "Preserve a second Trojan Pergama" (*serva altera Troiae | Pergama*, 3.86–7),[82] and, when he arrived on Crete, he called his city Pergama and his men rejoiced in the name (3.133). The name of this settlement hinted that it, like Buthrotum, would commemorate Troy through attempting to replicate it. Aeneas' Cretan settlement failed, another indication that this concrete and static mode of commemoration is not suitable for Aeneas. Aeneas can, and must, embark on a new path that will enable him to restore Troy's greatness by producing an original commemoration of the city, not a monument to a lost past.

In his farewell speech Aeneas elaborates on Helenus' indication of this potential mode of commemoration. Aeneas' final words evoke the challenge and reward of a less literal memorial (3.500–5):

> si quando Thybrim vicinaque Thybridis arva
> intraro gentique meae data moenia cernam,
> cognatas urbes olim populosque propinquos,
> Epiro Hesperiam (quibus idem Dardanus auctor
> atque idem casus), unam faciemus utramque
> Troiam animis: maneat nostros ea cura nepotes.

[81] I follow Conington 1884, ad 3.462, in taking *ingentem* as proleptic.

[82] This translation is from Horsfall 2006, 7. As Horsfall 2006, ad loc. notes, *altera* gives the idea of "Troy re-born."

> If ever I will have come to the Tiber and its neighboring fields and I will see the walls given to my race, then, on that day, our kindred cities and our related people, we will make Hesperia one with Epirus (they have the same Dardanus as founder and the same disastrous story), a single Troy in our spirits; may that care remain for our descendants.[83]

These lines outline the idea of an innovative commemoration of Troy that still honors the original.[84] Beginning with a tentative hope that he will one day found a new city, Aeneas moves from a recognition of the background that his city and Helenus' will share to the vision of a joint Troy that will live on into the future. "Spirits" (*animis*) and "descendants" (*nepotes*), two key words in the speech's final line, bring out this idea. Aeneas envisions a city that will not pay homage to Troy through its physical construction or geographical layout, but will instead be part of a joint commemorative venture furthered by humans living in a certain way.[85]

This speech, along with Aeneas' characterization of his visit to Buthrotum, does not signify his "abandonment of Troy,"[86] but rather a decision to pay tribute to its existence in a new way. These differing approaches to commemorating Troy show the variation in ideas about how to honor the past. Commemoration, like memory, is an intensely personal and emotional phenomenon; here each group searches for a degree of fulfillment through honoring the past in the way they deem most appropriate. Although Aeneas sees how Buthrotum satisfies Helenus and Andromache and he too takes some pleasure in that city, his choice to commemorate Troy in his own, less literal way reflects a judgment about what type of memorialization will prove most fulfilling for him.

Looking to the future

In these early scenes in the *Aeneid*, Aeneas struggles to understand how he should relate to Troy. His engagement with memory is an ongoing and imperfect process, one that involves self-deceit and delusion as well as hope and belief: Aeneas tries to cheer his men with words that he does

[83] For the translation of this passage, see Conington 1884, ad 3.502 and Horsfall 2006, ad 3.500f.

[84] E. Henry 1989, 53 is correct to note that Aeneas "at this point has ceased to envy the dead at Troy, but he does envy those who live in some kind of second Troy and do not have to face more struggles." This is true enough, but it does not reflect Aeneas' desire to commemorate Troy while moving forward.

[85] As Putnam 1995, 59 notes, while Andromache still thinks of the past even in parting, Aeneas is "capable of peering ahead in time."

[86] Cairns 1989, 117.

not himself hold true, while the narrator calls into question the comfort Aeneas draws from the commemoration of the Trojan War on Juno's temple. It could even be argued that Aeneas' first speech (1.94–101), where he yearns to secure commemoration by having died like those who fell "before their fathers' faces" (*ante ora patrum*, 1.95), presents social memory as an unrealistic comfort for his death. While Aeneas imagines taking comfort from the prospect of being remembered by his father, a series of parental reactions to the deaths of their children in the epic's second half showcases the bitter grief and anger that remain for those who are left to remember.[87] Yet, at this point in the epic, Aeneas is not thinking from the perspective of those who might remember him. Instead, he is thinking from his own vantage point, and foremost in his mind is the goal of ensuring that both he and his city are not forgotten. This is certainly not an odd desire for a hero to hold, but what makes Aeneas unique is that he is acutely aware of the tenuous nature of memory. Responsible for transforming the ending of one society into the beginning of another, he understands that failure at this task means failure at ensuring his own and Troy's memory.

What makes his charge all the more challenging is that he has come to accept that, even though he is still strongly pulled back to Troy, a return to that city is precisely what the fates forbid. As he tells Dido, if it were up to him, he would go back and rebuild. Instead, prophecies drive him to Italy (4.340–7). Perhaps it is no coincidence that the Cretan settlement Aeneas names after Troy ends miserably, besieged by disease and famine. It is only when Aeneas realizes that he must honor Troy in an innovative way by striking out anew that he can begin to move toward founding a new city. This lesson, seen in Aeneas' recollection of his visit to Buthrotum, appears to be an early indication of how he will come to use his memory upon arrival in Italy. Its effect might even be felt before that time: when Aeneas founds a city on Sicily and names it Ilium and its location Troy (5.756–7), this settlement pointedly is not for him. Rather, it is for those Trojan refugees who have decided to settle in Sicily instead of making the journey to Italy. Going against the advice that he should name the settlement after Acestes (5.718), Aeneas redirects the settlement's force toward Troy in a way that implies that this new city will commemorate the old one through repetition. This action reflects a tension between Aeneas' need to remember his obligations to his fated future and his dedication to commemorating

87 See the discussion of the reactions of Euryalus' mother, Mezentius, and Evander on pp. 143–5, 147, and 152–4. Also, Turnus' focalization of Pallas' death through the eyes of Evander brings out the assumption that a son's death is particularly different for a father to bear (see pp. 148–9).

the past. A bit earlier, Aeneas had pondered whether he should head to Italy or whether he should settle in Sicily, "paying no attention to fate" (*oblitus fatorum*, 5.703). If Aeneas had stayed in Sicily and settled in a city named after Troy, he would have memorialized that city but forgotten his fate. Instead, he remembers his obligations and leaves behind a commemoration of Troy for others to inhabit, a literal move toward Italy that signals a metaphorical abandonment of his own desire to inhabit an exact recreation of his past.

Even while one point of tension moves toward resolution as Aeneas slowly comes to an understanding of how he might commemorate Troy, his opposition with Juno remains just as stark. The two work toward opposite aims in *Aeneid* 1, where the goddess attempts to erase any memory of Troy by drowning the Trojans in the ocean's oblivion and Aeneas is determined to ensure that his men and their struggles are remembered. As if to underscore the depth of their commitment to their respective mnemonic goals, just as *Aeneid* 5 shows Aeneas commemorating Troy for the followers he will leave behind, that book simultaneously underlines the persistence of Juno's memory as a motivating factor in her behavior. As part of the episode centered on Iris' burning of the Trojan ships on Sicily's coast, Juno is described as "not yet sated in her ancient resentment" (*necdum antiquum saturata dolorem*, 5.608) and Venus dismisses any attempt to understand the origins of Juno's fury: "Let that one know the causes of so great a fury" (*causas tanti sciat illa furoris*, 5.788). These phrases recall the narrator's first description of Juno's memory and rage in the epic's proem. "Resentment" (*dolorem*) brings to mind the "violent resentment" (*saevi . . . dolores*, 1.25) of Juno which is tied up in and sparked by her memory,[88] while Venus's mention of "causes" (*causas*) links to the word's two early appearances, both of which are associated with Juno's recollections and rage (*causas*, 1.8 and *causae*, 1.25). These connections are only reinforced by Venus' description of Juno's fury as "so great" (*tanti*), a word which recalls the narrator's opening question about the depths of Juno's memory-fueled rage: "Can there be a wrath so great in the hearts of the gods on high?" (*tantaene animis caelestibus irae?*, 1.11). With Juno's rage and memory still firing her on to destroy the Trojans just as much as they did in *Aeneid* 1, the goddess remains at odds with Aeneas. Their fundamental opposition charges the epic with much of its narrative force, as Aeneas must figure out a way to survive in the face of the considerable obstacles she raises.

[88] *Necdum* appears in 1.25 and 5.608 as well.

Aeneas uses personal connections with other characters in his attempts to meet these challenges, and his relationship with Dido, the subject of the next chapter, shows how he strives, sometimes with success and sometimes with failure, to manage such connections through acts of recollection and commemoration.

CHAPTER THREE

A personal affair
Memories of Dido

Aeneas' interpersonal relationships are crucial to his ability to ensure the Trojans' survival, and no relationship in the *Aeneid* fist aids and then threatens the Trojans' quest as much as Aeneas' dalliance with Dido. Through a case study of Aeneas' interaction with the Carthaginian queen, this chapter explores how Aeneas leverages memory in his dealings with other people on a personal level. His interaction with Dido offers excellent material for such an investigation. The complex and changing currents of their affair are related in greater detail than any other relationship in the *Aeneid*, and recollection and commemoration are central to every one of its stages, from the flattering statements that grace its early conversations to the calculated recriminations and attempts at reconciliation that punctuate Aeneas' departure. An examination of their interactions reveals that Aeneas is fully aware of the rhetorical and emotional force he may gain from appealing to memory, as well as of the fluidity and opaqueness that attend a recollection's status as a representation of the past. This awareness, though, does not always translate into a mastery of memory's ramifications. This chapter argues that Aeneas initially lures Dido into engaging with memory in much the same way as he does, yet he soon finds that their relationship's commemoration outstrips his control, as Dido exercises her own considerable ability to influence how she and Aeneas will be remembered.

A consideration of the pair's interactions calls attention to the power that Aeneas can exercise over memory as well as the power that memory can exercise over him. In his conversations with Dido in *Aeneid* 1, Aeneas turns to memory in order to forge a bond with his host, and he finds success when Dido does the same. The emotional potential of memory, already latent in the pair's interactions, truly comes to the fore after Dido asks Aeneas to tell her of his past, as his metanarratival remarks in *Aeneid* 2 and 3 demonstrate the psychological toll remembering exacts and raise the question of how this narrative will affect Dido. Alongside this, Aeneas' depiction of Sinon's false tale opens up issues of representation and desire. As related to Dido, this episode reveals the potential for a false memory, perfectly calibrated to meet its listeners' needs, to be welcomed with happy belief. In doing so, it serves as an important backdrop to a consideration of the pair's understanding of personal memory, especially in regard to *Aeneid* 4. Here, after Dido first becomes closer to Aeneas because of recollection, she strives to undo any mnemonic ties that link her with the Trojans when she learns that he is set to depart. In the face of this rejection, Aeneas again turns to commemoration, but his efforts ultimately fail against Dido's concerted opposition, raising questions about what his remarkable dedication to memory, coupled with his lack of control over it, portend for his future.

A yearning for solidarity

In Aeneas' first interactions with Dido, he builds on the belief that memories of earlier events can bring a measure of solace and reinforce personal bonds. Aeneas advanced these beliefs in his speeches and his reaction to the seemingly sympathetic commemoration of the Trojan War on Juno's temple. Now, enveloped in a mist that conceals him, Aeneas hears Dido promise to help the Trojans. Having gained some confidence that the situation is safe, Aeneas steps out from the concealing mist and stands before the queen. He promises her that she will always remain with him, even if he must leave her shores (1.607–10):

> in freta dum fluvii current, dum montibus umbrae
> lustrabunt convexa, polus dum sidera pascet,
> semper honos nomenque tuum laudesque manebunt,
> quae me cumque vocant terrae.
>
> So long as rivers will run to the sea, so long as shadows on the mountains will play over the slopes, so long as heaven will feed the stars, your honor and name and praises will always remain, whatever lands call me.

Aeneas promises a mnemonic tie that will outlast any physical connection. In his imagination of the future, Aeneas' bond with Dido will be honored even as the distance between them grows. Aeneas links his dedication to Dido with three everlasting natural processes, thus casting his promise of remembrance as the expected path for him to take. At the same time as his rhetoric implicitly declares that he will not stay at Carthage, it also sets up memory as a process predisposed to bring people closer together and to overcome geographical distance.

Dido picks up on the purpose of Aeneas' words a few verses later. Here she shares an incident from her past (1.619; 623–26):

> atque equidem Teucrum memini Sidona venire . . . 619
> . . . tempore iam ex illo casus mihi cognitus urbis 623
> Troianae nomenque tuum regesque Pelasgi.
> ipse hostis Teucros insigni laude ferebat
> seque ortum antiqua Teucrorum a stirpe volebat.

> And I indeed remember that Teucer came to Sidon . . . Already from that time Troy's fall was known to me, along with your name and the Pelasgian kings. Teucer himself, although an enemy, used to say that the Trojans were of noteworthy renown, and he maintained[1] that he had been born from the Trojans' ancient race.

Dido represents her earlier memory of Trojan fame as predisposing her to help Aeneas now. Relying only on Dido's words, it is impossible to ascertain exactly what relationship there is between her representation of the past and her interaction with Teucer years ago. Did she ever meet this warrior? If so, did he say these things about the Trojans? Much easier to grasp than Dido's experience is how her current representation of Teucer's visit introduces her own wish for a connection with the Trojans. Her depiction of Teucer centers on his admiration for the Trojans and his belief that he actually sprang from Trojan ancestry. In Dido's speech the confusion of names between Teucer (*Teucrum*, 619) and Trojans (*Teucros*, 625) extends to a confusion of identities, as a Trojan enemy claims to be a Trojan himself. Dido's exposition of this confusion hints at how she too blurs her own identity by means of this recollection: her long-ago interaction with Teucer stands as a proxy for the personal connection with Aeneas she lacks.[2]

Dido soon brings up another memory in her bid to convince Aeneas that she understands his plight. She tells him the she has also experienced the pain of having to flee her homeland (1.628–31):

> "me quoque per multos similis fortuna labores
> iactatam hac demum voluit consistere terra;
> non ignara mali miseris succurrere disco."
> sic memorat.[3]

[1] For this interpretation of *volebat* see Conington 1884, ad loc.; Austin 1971, ad loc.; and *OLD* 18.

[2] Hardy 1991, 185 notes that Dido and Aeneas "share, at first, no direct, personal connections" and that their relationship "begins . . . with memory that forges connections."

[3] Although *memorat* in line 631 is explicitly used to indicate Dido is speaking, the verb may also call attention to memory's role in her decision to help the Trojans. See pp. 11–13.

> "Fortune wished that I also, tossed about through many similar toils, stand on this land at last. Not unacquainted with hardship, I am learning to help the wretched." Thus she speaks.

Dido's representation of her past is strikingly similar to Aeneas' own history. It is not likely that she gives herself such a history by chance. She already claimed knowledge about Aeneas' race and Troy's destruction prior to the Trojans' arrival, and she presently crafts a memory that draws upon details from two Trojan speeches, one spoken by Ilioneus, the other voiced by Aeneas and partially quoted above. Both these speeches describe what the Trojans suffered in the past and are suffering now, and Dido endows her story with a series of details which match up with the Trojans' past: the role of fortune or fate, the multitude of labors, the trials at sea, and the eventual arrival upon land.[4] In addition to presenting memories with content quite close to the Trojans' pasts, she also puts her recollection to a purpose very similar to Aeneas. Although she could not know it, her assertion that she is "not ignorant of hardship" (*non ignara mali*) echoes Aeneas' statement to his men that "we are not ignorant of earlier disasters" (*neque . . . ignari sumus ante malorum*, 1.198), and it advances memory as a force to bring people together who have experienced like misfortunes.

While Dido adroitly and actively fashions the themes of her past to match those of the Trojans, the narrator also reveals how her memory is manipulated by someone close to Aeneas. Concerned for her son's safety at Carthage, Venus moves to secure the queen's love for him. As part of her plan, she tells Cupid to go to Dido in the guise of Ascanius. Once the god arrives in Dido's palace, she is immediately taken with the boy she supposes to be Aeneas' son (1.717–22):

> haec oculis, haec pectore toto
> haeret et interdum gremio fovet inscia Dido
> insidat quantus miserae deus. at memor ille
> matris Acidaliae paulatim abolere Sychaeum
> incipit et vivo temptat praevertere amore
> iam pridem resides animos desuetaque corda.

> Dido clings to him with her eyes, with her whole heart, and now and then caresses him in her lap, not knowing how great a god

[4] The links are many: Fortune/fate – Ilioneus: 1.546; Dido: 1.628. Labors – Aeneas 1.597; Dido: 1.628. Trials at sea – Ilioneus 1.524, 1.535–8, 1.551; Aeneas: 1.596, 1.598; Dido 1.629. Arrival on land – Ilioneus: 1.528, 1.538; 1.541; Dido: 1.629. Particular emphasis is given to the link between Dido's and Ilioneus' references to landfall; both use the same words to express this action (*consistere terra*, 1.541=1.629) and both phrases appear in the same metrical seat.

> sits upon her, to her sorrow. But that one [Cupid], since he is mindful of his Acidalian mother, begins to efface the memory of Sychaeus bit by bit and tries to preoccupy her long listless spirit and her long unaccustomed heart with a living love.

Cupid causes Dido to forget her dead husband Sychaeus, a forgetting that directly contradicts the queen's wishes.[5] Through a cunning verbal play the narrator emphasizes Dido's lack of control over her memory. Lines 718 and 719 both end with an adjective followed by a noun, a parallel structure that calls attention to an important difference. While Dido lacks knowledge, Cupid is mindful of his mother's orders.[6] He knows and remembers them. The play continues in line 720, where Cupid causes Dido to forget. The lack of an explicit word referring to Dido's memory contrasts with the narrator's use of such language to note Cupid's mindfulness of his mother. This transfer of the language of memory from the place where it is expected (Sychaeus) to where it is not (Cupid) is emphasized by the narrator's innovative use of *abolere*: this is the first time the verb denotes the erasure of a person from memory.[7] If Cupid may be allegorized as Dido's desire, then the narrator points out how her old passion returns, but not its object.[8] In the narrator's depiction of this change, Dido is incapable of contesting this forgetting, an oblivion which she would never choose and which leads to her suicide.[9]

The fatal repercussions of Dido's engagement with memory resurface at the end of a feast welcoming the Trojans. Having already knit her past together with the Trojans', Dido now attempts to do the same with their future. Circling back to Aeneas' original vow that her name will forever remain with him, Dido prays to Jupiter: "May you wish this day to be a happy one both for the Tyrians and for those who set out from Troy, and may you wish for our descendants to remember it" (*hunc laetum Tyriisque diem Troiaque profectis* | *esse velis, nostrosque huius meminisse minores*, 1.732–3). Just as Aeneas hopes that his men would one day recollect their earlier trouble with pleasure, Dido looks to a time when the present will be remembered. She envisions a future when the descendants of the Trojans

[5] 4.321–3 shows how Dido yearned to be remembered for her singular devotion to Sychaeus alone.

[6] Line 719 is unusual in that ictus and accent do not coincide in the fifth and sixth feet. (See Austin 1971, ad 1.199; and R. F. Thomas 1988, 30–1.) This, along with the bucolic diaeresis after *deus*, give *at* ("but") a strong emphasis.

[7] See *OLD* 3 and *TLL* 117.34–6.

[8] This is consistent with Dido's recognition of the return of her earlier feelings of love in *Aeneid* 4: "I recognize the traces of the old flame" (*agnosco veteris vestigia flammae*, 4.23).

[9] See Hill 2004, 111 on the evidence that Dido sees herself at fault for breaking her promised fidelity to Sychaeus and that this is a significant reason for her suicide.

and Carthaginians will honor the day she welcomed the Trojans to her court. Her imagined future captures the idea that memory may offer the opportunity for happiness and the formation of communal bonds. The very next line, though, casts a shadow over her request: "May Bacchus, the giver of joy, be present and gracious Juno" (*adsit laetitiae Bacchus dator et bona Iuno*, 1.734). Dido's wish for Juno's presence does not augur well for this shared memory, and the same could be said of her request to Bacchus. The goddess' hatred of the Trojans is explicit, and Dido's prayer may even foreshadow the role, disastrous for her, that Juno will play in effecting her "marriage" to Aeneas in *Aeneid* 4. The queen's request for Bacchus' presence foreshadows her mad run through the city in *Aeneid* 4; here, Aeneas' departure dooms Dido's wish that his day of arrival be remembered as happy one, and her reaction to this knowledge is likened to that of a Bacchant (4.300–3). Furthermore, the audience's knowledge of the three Punic Wars to come likewise undercuts her prayer. Through a potent mixture of her desire and Aeneas' charismatic fame, Dido gladly mirrors his approach to memory, but, at the end of *Aeneid* 1, there is already doubt about the repercussions of her decision.

Re-experiencing the past

At the close of *Aeneid* 1, Aeneas is forced to confront his past. Inflamed with love for the Trojan, Dido wants to hear about the Greeks' treachery, Troy's fall, and Aeneas' search for a new home. What Aeneas says to Dido reveals much in terms of his attitude toward remembering and sharing the past with another. Most essentially, his introduction of his story and the comments that he intersperses throughout show that he regards retelling his past as an act of recollection and that emotion is central to this process. He characterizes himself as re-experiencing the earlier pain once caused by these past traumatic events as well as the new pain provoked by remembering them. This focus on emotion nearly makes the events secondary to the telling.

The opening words of Aeneas' reply showcase the fresh hurt that springs from retelling a horrible past. At first Aeneas tells Dido that he simply cannot comply with her request (2.3–8):

> infandum, regina, iubes renovare dolorem,
> Troianas ut opes et lamentabile regnum
> eruerint Danai, quaeque ipse miserrima vidi
> et quorum pars magna fui. quis talia fando
> Myrmidonum Dolopumve aut duri miles Ulixi
> temperet a lacrimis?

> Unspeakable, queen, is the grief you order me to renew, how the Greeks destroyed Trojan power and Troy's lamentable kingdom, most wretched things which I saw myself and of which I was a great part. Who of the Myrmidons or Dolopes or what soldier of harsh Ulysses could refrain from tears in the telling of such events?

Infandum – "unspeakable" – is a strange word with which to begin a story, as it suggests that there will be no story at all.[10] The events of the Trojan War evoke emotions so painful that Aeneas is unwilling to re-experience them. At the epic's beginning Juno used her memories to stoke her own "violent resentment" (*saevi . . . dolores*, 1.25), but now, when *dolor* again appears in connection with memory, it signifies a mixture of anguish and grief.[11] These emotions, known only to those who have lived through trying times and now remember them, hold Aeneas back.[12] Primo Levi, writing on memory and trauma, evokes the challenges that face someone like Aeneas who is asked to tell of a difficult past: "The memory of a trauma suffered . . . is itself traumatic because recalling it is painful or at least disturbing: a person who was wounded tends to block out the memory so as not to renew the pain."[13] The Trojan War was so traumatic that even the victors would take no pleasure in recounting it: Greek soldiers, Aeneas say, would weep when recalling its events.

So why, then, if remembering the war is an exercise in sorrow for victor and vanquished alike, does Aeneas tell his story? He does so, he says to Dido, for her sake (2.10–3):

> sed si tantus amor casus cognoscere nostros
> et breviter Troiae supremum audire laborem,
> quamquam animus meminisse horret luctuque refugit,
> incipiam.

> But if you feel so great a yearning to learn about our defeat and to hear in brief Troy's final struggle, although my mind shudders to remember and has recoiled in grief, I will begin.

[10] There is a tension here, sparked by the etymological links between *infandum* and *fari*, centered on the need to say something that cannot be rendered in words. See Conington 1884, ad loc. and ad 1.525; and Commager 1981, 102 on this wordplay. Aeneas already described Troy's sufferings with this same word in his first interaction with Dido: "Troy's unspeakable labors" (*infandos Troiae . . . labores*, 1.597).

[11] For the meaning of *dolor* at 1.25, see *OLD* 3; for 1.3, see *OLD* 2.

[12] MacDonald 1987, 23–4 comments on the emotional involvement shown by this beginning.

[13] Levi 1988, 12.

Dido's desire overcomes Aeneas' reluctance to share his past. The relationship between Aeneas and Dido is just beginning, and its erotic potential, if sensed at all by either person, is still unexpressed. Yet by connecting Dido's yearning with his own past, Aeneas picks up on how she has already used her memories of Teucer to forge a personal connection between the two. Now, she wishes to hear his memories. These memories will also help to build a bond.

When Aeneas at last declares that he will tell his story, the dramatic verb "I will begin" (*incipiam*) itself begins a line, and it cuts off Aeneas' lingering portrayal of the emotional trauma remembering entails. Although Aeneas agrees to Dido's request, the construction of this passage questions whether he can satisfy her wish. The first and last words of Aeneas' reply encapsulate the challenge of remembering a horrific past: *infandum* (2.3) and *incipiam* (2.13). Linked by their shared metrical seat and common initial syllable, Aeneas' signal that he will begin (*incipiam*) recalls his indication that he could not (*infandum*), a connection that paradoxically grounds his story on the impossibility of verbalizing his memories. Dido will hear Aeneas' story, but the emotional pain of that experience and its recollection is simply incommunicable.

Right before Aeneas tells Dido he will begin his tale, he frames his narrative as one grounded in memory and grief: "My mind shudders to remember and has recoiled in grief" (*animus meminisse horret luctuque refugit*, 2.12). The different tenses of these two verbs offer a precise portrait of Aeneas' relation with earlier events and the emotions they inspire.[14] The perfect *refugit* shows that Aeneas has moved away from the past,[15] while the present *horret* indicates that he recognizes what a fresh engagement with these events may mean for him. Aeneas inverts the chronology of the two actions, setting the later action (*horret*) first since he now faces it directly and it occupies his mind to a greater extent than the earlier action (*refugit*). It is revealing that Aeneas chooses *meminisse* to characterize the process that lies at the heart of narration. When Dido asked him to relate his story, she did so with a simple verb of speech, "tell" (*dic*, 1.753). Now

[14] Contra Servius, who claims that "Vergil used the perfect tense in place of the present tense on account of meter" (*propter metrum pro praesenti praeteritum*). Austin 1964, ad loc. also argues that a difference in time and aspect should be understood between *horret* and *refugit*, although he minimizes the temporal difference between the two actions: "the spirit 'has started back' and 'is shivering', but both actions are so close in time and in relation that it makes no difference which is mentioned first."

[15] The object of *refugit* is left vague; it is likely Aeneas' past or the activity of recollecting that past. A parallel exists for the verb to take the infinitive (Sen. *Ag.* 417), although that construction is rare (see *OLD* 6). Conington 1884, ad loc. construes the infinitive *meminisse* with both *horret* and *refugit*.

Aeneas demonstrates that, in his eyes, his task depends on recollection. The injunction "tell" is simple and flavorless, devoid of any implication; Aeneas rebuts this characterization of his narration, instead grounding it in emotion and recollection.[16]

The details of this process are elaborated in a series of remarks in Aeneas' tale. Coming in the forms of apostrophes and metanarratival comments, these authorial interventions give Aeneas' narrative a certain focus and tinge it with a particular emotional coloring. His representation of earlier events becomes as much about how Aeneas feels as it is about the events themselves. His audience can only regard Aeneas' past through the lens of his storytelling, and Aeneas' emotional emphasis falls squarely on the horrendous events that shook him the most, not on the hopeful signs he received along the way through prophecy or divine intervention.

Several apostrophes reveal how Aeneas remembers and re-experiences the emotions associated with his past. The emotions Aeneas attaches to these events do not change the facts, but they do make his feelings as much a focus of his narrative as the events themselves. One apostrophe comes near the beginning of his story, when Aeneas imagines what could have been if the Trojans had uncovered the Greeks' ruse (2.54–6):

> et, si fata deum, si mens non laeva fuisset,[17]
> impulerat ferro Argolicas foedare latebras,
> Troiaque nunc staret, Priamique arx alta maneres.

> And, if the will of the gods had not been hostile, if our mind had not been blind, then Laocoön would have driven us to befoul the Greek hiding places with swords, and Troy would now stand, and you, high citadel of Priam, would remain.

Invoking the presence of Troy and its leader, Aeneas' address of Priam's citadel vocalizes the futile wish that this destruction would not have occurred. The verb *impulerat* in line 55, which literally means "he had driven," reveals Aeneas' bitter anguish. Its indicative mood represents the event as actually having happened, yet Aeneas and his audience know that it did not: Laocoön was killed by a pair of snakes before he could convince the Trojans to destroy the horse.[18] The apostrophe casts a feeling of fresh pain over Troy's irrevocable destruction, bringing the audience's perception of the events closer to Aeneas'.

[16] Gasti 2006, 116 also notes how 2.1–13 makes Aeneas' narrative dependent on memory.

[17] For a bibliography and discussion of the syntax, meaning, and translation of line 54, see Horsfall 2008, ad loc.

[18] See Austin 1964, ad loc. and Horsfall 2008, ad loc. on this verb.

Another apostrophe in Aeneas' narrative likewise places the emotion, and not the event, at the center of his memory. Much later in his story, with the Trojans in the seventh year of their search for a new home, Aeneas' father dies (3.708–11):

> hic pelagi tot tempestatibus actus
> heu, genitorem, omnis curae casusque levamen,
> amitto Anchisen. hic me, pater optime, fessum
> deseris, heu, tantis nequiquam erepte periclis!

> Here, having been driven by so many sea-storms, alas, I lost my father Anchises, solace of all my cares and trials. Here, best father, alas you desert me in my exhaustion, you who were snatched in vain from so many dangers!

Again, an apostrophe forms the peak of an emotionally charged recollection. The feelings it captures – loss tinged with frustration, a hint of angry bewilderment directed at fate – become the center of Aeneas' narrative, with the events that caused them relegated to a secondary importance. The focus on Aeneas' feelings hints at an ongoing process of selection and emphasis.[19] Aeneas focuses, consciously or not, on the events from his past that exert a great emotional force upon him.

Aeneas' comments on his narrative also call attention to the selective nature of his story and the emotional demands he feels while representing the past. Aeneas usually voices these metanarratival remarks right before particularly dreadful moments in his narrative, and they testify to the challenge involved in retelling the past.[20] As twin snakes glide toward Laocoön and his sons, Aeneas exclaims: "I shudder at recalling these things" (*horresco referens*, 2.204);[21] as Troy's destruction nears its grim climax, he asks: "Who could unfold the disaster of that night, who could unfold the deaths in speech or be able to equal the suffering with tears?" (*quis cladem illius noctis, quis funera fando | explicet aut possit lacrimis aequare labores?*, 2.361–2);[22] and as Aeneas hesitates before describing how blood issued forth

[19] There are two other apostrophes in Aeneas' narrative, both of them addressed to Troy (2.241–2 and 2.431–4) and both of which function in much the same way as the ones addressed above.

[20] Lynch 1980, 170 writes of *Aeneid 2* that "Aeneas' narrative . . . is fast-paced, almost breathless; it has the flavour and emotional intensity of an eye-witness account rather than a retelling of a past experience." Lynch is correct to note the eye-witness nature of Aeneas' tale (see especially p. 178 n. 1), but Aeneas' comments on his narrative and inclusion of later knowledge make clear that he is remembering past experiences.

[21] For this meaning of *referre*, see *OLD* 17 and 18.

[22] Gasti 2006, 117 remarks how this passage brings up "doubts about the communicative power of poetic language." In doing so, it hearkens back to Aeneas' statement about the impossibility of telling his story to Dido.

from a bush at Thrace, he wonders, "Should I speak or be silent?" (*eloquar an sileam?*, 3.39).[23] These comments focus on Aeneas' process of recalling the past and the emotions he experiences while doing so.

Along with the apostrophes in his narrative, such remarks call attention to the singularity of Aeneas' story. The precise transformation Aeneas effects between the events he experienced and his representation of them will be forever unknown, but these comments offer traces of his struggle with that transformation. Ultimately, Aeneas' story represents what he deems worthy of remembering and reflecting upon.[24] Although Dido and the Trojans have certain expectations about the general outline of Aeneas' story, he enjoys a considerable amount of latitude in his selection, emphasis, and perspective, and his choices construct a unique memory that represents his past differently from how another person would. Even if Aeneas desired, it is unlikely that he could relay a memory that completely and accurately represents the events as he originally underwent them and that would match another person's recollection in every detail. The singularity of each individual makes that impossible,[25] along with the challenge of remembering every detail that occurred.[26]

In one sense, this inevitable failure to accurately portray the past makes Aeneas' memory false.[27] In another sense, though, Aeneas' selection and shaping of the events make his story a remarkable indication of who he desired to be in the past and who he wishes to be now. At the core of Aeneas' construction of his personal history is his self-representation. From Dido's perspective, he portrays himself to be one who is reluctant to comply with her request, but eventually fulfills it in its entirety. The bare contents of his story, in its halting but ineluctable progress from Troy's ashes to a location for a new city, show that he is now directed toward Hesperia and finding

[23] See 2.506, a verse introducing Aeneas' narration of Priam's death, for another example.

[24] See Casey 1987, xii and Fentress and Wickham 1992, 32 on the transformation of experience via memory. From a narratological perspective Chatman 1978, 37 notes the consequences of the representation of any sequence of events: "Story . . . exists only at an abstract level; any manifestation already entails the selection and arrangement performed by the discourse as actualized by a given medium. There is no privileged manifestation."

[25] Fentress and Wickham, 1992, 36 point out the basic conclusion of early twentieth-century research that "Different individuals remembered differently, using different details as their governing ideas and differing strategies to memorize them." Compare this statement with the claim of Bowie 2008 that Aeneas is an objective narrator in *Aeneid* 2 and 3.

[26] For fictional and non-fictional considerations of a person endowed with such a memory, see Borges 1964 and Luria 1968, respectively.

[27] As Fentress and Wickham 1992, 40 observe, memory has a "subjective and conceptual character. Memory is ordered not like a physical text, but . . . like thinking itself. It is not a passive receptacle, but instead a process of active restructuring, in which elements may be retained, reordered, or suppressed." See also Halbwachs 1992, 39–40.

an appropriate way to commemorate Troy. Yet, while the contents of his story do not explicitly mislead Dido and they certainly communicate that Carthage cannot and will not be his final stop, Aeneas focuses his energy upon where he has been and what he has lost along the way.

The authorial comments that both begin his tale and appear within it set the emotional energy of his recollection upon the pain involved in remembering crucial moments when his losses were cemented with a dread finality. His story's emotional markers, both apostrophes and metanarratival comments, are set almost exclusively in *Aeneid* 2 and its story of Troy's downfall, with the only exceptions coming in his narration of a bloody apparition at Thrace (3.39) and Anchises' death (3.708–11). No equivalent markers, for instance, punctuate the moments in Aeneas' voyage where he makes tangible progress and finds relief, such as when he at last learns the Trojans' destination from the Penates (3.172–9); when he makes his way through a series of Greek islands (3.276–7); or when he finally sights Italy on the horizon (3.521–3). Each of these moments surely could merit a positive emotional reflection as part of Aeneas' retelling, but each receives none. Instead, Aeneas focuses his and his audience's energy on the trauma that first set him on his path and then continued to follow him along his way. Fate may compel him to move on, but Aeneas focuses on the human costs of doing so, not on the headway, hard-won but real, that the Trojans make in their journey. The part of Aeneas' narrative that looks ahead to his founding a new city is de-emphasized, and he establishes an identity for himself, interlaced with the collective identity he constructs for the Trojans, that leaves Dido with a portrait of a suffering man and people, buffeted both by past storms and by the toll of remembering them now, who deserve her sympathy and help.[28]

Sinon's false tale

Early in his narrative of Troy's destruction, Aeneas tells how Sinon convinces the Trojans to bring the large wooden horse left by the Greeks within their city walls. Although only one memory-related word occurs in Aeneas' rendition of this episode, Sinon characterizes his story as a personal account of events he has lived through, and such depictions of one's past are consistently characterized as recollections by the *Aeneid*.[29] One of the most relevant illustrations of this tendency comes a mere sixty lines earlier in Aeneas' introduction to his own story (2.3–13); the conception Aeneas

[28] For more on individual and collective identity, see J. Assmann 2006, 16ff.

[29] See pp. 12–13.

advances there of a personal narrative as an act of memory implies that the Trojans regarded Sinon's story as an act of memory when they heard it. Viewed as such, Sinon's relation of his personal history would encourage certain expectations, not the least of which would be that his story is based on the memory of events that he actually experienced. This, though, is nowhere near the truth. His story is not a recollection at all, but rather a false tale largely unrelated to his past.[30]

On the one hand, Aeneas' description of this episode highlights a costly lesson: that what matters is not the relationship between what is remembered and what occurred, but rather the use to which a "memory" is put within a present context. Yet, at the same time, Aeneas' tale creates a tension around the relationship between memory and knowledge. Even as he reveals how the Trojans were duped by Sinon's false memory, Aeneas' story shows how he has gained knowledge through looking back at the past. At some point before he tells this story to Dido, Aeneas recognized via hindsight how Sinon's tale was utterly false. There are no explicit clues as to when this realization occurred, but it must have somehow been achieved from Aeneas' reflections on his memories.[31] Now, as he remembers this story one more time and commemorates it for the future, Aeneas' narrative reflects the knowledge he has gained from thinking over his memory. His story thus presents two contrary yet coexisting aspects of recollection: a memory of the past can mislead the audience, with disastrous consequences, and a memory of the past can help to uncover a previously unseen reality.

While the Trojans are debating what to do with the mysterious wooden horse on their shore, a group of farmers capture Sinon. The Trojans set to questioning him right away: "We urge him to say from what race he is born, or what he brings" (*hortamur fari quo sanguine cretus, | quidve ferat;* 2.74–5). In orders typical of those given to an unknown stranger, the Trojans demand Sinon's personal history and present purpose. While the theme of memory is certainly not explicit in these questions, the Trojans' next command hints at an assumption that remembering will underlie Sinon's reply: "We urge him to state what trust there is for a captive"

[30] Vergil innovated widely in his depiction of Sinon (Scafoglio 2008), and he may have been the first to depict Sinon as sharing a long and complex false memory.

[31] As part of a larger argument that hindsight yields a measure of self-understanding and the possibility for improvement of one's moral life, Freeman 2010 argues that remembering, while it may sometimes falsify the past in its reconstruction, can also yield a more complete understanding of what actually occurred: Hindsight has a "capacity to yield insight and understanding, indeed *truth* of a certain sort that *cannot* occur in the immediacy of the present moment" (emphases original, p. 173). For more on this idea, see Freeman 2010, 42, 154, 177–8, 180–1, and 185.

(*hortamur... | ... memoret quae sit fiducia capto*, 2.74–5). Context dictates that *memoret* most likely has the surface meaning "to say," but the verb is associated with the idea of remembering through its etymological link with *memor* as well as through its frequent connection in the *Aeneid* with the vocabulary of memory.[32] Aeneas' use of *memoret* leaves the impression that the Trojans were expecting Sinon to recollect what he had actually experienced.

The opening of Sinon's reply picks up on the idea that he will reveal his own past. He seeks to earn the Trojans' trust by stating that what he is about to say is personal and real (2.77–80):

> "cuncta equidem tibi, rex, fuerit quodcumque, fatebor
> vera," inquit; "neque me Argolica de gente negabo.
> hoc primum; nec, si miserum Fortuna Sinonem
> finxit, vanum etiam mendacemque improba finget."

> "I will tell you the whole truth, king, whatever occurred," he says; "and I will not deny that I am of the Greek race. This is the first thing; indeed, if Fortune has made Sinon wretched, she will not also shamelessly make him out to be false and lying."

Sinon prefaces his answer by stating that he will tell everything (*cuncta*) and that it will all be true (*vera*), words highlighted by their placement at the beginning of consecutive lines and the extraordinary hyperbaton generated by these positions. To emphasize once again that he is telling the truth, he denies the possibility that he could be speaking falsely: his is not the character of a liar or charlatan, even if Fortune has set him in a wretched spot. Sandwiched between these claims of veracity is an admission so damning that it could never be made up: Sinon is Greek.[33] By starting his story with this confession, Sinon predisposes his captors to believe whatever he will say. For if Sinon admits he is Greek, the thinking goes, then he cannot be a liar; no Trojan captive would willingly sign his own death warrant by falsely claiming to be an enemy. In setting up his speech as a rendition of his personal experience, Sinon fosters the belief that the events he recalls actually occurred and that a reference point exists for them.

Sinon's speech builds on this opening. He crafts an entrancing explanation for his predicament, the precise details of which – how his poor

[32] See pp. 11–13 and the comment from Servius quoted on p. 13 n. 47.

[33] Hexter 1990a argues that Sinon plays with the truth in his speech and nearly lets the Trojans in on his duplicity. While Sinon flirts with revealing his actual situation, his speech's surface is almost completely composed of lies.

father sent him to accompany Palamedes to Troy, how he kept on recklessly bemoaning his companion's unjust death, how he narrowly escaped Odysseus' plan to have him killed – dress his story in the garb of a trustworthy personal narrative. Sinon renders this masquerade all the more believable by vouching for his words at a critical point in his story. As he draws tantalizingly close to revealing the horse's purpose, Sinon asks for the Trojans' faith: "Only may you, Troy, stand by your promises and, saved, maintain your faith, if I will bear the truth and make a large return" (*tu modo promissis maneas servataque serves | Troia fidem, si vera feram, si magna rependam*, 2.160–1).[34] This request adroitly plays on an order Priam just gave Sinon: "Explain these things to me truly when I ask" (*mihi . . . haec edissere vera roganti* (2.149). Priam sets a premium on receiving true answers to his questions, and Sinon cleverly links the truth with Troy's safety. The salvation he offers exploits the Trojans' willingness to think that their city can be saved, and, thus, he induces them to stand by their word and believe that he does the same.

Sinon's story exploits the Trojans' willingness to assume the legitimacy of a supposedly personal recollection. His success is ultimately grounded in a simple belief about the history of another. As Iwona Irwin-Zarecka writes, "When the past we attend to is not ours, the experiential base principle translates into the common sense idea that 'memory' has a reference, a reality it connects us to."[35] In Aeneas' re-telling, Sinon takes advantage of this "experiential base principle." His trickery, predicated upon the Trojans' assumption that a representation of one's past is grounded in reality, allows him to pass off a false story as an account of actual experience. Looking back on these events as he narrates the story to Dido, Aeneas knows that this pivotal speech was entirely constructed and that Troy fell because there was a gulf between the past that Sinon claimed for himself and the events that preceded his capture. In narratological terms, Sinon uses his story to construct a supposed reality (a "fabula") that in fact has little connection with the events that he experienced.[36] This stretch of Aeneas' own personal history, now so vividly recollected, surely has an impact on his and his audience's understanding of how the past can be misrepresented in the service of a particular aim. At the same time, though, Aeneas' story also

[34] This echoes another appeal Sinon made for the Trojans' pity just a bit earlier, where he implicitly claimed his story to be true by appealing to "divinities, knowing of the truth" (*conscia numina veri*, 2.146).

[35] Irwin-Zarecka 1994, 18. On the same page, Irwin-Zarecka offers another observation that could certainly apply to Sinon's fabrications: "Even, or perhaps especially, stories with no base in reality would frequently represent themselves as accounts of actual events."

[36] See Culler 1980, 32 and Bal 1997, 5.

reveals how he now understands Sinon's manipulations, a comprehension which he and the rest of the Trojans originally lacked.

Unraveled memories

Aeneas' two-book-long narrative constructs both his and the Trojans' past. When he brings his story to a close at the end of *Aeneid* 3, there is no doubt that he has fulfilled Dido's request to hear his history and to have the chance to become closer to him through doing so. In this respect, Aeneas' story is not unlike Sinon's, in that each offers his audience a constructed recollection of the past that they want to hear. While Aeneas, unlike Sinon, does not baldly lie about major events in his personal history (Aeneas is constrained by Dido's knowledge of the Trojan War),[37] he nonetheless does shift how his past is perceived by throwing an emotional spotlight on only some of its aspects.[38] This emotional intensity inherent in Aeneas' act of remembering guides Dido's reaction. Its energy soon spreads to the queen: "Aeneas' face and words linger in her heart, fixed there, and care does not give her limbs peaceful rest" (*haerent infixi pectore vultus | verbaque nec placidam membris dat cura quietem*, 4.4–5).[39] As time passes, Dido yearns to hear Aeneas recite his story again (4.77–9):

> nunc eadem labente die convivia quaerit,
> Iliacosque iterum demens audire labores
> exposcit pendetque iterum narrantis ab ore.
>
> Now with the day ending she seeks the same banquets, and again in a frenzy she demands to hear the labors of Troy and again she hangs upon every word of his tale.

Dido wishes to recapture her initial experience of hearing Aeneas' recollection, a memory of him reciting his memories. A clear marker of what aspect of those memories exercised the greatest impact on her, the phrase "the labors of Troy" (*Iliacos . . . labores*, 4.78), specifically asks for another telling of the story of Troy's destruction,[40] those devastating experiences emphasized by Aeneas' emotional markers in *Aeneid* 2, not the unmarked

[37] This knowledge is evident in the scenes of that war on Juno's temple (1.446–93), and Dido states herself that she knows about Aeneas' race and Troy's destruction (1.565–8).

[38] See also Biow 1994 on how Aeneas may reshape the contents of his story.

[39] Most 2001, 162 notes the formative effect of Aeneas' own emotions on his listeners. Baraz 2009, 319 observes that these lines show Dido's "inability to separate herself from the agent of destruction."

[40] As Conington 1884, ad loc. notes, these words recall the phrase "Troy's final struggle" (*Troiae supremum . . . laborem*, 2.11), which designates Troy's final day.

events of *Aeneid* 3 which paced the Trojans' slow but steady progress in their search for a new city.

Dido's relationship to Aeneas' memories is not entirely dissimilar from what Marianne Hirsch terms "postmemory." Hirsch writes that postmemory describes the "relationship of children of survivors of cultural or collective trauma to the experience of their parents, experiences that they 'remember' only as the stories and images with which they grew up, but that are so powerful, so monumental, as to constitute memories in their own right."[41] While Dido and Aeneas are not parent and child, Aeneas' rendition of the Trojans' trauma has the potential to become a memory in its own right for Dido. Aeneas has portrayed Troy's downfall as the most traumatic aspect of his past, and this is what Dido wants to hear again and again, searching for a way to make his memories hers, a postmemory as Hirsch terms it. Dido's earlier story of her interaction with Teucer already blurred the line between her identity and Trojan identity. Now that she has heard the Trojans' story, she asks to hear it again so that the Trojans' experiences may become her memories and their identities may meld further.

As Dido's interest in Aeneas' memories builds, she learns that he is preparing to leave. Soon the couple's interactions change drastically. Aeneas, who earlier had manipulated his men, Dido, and perhaps even himself in advancing the belief that memory can build a bond and offer solace, comes to find that these sorts of promises fail him now. Memory devolves from a mechanism of communication and empathy to a locus for misunderstanding and animosity, a change embodied in two disagreements. Both disagreements center on Aeneas and Dido's relationship, the first on its precise meaning in the present, the second on its significance in the future.

While the question of whether or not Aeneas and Dido are married has long been a crux of Vergilian scholarship,[42] the focus here is not so much on establishing the status of their relationship as on exploring how they offer different renditions of a specific incident that may have resulted in their marriage. As each puts forth a claim, the line between recollection and interpretation becomes heavily blurred. Dido and Aeneas' understanding of their shared experience influences what they remember about it, and, conversely, their memories of the event impact their understanding. This

41 Hirsch 1999, 8.

42 For recent bibliography on this question, see Gutting 2006, 272 n. 33. Gutting argues that the couple's relationship is ambiguous and problematic since it challenges the polarization of "the conjugal and erotic worlds" (278).

reciprocal process means that, even if neither is lying, the only conclusion each can come to is that the other is not telling the whole truth.

The result of Dido and Aeneas' meeting in a cave is unclear from the start, and such ambiguity provides fertile ground for the growth of opposing memories and interpretations. As part of a plot to keep Aeneas in Carthage, Juno tells Venus of her plan for Dido and Aeneas to arrive at the same cave in order to escape a rainstorm. Once they are inside, Juno says (4.125–7):

> adero et, tua si mihi certa voluntas,
> conubio iungam stabili propriamque dicabo.
> hic hymenaeus erit.

> I will be present and, if your will is resolved, I will join them in a steadfast marriage and I will give Dido over as his. This will be their wedding.

Juno envisions a wedding that results in a marriage. Venus' reaction, however, implies that she might not allow this to occur: "Venus nodded, not opposed to what Juno was seeking, and she laughed at the discovered treachery" (*non adversata petenti | adnuit atque dolis risit Cytherea repertis*, 4.127–8).

When Aeneas and Dido do make their way into the same cave, the narrator's description of what ensues is far from clear-cut (4.166–72):

> prima et Tellus et pronuba Iuno
> dant signum; fulsere ignes et conscius aether
> conubiis summoque ulularunt vertice Nymphae.
> ille dies primus leti primusque malorum
> causa fuit; neque enim specie famave movetur
> nec iam furtivum Dido meditatur amorem:
> coniugium vocat, hoc praetexit nomine culpam.

> Primal Earth and nuptial Juno give a sign; fires blazed and heaven was a witness to the marriage and the Nymphs yelled from the highest peak. That day was the first day of her death and that first day was the cause of her woe; for neither is Dido moved by outward appearance nor by rumor, nor does she any longer think of her love as clandestine: she calls it marriage, she disguises her affair with this name.

Lines 166–8 give this event every appearance of a marriage: Juno and Earth inaugurate the couple's joining, heaven stands as a witness, and the

Nymphs sing.[43] Yet the narrator's remarks in 172 belie this implication: he pointedly says that Dido covers her adultery with the name of marriage. This conflict between the divine actions and the narrator's interpretation cannot be easily resolved. To compound this problem, the event lacks any human witnesses who could offer a common memory of what occurred.

No agreement exists between Aeneas and Dido about what happened in the cave. While the narrator's account fosters ambiguity, that quality is missing from the couple's recollections. In conversations with Aeneas, Dido matter of factly characterizes their relationship as a marriage. When she calls on the Trojan to remain in Carthage, she begs him "by our wedding, by the marriage we have begun" (*per conubia nostra, per inceptos hymenaeos*, 4.316). As Dido's outrage grows, she pointedly uses the word "guest" and "husband" to contrast Aeneas' present treatment of her with how he ought to behave: "To whom do you leave me at my death, guest (since only this name remains from the name of husband)?" (*cui me moribundam deseris hospes | (hoc solum nomen quoniam de coniuge restat)?*, 4.323–4).[44] Aeneas flatly refutes this. He tells Dido, "I never held out the marriage torches nor did I enter into such an agreement" (*nec coniugis umquam | praetendi taedas aut haec in foedera veni*, 4.338–9). Aeneas and Dido interpret and remember an ambiguous event in entirely different ways.[45] There is a close relationship between their interpretation and memories, and these mental actions are also influenced by the characters' aims to bolster their respective arguments: Aeneas that he must leave Carthage, Dido that he ought to remain. While Dido and Aeneas surely agree on certain things (e.g., that they met in a cave during a rainstorm), it is the details about which they disagree, and, in this case, it is the details that matter.

A second major disagreement between Aeneas and Dido centers on how their relationship ought to be remembered. This argument showcases

[43] See Conington 1884, ad 4.166 and 4.1667 on the aspects of a marriage ceremony these actions might represent.

[44] Dido also characterizes her relationship with Aeneas as a marriage in conversations with other characters; see her words to her sister Anna at 4.431 and 4.496, as well as her complaint in a monologue at 4.550–1, which likely alludes to both of her marriages. While it could be said that Dido's claims of marriage in her conversations with Aeneas and Anna are purely rhetorical and do not reflect her actual belief, Dido speaks these words at 4.550–1 to no one but herself (see 4.533). (For more on the implications of 4.550–1, see Nappa 2007.)

[45] A somewhat similar disagreement can be found in the juxtaposition between Palinurus' recollection of his death and the narrator's. While the narrator describes Palinurus' death as the result of divine action, the character attributes it to the accidental breaking off of a part of the ship. As Bandera 1981, 227 writes, if Palinurus "is not really lying but reporting the event as he could perceive or remember it, . . . [h]is knowledge then would not be downright false but only insufficient." If Aeneas and Dido are not lying, then, like Palinurus, each may simply be relating the event as he or she remembers and understands it.

Aeneas' efforts to convince Dido that he will remember her even as his mental attention turns elsewhere. Dido and Aeneas' dispute strongly recalls the depiction of Ariadne and Theseus in Catullus 64, and a comparison between these two couples illuminates the positions Aeneas and Dido take as the Trojans' parting grows closer.[46] A quick glance at the earlier poem shows that its major plot points confirm this connection. Just as in the *Aeneid*, a woman saves a man's life, believes that she enters into a marriage with him, and feels unjustly abandoned when her "husband" sails off. Memory is likewise central to the pair's actions. In Catullus 64 both Ariadne and the narrator label Theseus as "forgetful" (*immemor*).[47] His mental state is part and parcel of his morally suspect act of abandoning Ariadne on Naxos, and the narrator specifies that Theseus later receives a just reward for his behavior, as he forgets his father's instructions on how to signal his safe return. Aegeus had ordered Theseus to remember to raise a white sail to indicate that he was alive,[48] but "Theseus let all things slip away, in a state of forgetfulness" (*oblito dimisit pectore cuncta*, Cat. 64.208). When Theseus comes home under a black sail, Aegeus commits suicide. The narrator makes clear just what caused Theseus' deadly mistake: "Theseus himself took back such a sorrow as he himself inflicted upon Ariadne with his forgetful mind" (*Theseus, qualem Minoidi luctum | obtulerat mente immemori, talem ipse recepit*, Cat. 64.247–8).[49]

[46] For links between the two poems, see Kepple 1976, 356–7; Hamilton 1993, 252–4; and Nappa 2010, 383–5 and see n. 50 for a verbal echo that connects the two poems as well. Another significant influence on *Aeneid* 4 is Apollonius' *Argonautica*. Memory comes to the fore in Jason's relationship with Hypsiple and Medea, each of whom asks Jason to remember her (1.896–8, 3.1069–71). Jason promises Medea that he will never forget her (3.1079–80), but then she accuses him of having done just that (4.356). (For discussion of the thematization of memory in Apollonius' work, see Fantuzzi and Hunter 2004, 117–26.) With regard to the *Argonautica*, Vergil compresses and complicates the portrait of memory by having two characters construct competing memories.

[47] The narrator describes Theseus as "the forgetful youth" (*immemor . . . iuvenis*, 64.58) and says that Theseus left Ariadne "with a forgetful breast" (*immemori . . . pectore*, 64.123), descriptions echoed by Ariadne's labeling of him as "forgetful" (*immemor*, 64.135). In addition to indicating that Theseus is forgetting Ariadne (and this is surely the basic meaning of *immemor* here, rightly catalogued at *TLL* 447.40–2), the adjective can also imply that one is ungrateful (see *TLL* 447.21–7), a charge which fits Theseus as well. Fordyce 1961, ad 64.58 notes that "*immemor* regularly implies not mere absentmindedness but indifference to one's obligations, ingratitude, or treachery."

[48] "Be sure that these orders remain, buried in your remembering heart, and do not let time erase any of them" (*facito ut memori tibi condita corde | haec vigeant mandata, nec ulla oblitteret aetas*, Cat. 64.231–2).

[49] Confirmation of the connection between the forgetting that leads to Aegeus' death and the forgetting that leaves Ariadne deserted comes in the description of Aegeus' house as "sorrowful" (*funesta*, Cat. 64.246). This adjective recalls Ariadne's use of the related verb *funestet* (64.201) in her prayer that Theseus' homecoming be disastrous: "But, goddesses, may Theseus desecrate himself and his people with such a mind as with which he left me here, alone" (*sed quali solam Theseus me mente reliquit, | tali mente, deae, funestet seque suosque*, 64.200–1).

In Catullus 64, Theseus is justly punished for his immoral forgetting of Ariadne, and this characterization of his behavior and its consequences stands as an important backdrop to Aeneas and Dido's disagreement about what role memory plays in their relationship. Unlike Theseus, who flees while his paramour sleeps, Aeneas, although he initially hides his plans to leave and only approaches Dido once she learns of them, tries to convince her that his commitment to remembering her should soften the blow of this departure. After first appearing open to remembering Aeneas in a positive manner, Dido charges him with forgetfulness and yearns to destroy every pleasant memory of their relationship. To complicate this depiction, the *Aeneid*'s narrator labels Aeneas as forgetful, just as the Catullan narrator does with Theseus, but the specific charge is not that Aeneas forgets Dido, but rather that he does not remember his obligations as a ruler.

Once the queen learns of Aeneas' plans to leave, she tells him of her impossible wish for a living, tangible marker of their relationship (4.327–30):

> saltem si qua mihi de te suscepta fuisset
> ante fugam suboles, si quis mihi parvulus aula
> luderet Aeneas, qui te tamen ore referret,
> non equidem omnino capta ac deserta[50] viderer.
>
> At least if I had conceived some child with you before your flight, if some little Aeneas were playing in my courtyard who could, in spite of it all, recall you by his face, then I would not seem to be completely caught and deserted.

At this point in their discussion, Dido still hopes that she can convince Aeneas to stay, even if only for the winter. The verb *referre* invokes the idea of recalling something from the past, and it reveals Dido's desire to remember Aeneas in a positive way.[51] A living monument of the man who has sailed away, a child fathered by Aeneas could almost cushion the blow of his departure.[52] Dido's method of commemoration is stunningly

[50] *Deserta* further links this passage with Catullus 64, as the adjective *desertus* is used to describe Ariadne's situation at 64.57, 133, and 187. Without knowing it, Dido is portraying herself as Ariadne and Aeneas as Theseus.

[51] See 10.281 where the verb is used with the meaning "to recall" and *OLD* 17. For the idea that memory of an absent person has the power to lessen a lover's pain, see Sappho 94V and 96V, where recollection comforts a lover whose paramour is absent (see Burnett, 1983, 277–313 on these two poems).

[52] Ascanius himself, although the son of Aeneas and Creusa, has already begun to perform such a function at the start of *Aeneid* 4, as Dido appears to take his presence as a consolation for the times when she is not in Aeneas' company (see 4.83–5). (For an opposite view, that Ascanius is not present, but is merely an imagined presence like Aeneas, see Austin 1955, ad 84.)

similar to that of Andromache and Helenus, who construct Buthrotum as a miniature version of Troy. Having heard Aeneas' recollection of his visit to this city and recognized his compassion toward Andromache and Helenus' project, Dido wants to mimic their attempt to recreate an original object on a smaller scale, ineffectual as it might have been.

In his response Aeneas explains why he must go. Scholars often fault Aeneas in these exchanges, arguing that he lacks sympathy and does not at all try to console Dido.[53] While Aeneas' sympathies are difficult to determine[54] and his attempts to communicate with Dido can be termed clumsy, he does make an effort to connect with her. He replies to Dido at length, beginning with an appeal to memory (4.333–6):

> ego te, quae plurima fando
> enumerare vales, numquam, regina, negabo
> promeritam, nec me meminisse pigebit Elissae
> dum memor ipse mei, dum spiritus hos regit artus.

> I will never deny, queen, that you deserve the greatest number of things you can count out in speech, nor will I ever regret remembering Elissa, so long as I remember myself, so long as my spirit controls these limbs.

This is a profound statement. Aeneas crafts an unbreakable link between himself and the Carthaginian queen, making his memory of her coeval with and, implicitly, equivalent to his memory of himself. This speech rebuts any arguments that his leaving of Dido represents a morally faulty instance of forgetting, like that which Theseus committed. Aeneas can and will remember Dido even though he does not stay with her. For him, memory is a tool to confer honor and pleasure through recollecting an old connection.[55]

Echoing a promise Aeneas made to Dido at their initial meeting, this vow, though, may actually undermine Aeneas' argument and irk Dido all

[53] Scholars critical of Aeneas include Page 1893, 417; R. D. Williams 1971, 423; and Lyne 1987, 165. Austin 1955, 106; E. L. Harrison 1989, 20; Feeney 1983, 219; and Reckford 1995/96, 24 argue that Aeneas does the best he can, given the situation.

[54] The narrator makes Aeneas' feelings difficult to judge. For instance, after Anna begs Aeneas to stay and he refuses, tears are shed: "His mind remains unmoved, the tears fall in vain" (*mens immota manet, lacrimae volvuntur inanes*, 4.449). It is unclear whether these tears are Aeneas or Anna's; as Austin 1955, ad loc. comments, "Virgil is purposely ambiguous."

[55] Rodgers 1992, 25 and n. 11 perceptively remarks how Aeneas' vow and, in particular, his characterization of Dido as "deserving" (*promeritam*) try to respond to her earlier claim, "If I did you any service" (*si bene quid de te merui*, 4.317). Even though Dido asked for Aeneas to stay in recognition of all her help, he portrays his promise as a sufficient recognition of his debt to her.

the more. In 1.607–10 (quoted on p. 97), Aeneas linked the duration of his memory of Dido with the presence of a series of natural phenomena, such as the flowing of rivers to the sea or the play of shadows on mountains. His claim implies that it is natural for the person who leaves to remember and praise the one left behind. Now, when Aeneas says that he will remember Dido, he draws upon his earlier promise and implies that this memory will likewise be linked to praise. The striking similarities between these two promises testify to Aeneas' conviction that memory, powerful enough to bring him and Dido together when they first met, can calm her anger and sate her desire for him to physically remain in Carthage. Considered in and of itself, this is a powerful idea, but within the present context of Aeneas and Dido's relationship, it is a potentially thoughtless and hurtful one. Aeneas suggests that he will remember Dido and remain true to her forever, something Dido aspired to do with Sychaeus (4.24–30) but ultimately fell short of accomplishing. Along with reminding Dido of her own failure to remember Sychaeus and her obligations to him, the repeated promise also implies that their relationship is closer to a marriage than Aeneas has acknowledged. Yet this raises more difficulties, as Aeneas' vow to remember Dido would already appear doomed in Dido's eyes. She learned from Aeneas' story, in a speech made by none other than the shade of his recently dead wife Creusa, that Aeneas is destined to find "both reign and royal wife" in Hesperia (*regnumque et regia coniunx*, 2.783).[56] Aeneas attempts to communicate a sense of obligation with this promise, but it has the potential to anger Dido all the more.

After Aeneas goes on to reveal that fate and the gods compel him to depart, Dido responds with rage. Earlier she yearned for a little Aeneas to run about her halls, but now she wants their relationship to have a darker significance. She orders Aeneas (4.381–4):

> i, sequere Italiam ventis, pete regna per undas.
> spero equidem mediis, si quid pia numina possunt,
> supplicia hausurum scopulis et nomine Dido
> saepe vocaturum.
>
> Go, pursue Italy by the wind, seek your kingdom over the waves. Indeed I hope that, if the pious gods have any power, in the middle of the rocks you will drain your punishments and often call out the name Dido.

[56] Dido might also be further discouraged in believing or appreciating Aeneas' offer by the tale she heard Aeneas tell of his loss of Creusa. For in Aeneas' telling forgetfulness played a large role in his loss of his wife (Grillo 2010).

Dido cleverly changes the role of memory. She goes above and beyond severing any link between remembrance and praise by constructing a mnemonically perverse end to Aeneas' life. In hoping that Aeneas calls out her name in the midst of a watery death, she prays for him to remember her at a moment in which he himself will effectively become anonymous, drowned in the waves and never buried.[57] Her prayer, in its address to the gods and hope for a fitting punishment, recalls Ariadne's prayer that Theseus suffer in the same way that she does.[58] Here Dido aims to strip the commemoration of their relationship of any notion of happiness and to leave it linked only with enmity and suffering.[59]

Now, after Dido's conversation with Aeneas ends and she is alone in her palace, she works to further undo the promise Aeneas made at their initial meeting (1.607–10). As part of a plan to conceal her suicide preparations from her sister, Dido tells Anna that she knows magical arts that will either win Aeneas back or rid her of any feelings for him. These arts are so powerful, Dido says, that the one who wields them is able "to stop water in the rivers" (*sistere aquam fluviis*, 4.489).[60] This impossibility is an exact reversal of what Aeneas described in 1.607, where he vowed that Dido's name will remain with him "so long as rivers will run to the sea . . ." (*in freta dum fluvii current . . .*). Two subsequent passages underline Dido's desire to disprove Aeneas' earlier vow. She closes her speech by specifically referencing memory: "It helps to destroy all the monuments of that wicked man" (*abolere nefandi | cuncta viri monimenta iuvat*, 4.497–8).[61] Literally calling Aeneas "unspeakable" (*nefandi*), Dido states that no monuments of him should remain.[62] By ridding herself of any tokens that would influence her future remembrance of Aeneas, Dido is more easily able to enforce her

57 Dido later reaffirms this wish in a curse spoken shortly before her suicide. If, Dido says, Aeneas must reach Italy, then she hopes he dies "unburied in the middle of the sand" (*media . . . inhumatus harena*, 4.620). Kepple 1976, 356–8 considers textual clues which hint that Dido's wish may be fulfilled.

58 See Cat. 64.200–1, spoken by Ariadne: "But, goddesses, may Theseus ruin himself and his people with the sort of mind by which he left me alone" (*sed quali solam Theseus me mente reliquit, | tali mente, deae, funestet seque suosque*).

59 Dido reaffirms this desire at 4.624–9, where she wishes that their relationship be commemorated by enduring enmity between Rome and Carthage.

60 There is no way to know if Dido invents this memory of her visit to the Massylian priestess or if she tailors it to her current purposes. Given that it is part of her manipulation of Anna, it has the look of a fabricated memory.

61 *Abolere* recalls 1.720; there Cupid made Dido forget Sychaeus, and now Dido wants to abolish Aeneas from her memory.

62 The word also recalls Aeneas' description of the effect of telling Troy's story as "unspeakable grief" (*infandum . . . dolorem*, 2.3), an allusion that hints at the pain and anger Dido might feel from remembering Aeneas.

own commemoration of their relationship.[63] Secondly, as Dido draws even closer to her suicide, she sarcastically asks if she ought to sail away with the Trojans "because the gratefulness for an old deed steadfastly remains among the mindful?" (*quiane . . . | et bene apud memores veteris stat gratia facti*, 4.538–9). Here Dido plays upon both meanings of *memor*, as she implies that Aeneas remembers neither her nor his obligations to her.

With this use of "mindful" (*memores*), Dido seeks to undo any claim on Aeneas' part that he can honor her and their relationship via memory. It is as close as Dido comes to leveling the sort of charge of forgetfulness against Aeneas that Ariadne levels against Theseus. Yet what is remarkable in the *Aeneid* is that the narrator depicts Aeneas as forgetful of his obligations to his reign, not of his obligations to Dido. As Aeneas becomes more and more infatuated with Dido and appears closer to remaining in Carthage, his forgetfulness is indicated three times: Rumor (*Fama*) travels around Africa with news of how Aeneas and Dido are "forgetful of their reigns and captured by degrading desire" (*regnorum immemores turpique cupidine captos*, 4.194); Jupiter himself notices that "because of their love, they have forgotten their better reputation" (*oblitos famae melioris amantis*, 4.221); and Mercury, acting on Jupiter's orders, chastises Aeneas: "Alas, forgetful of your reign and your situation!" (*heu, regni rerumque oblite tuarum!*, 4.267).[64] Society at large (indicated by Rumor's wide-ranging journeys), as well as the gods, focuses on how Dido and Aeneas forget their obligations as rulers[65] even as memory plays a very different role in their relationship. Since Aeneas chooses to leave after Mercury informs him of his forgetfulness of his responsibilities as a ruler, his departure can even be characterized as an act of remembering. Unlike Theseus, who was shown to be forgetful of Ariadne, Aeneas, according to the gods and *Fama*, was forgetful of his larger obligations to his reign and, ultimately, to Rome itself. By transferring this charge of forgetfulness to Aeneas' rule, the narrator partly exculpates him for his leave-taking.

Yet Dido fights, powerfully and dramatically, against any suggestion that Aeneas remembers or that he ought to be remembered. In her mind, when

[63] As Goud and Yardley 1988, 386 note, Dido claims to Anna that she builds the pyre in order "to erase the memory of Aeneas by a symbolic funeral." This will effect a clean slate onto which Dido can project her own commemoration.

[64] For a use of *oblitus* similar to those cited above, see 5.703: here Aeneas wonders if he should give up his quest and settle in Sicily, "paying no attention to fate" (*oblitus fatorum*). See also 5.174, where Gyas is labeled as "forgetful both of his own honor and his companion's health" (*oblitus decorisque sui sociumque salutis*). See P. Hardie 2012, 91–5 on the role of *fama* in these passages.

[65] This theme is picked up after Aeneas remembers those obligations and decides to leave. In a simile comparing the Trojans to a band of ants, the narrator says the insects bustle about bringing in food, "mindful of winter" (*hiemis memores*, 4.403).

she thinks of the obligation memory may carry, she hopes for "a just and remembering divinity" that cares for wronged lovers (*numen . . . iustumque memorque*, 4.521). Undermining the Trojan's promises, destroying everything he left behind, and proposing different monuments for their romance – she acts to establish how their relationship will be remembered and commemorated. Nothing proves this more strongly than her final action, a suicide committed with Aeneas' sword (4.646–7 and 663–5). When Dido selects his sword for her death, she makes her end a conclusive marker of Aeneas' role in her life. As Daniel Gillis points out, Aeneas' sword is highly suggestive of his penis, which "should give life, not take it."[66] Dido's use of his sword for this deadly purpose consummates their relationship in a new and terrible way. Deaths are often linked with the commemoration of the deceased in the *Aeneid*,[67] and by choosing to die in this manner, Dido ties her death and commemoration to Aeneas.[68] Her suicide becomes a monument of their relationship, a funereal display that makes him responsible for her fate and mocks his promise to remember her as long as he lives.[69] Dido's extraordinary efforts to end her life in this way only confirm how powerful commemoration can be, as she struggles to the last to ensure that her depiction of her relationship with Aeneas overwrites his.

Backward and forward

In *Aeneid* 1–4, Aeneas and Dido both turn to memory to accomplish their goals in their relationship, and, in the process of doing so, each casts a light on the other's actions. Aeneas tailors his interactions with memory to whatever situation confronts him. His behavior shows more than a hint of subtlety and manipulation, as he strives to influence those around him to share his view of memory, and, in so doing, to secure safety for himself and his men at Carthage. Yet his extensive interaction with memory in a manner encouraging hope and bonds reveals something about his

66 Gillis 1983, 47. For more on this idea, see ibid. 46–52 and Syed 2005, 129. Adams 1982, 19 points out the frequency of *ad hoc* weapon metaphors for the penis in Latin. Ovid alludes to the risqué overtones of Aeneas' stay at Carthage, where he brings to mind specific parts of the body while discussing what is the most read scene in the *Aeneid*: "And no part from the whole corpus is more read than that love joined in an improper union" (*nec legitur pars ulla magis de corpore toto | quam non legitimo foedere iunctus amor*, *Tr*. 2.535–6).

67 See the deaths of Caieta, Nisus, Euryalus, Lausus, and Pallas, all discussed in pp. 137–54.

68 Hill 2004, 119–20 is correct to point out the disorganization that marks Dido's ending, characteristics brought out further by the narrator's revelation at the end of *Aeneid* 4 that this particular death was not fated for the queen. Yet, in spite of the fury that possesses her, Dido still is able to construct her suicide so that it at least aims at influencing how she and Aeneas will be remembered.

69 See Syed 2005, 95 on Dido's effort to set herself up as a spectacle upon her death.

character beyond a grim practicality and a struggle for survival. Occurring in a programmatic location, Aeneas' engagement with memory in *Aeneid* 1 shows him in the process of discovering how to turn a weakness into a strength. His past having been destroyed, remembering ought to be a purely painful phenomenon. Yet Aeneas displays a remarkable determination in trying to find ways to approach the past in a positive manner. Dido, partly influenced by Aeneas' behavior and divine machinations, partly by her own inclinations, likewise turns to recollection and commemoration as tools to bring the Carthaginians and Trojans closer together in *Aeneid* 1. She, too, accentuates certain aspects of her past to appeal to the Trojans and holds out the idea of a communal commemoration from a future perspective, even though she, like Aeneas, is burdened with a traumatic past. In *Aeneid* 1, the pair's relationship begins, and it begins well.

In *Aeneid* 2 and 3, Aeneas sets emotion at the center of his narrative. Highlighting certain aspects of his experiences, Aeneas' metanarratival comments cast him as a nearly broken man, who deserves and needs sympathy. In this aspect, his narrative may not be so different from Sinon's. He does not lie to the extent that the Greek does, but he does present Dido with a portrait that emphasizes his need for the sort of help she has already offered, all the while playing down his future journey to Hesperia. His memory, like Sinon's, fulfills a need of its audience, and he is so successful that Dido hungers to hear his narrative time and time again. Yet here, as memory brings the pair closer, the result outstrips Aeneas' wishes. He hopes to forge a bond between himself and Dido, but in sharing his entire past with her he leaves her obsessed with hearing it repeatedly. Their relationship comes to threaten his fated mission, and the two characters, each endowed with the ability and willingness to advance his or her position though appeals to memory, are now at odds with one another. Aeneas offers various commemorations of their relationship in an attempt to placate Dido upon his leaving, and Dido presents counter-commemorations of her own, ones that will not let Aeneas' memorial of their relationship come to define it.

What all of these personal interactions with Dido demonstrate is that Aeneas possesses a deeply held belief that he can control how people engage with memory. Whether it ought to be called bravery or foolishness, boldness or naïveté, it reflects just as much a rhetorical strategy as it does a dedication to the idea that memory can form bonds between people and offer them solace. Aeneas' readiness to believe in this power reflects a supremely individual and human aspect of his character, one that is intertwined with his uneasy acceptance of a destiny he does not entirely know and will perhaps never completely embrace. All the while that fate drives him to found a city and bring his gods to Latium, Aeneas is engaged in a battle about self-identity, self-worth, and self-preservation. Memory allows him some degree of control in his imaginings of the past and future.

Yet if the challenges Aeneas faces are so great that he can go forward with nothing less than a supreme confidence in his control of memory, then this confidence is misplaced. This same determination to remember and to be remembered in a specific way, while it will prove essential to Aeneas' success, also has the potential to make him into memory's victim. This is hinted at not only in his viewing of the temple paintings in *Aeneid* 1, where the narrator points out that Aeneas deludes himself by drawing consolation from an "empty picture" (*pictura . . . inani*, 1.464), but also in *Aeneid* 4, where his recollections of the past entrap him in Carthage and his attempts to palliate Dido's anger with promises of remembrance enrage her all the more. Aeneas' determination to engage with memory ensures that these complications only build with the progression of his journey, and, as the *Aeneid*'s second half begins, these problems of control, emotion, and identity come to impact the epic's narrative audience as well.

CHAPTER FOUR

The narrator's song

The *Aeneid*'s narrator relates a past several hundred years removed from his own time.[1] Yet this temporal gap does not stop him from attempting to link his audience with the events he describes. This chapter argues that the narrator shapes his audience into a remembering community and strives to establish the standardized version of their past. The narrator grounds this project in his own unique command over memory, a command that he differentiates from that of the Muses and his characters. In a series of apostrophes to the Muses he appropriates the ability to create a memory of Aeneas' story, while in several scenes involving the *Aeneid*'s mortal characters he distinguishes his all-encompassing comprehension of memory's intricacies from their lack of understanding. Altogether he marks himself as one who, on a grand temporal scale and from a nearly omniscient perspective, creates a lasting memory of the events of which he sings.

The narrator takes advantage of these talents to gather his audience around the story of the origins they share with him and with each other. In several of his aetiological explanations of Roman customs and place names, he bridges the centuries between his audience and the Trojans, showcasing the ties between past and present. The narrator brings these various factors – his links with his audience, his control over memory, the connections between Romans and Trojans – to bear in a series of apostrophes that punctuate the *Aeneid*'s second half. Since these apostrophes merge the present of the narrating instance with the present of the narrative,[2] the narrator includes his audience in these mnemonic focal points and engages them in remembering these characters as well. In these apostrophes, all

[2] The narrating instance is the time at which the narrator is singing; this can also be described as the "the generating instance of narrative discourse" (Genette 1980, 213).

directed at characters who are near death, the narrator attempts to define the essence of these characters and to compel the audience to share his commemorations' unique point of view. When the narrator advances an overarching and far-sighted commemoration of these characters' lives, the audience is invited to share his view of the past and remember these characters in the same way he does.

In spite of the narrator's effort to fashion the audience into a remembering community, there is no guarantee they will mimic his responses. A narratival apostrophe rarely stands as the only reaction to a character's death. Death presents a natural opportunity to reflect on the significance of a person's life. It often prompts the *Aeneid*'s characters to set out their own views of how a person ought to be remembered, each with the implicit goal of having his commemoration most effectively influence the group's social memory. The contradictions between the characters and narrator's commemorations give rise to a challenge for the *Aeneid*'s audience. They have been brought into the time of these events and prompted to remember these characters, but they must select an appropriate memorial from a profusion of contradictory apostrophes.

Invocations of the Muses

A Muse stands as the font of memory and song in the Greek and Roman epics that precede Vergil's, and generic expectations foster the assumption that she would play a similar role in this poem. The *Aeneid*'s narrator, though, reshapes the typical Muse–singer relationship.[3] It is not that the narrator never addresses a Muse or that he claims to independently remember every event of which he sings.[4] Rather, he appropriates one specific aspect of her talents: the ability to fashion a story that will be remembered in the future. At the beginning of *Aeneid* 1 and 7, in the epic's two most structurally and thematically significant invocations, the narrator elevates

[3] Block 1982, 11 writes that invocations of the Muse "direct the attention of the audience toward the significance of what is about to happen, and . . . ask for help in describing momentous events." This is certainly true, but it only tells part of the story. Every invocation in the *Aeneid*, particularly the longer and more structurally significant ones, also establishes the grounds of the relationship between the narrator and the Muse. On the ancient belief that the Muses enable and inspire the poet's song, see Coleman 1977; ad 7.19 and Clausen 1994, ad 7.19.

[4] The narrator invokes one or more Muses six times in the *Aeneid*: 1.8–11; 7.37–44; 7.641–6; 9.77–9; 9.525–8; and 10.163–5. Four of these invocations (7.641–6, 9.77–9, 9.525–8, 10.163–5) are relatively short and mostly concerned with the narrator's request for a specific piece of information. (Block 1982, n. 16 includes 6.264–7 as an invocation, but no Muse is addressed there. See Novara 1986, 8 on this passage.)

himself over the Muse as the dominant creator of memory.[5] She may pass on information about events she remembers, but the narrator forges those events into an originary social memory for his audience.

Perhaps the most distinctive characteristic of the *Aeneid*'s opening invocation is where it is not located. The first verses of both the *Iliad* and the *Odyssey* construct an unambiguous relationship between singer and Muse: "Sing, goddess, of the wrath of Achilles, son of Peleus" (Μῆνιν ἄειδε θεὰ Πηληϊάδεω Ἀχιλῆος, *Il.* 1.1)[6] and "Tell me, Muse, of the man of many ways" (Ἄνδρα μοι ἔννεπε, Μοῦσα, πολύτροπον, *Od.* 1.1).[7] While neither of these Homeric invocations foregrounds memory, both depict the Muse as supplying the narrator with the details of past events in a poetic form, ready for him to repeat to his audience.[8]

The *Aeneid* plays with the expectation that its opening verse will call upon the Muse in such a manner. Its first words, "Arms and the man" (*arma virumque*, 1.1), announce its subject, just as the initial words of the *Iliad* and *Odyssey* do. While the *Aeneid* likewise follows up this announcement with a verb denoting singing, Vergil's epic and Homer's diverge here. The *Aeneid*'s first verb is not a second-person imperative directed at the Muse, but rather a first-person indicative: "I sing" (*cano*, 1.1). The narrator's appropriation of the Muse's role draws attention to his active control and imaginative power.[9] Marco Fantuzzi and Richard Hunter note that "epic narration is always an act of memory, implying a past narrative worth telling."[10] As the singer, the *Aeneid*'s narrator commemorates past events on his own and therefore influences the memories others will have of them. While, in Gregory Nagy's words, the Homeric narrator is "an instrument . . . in the hands of the Muse,"[11] the *Aeneid*'s narrator does not simply pass on what the Muse tells him. His first words instead foreground his own creativity, leaving the Muse absent.

[5] G. Williams 1983, 165; Feeney 1991, 185–7; and Kyriakidis 1998, 166 remark on the prominent and independent voice in these two invocations. This is especially evident in comparison with Homeric invocations (Behr 2005, 200; 2007, 17–8; and Beye 2006, 230) and Apollonian invocations (Feeney 1991, 90–3; Hunter 1993, 195; and Nelis 2001, 275).

[6] Kirk 1985, ad loc. identifies the invoked goddess as the Muse. Detienne 1996, 39–52 writes in detail about the Muses in ancient Greek poetry and thought.

[7] In regard to the *Iliad*, DuBois 1982, 11 notes, "The role of memory is represented by the Muses who remind the poet of the details of his song, who give him inspiration and sight."

[8] Nagy 2007, 56 writes that the Homeric Muses grant "the absolute power of total recall" to the narrator.

[9] Servius ad loc. notes that *cano* has three significations: sometimes it means "to praise," sometimes "to prophecy," and sometimes "to sing," a meaning he says it holds in this instance. Yet the word surely also here endows the singer with a nearly divine power of his own through its association with prophecy.

[10] Fantuzzi and Hunter 2004, 122.

[11] Nagy 1979, 16.

No address to the Muse appears until the eighth verse: "Muse, tell me the causes..." (*Musa, mihi causas memora*... 1.8). By now, the narrator has already shown that he can craft an outline of his song, from the beginning of Aeneas' journey in Troy to its culmination in Rome. And, by describing the role Juno's remembering plays in these events, he expresses an understanding of memory's impact on his story.[12] The boldness of these opening verses is only partly tempered by the invocation that finally appears in line 8.[13] The alliteration of *Musa*, *mihi*, and *memora* grants urgency to the narrator's request while also implying a link between himself and the Muse, with memory as a conduit between them. The verb *memora* alludes to the Muse's relationship with memory. While the surface meaning of *memora* is "tell," the verb can also mean "remind" or "remember,"[14] and this secondary meaning is drawn out by its juxtaposition with "Muse" (*Musa*). The name itself is etymologically connected with "words for memory"[15] and the Muses are, after all, Memory's daughters. When he asks for assistance, he is asking the daughter of Memory for a reminder, and his request, late as it comes in the *Aeneid*'s proem, shows he depends on her for a reminder of the origins of his tale. The energy of the narrator's imperative comes to rest on "causes" (*causas*). After his characterization of Juno's memory as something that sparks a response (1.4), the narrator links memory and causality again, raising the question of what repercussions will arise from his song, itself a commemoration of the past.

The epic's second major invocation again raises a tension between the narrator and the Muse's command over the *Aeneid*'s story, but here the narrator's appropriation of the Muse's role is even more pointed. She is not invoked until thirty-six lines have passed in *Aeneid* 7 (7.37–45):

> nunc age, qui reges, Erato, quae tempora, rerum
> quis Latio fuerit status, advena classem
> cum primum Ausoniis exercitus appulit oris,
> expediam, et primae revocabo exordia pugnae.

[12] See *Aen* 1.4 and pp. 68–70 for discussion of this.

[13] As Spence 1988, 24 notes, the delay of the Muse's invocation to the eighth verse signals a new beginning.

[14] On the meanings of *memorare* see pp. 11–13. *Memorare* recalls "unforgetting" (*memorem*) from line 4, the epithet given to Juno's anger. This connection (also noted by A. Hardie 2007, 571–2) is reinforced by the lines' metrical patterns: both words follow a strong caesura in the third foot.

[15] O'Hara 1996, 115; on the same page, he also points out other instances of Vergilian wordplay that allude to the link between the *Musa* and memory words. See also Fordyce 1977, ad 41 on this connection and Paschalis 1997, 35 n. 6 on this present instance. See Feeney 1991, 121 and O'Hara 1996, 115 on the beginning of Livius Andronicus' *Odyssey*, which may have inspired this Vergilian wordplay.

tu vatem, tu, diva, mone. dicam horrida bella,
dicam acies actosque animis in funera reges,
Tyrrhenamque manum totamque sub arma coactam
Hesperiam. maior rerum mihi nascitur ordo,
maius opus moveo.

Now come, Erato, I will give an account of who were the kings, what were the conditions, what was the state of affairs in Latium, when the foreign army first brought its fleet to Ausonian shores, and I will recall the first battle's beginnings. You, goddess, you, remind your sacred bard. I will sing of dreadful wars, I will sing of armies and kings driven to death by their courage, and an Etruscan band and all Hesperia pressed into arms. A greater order of things is born for me, I start a greater work.

The narrator calls upon the Muse and describes the themes of his work's second half. Vergil's audience, drawing upon their familiarity with the *Eclogues* and *Georgics*, would have expected this passage to come at the very beginning of *Aeneid* 7, the poem's midway point,[16] and the narrator slights the Muse by postponing any mention of her until well after the book's opening verses.

Moreover, the narrator's treatment of the Muse in these nine lines challenges her for control over what is remembered or forgotten. Erato is apostrophized at line 37,[17] and the imperative "come on" (*age*, 7.37) indicates that another, more specific order is soon to follow.[18] The three indirect questions in lines 37 and 38 are tailor-made for the Muse to answer, and they raise the expectation that the narrator will soon command her to sing. Yet the verb which emphatically appears at the beginning of line 40 ("I will give an account" (*expediam*, 7.40))[19] has the narrator as its subject, as does the next verb ("I will recall" (*revocabo*, 7.40)).[20] These first-person verbs assert the narrator's creative primacy and encroach upon the Muse's talent

[16] On Vergil's "proems in the middle," see R. F. Thomas 1986 and Conte 1992. See Fraenkel 1945, 1; Kyriakadis 1998; and Horsfall 2000, ad 1–4 and 37–45 on the audience's expectations at the start of *Aeneid* 7.

[17] Kyriakidis 1998, 161 n. 1 provides an extensive bibliography on the question of why Erato is invoked. For the current discussion, it is relevant to point out that Apollonius invokes the same Muse in the first line of *Argonautica* 3, directly after his epic's midpoint; the invocation of Erato in the *Aeneid* recalls her appearance in the *Argonautica* and only makes the delay in Vergil's epic all the more noticeable.

[18] See *OLD* 24 a, b, c.

[19] *Expedio* is frequently used to indicate who will narrate a story (see *TLL* vol. 5, *pars altera* 1613.5–6 and this particular use at 1613.56–7); the narrator's selection of it gives an edge to his appropriation of the Muse's role.

[20] This is the first use of *revocare* meaning "to recall to mind" (*OLD* 13b). See Horsfall 2000, ad loc. on its use here.

for recalling past events. He will create his song, deciding what does and does not gain a place in it and, accordingly, what his audience remembers. He has appropriated the role of the Muse for himself, seizing a greater degree of control.[21] Yet he has done more than this, since he appropriates that role after pointedly invoking her presence. Amazingly, when line 40 comes to a close, the Muse has been left for four verses as a mere spectator; an awkward presence without a clear purpose, who was invoked as if to speak but instead merely left to listen.

The Muse, though, is not entirely forgotten: in line 41 the narrator picks up his earlier address: "You, goddess, you, remind your sacred poet" (*tu vatem, tu, diva, mone*). The verb "remind" (*mone*) asserts the Muse's link with memory, but also reveals that her only function is to remind the narrator of details of his story that he has forgotten.[22] Even though the narrator portrays himself "as the consulter of authorities,"[23] he claims still further control for himself, as all he needs from the Muse is the mere reactivation of a memory. He shows his need for the Muse's assistance, but he is equally adamant that he can ensure that those events are remembered in the future.[24] The narrator reiterates this claim near the end of the invocation by stringing together two more first-person verbs with a first-person pronoun: "I will sing" (*dicam*, 7.41, 42); "I start" (*moveo*, 7.45); and "for me" (*mihi*, 7.44). This division between the Muse and the narrator essentially reiterates the relationship first set out in *Aeneid* 1, but now even more power shifts to the narrator: the Muse offers the narrator a reminder of events, but he creates his song.

Each of the *Aeneid*'s four other invocations, all substantially shorter and appearing at less structurally marked locations, contains a request to the Muse for her assistance with memorializing specific past events.[25] In none of these does the narrator attribute to her responsibility for his entire song. The longest, coming directly before the catalogue of Italian forces in *Aeneid* 7, testifies to the narrator's need for the goddess to remind him of details from the past (7.641–6):

[21] Nelis 2001, 275, in an analysis of this invocation with an eye to the *Argonautica*, writes that the narrator shows himself to be "in sole command of the epic."

[22] *Mone* could also be taken as "instruct," but the meaning "remind," given the Muses' previous association with memory, is more likely here. (Fordyce 1977, ad 41 argues for this meaning as well, and he also notes the etymological connections between *Musa* and *moneo*.) Lastly, *mone* may pick up and elaborate on *memora* (1.8), where implications of reminding are already present, although that meaning is not so close to the surface there as it is here.

[23] Feeney 1991, 186.

[24] Kyriakidis 1998, 175 too notes how the narrator sets himself as "a composer in his own right."

[25] Kyriakidis 1998, 166 points out that the poet's role is underplayed in these four invocations.

pandite nunc Helicona, deae, cantusque movete,
qui bello exciti reges, quae quemque secutae
complerint campos acies, quibus Itala iam tum
floruerit terra alma viris, quibus arserit armis;
et meministis enim, divae, et memorare potestis;
ad nos vix tenuis famae perlabitur aura.

Open up Helicon now, goddesses, and undertake the songs that tell what kings were roused in war, which loyal armies filled the fields, with what men already then did the nourishing Italian land flourish, with what arms did it burn; for you, goddesses, both remember and are able to remind; the thin breeze of fame scarcely reaches us.

Of all the *Aeneid*'s invocations, this one claims most forcefully that the narrator needs the Muses. The narrator focuses almost exclusively on their power to remind him of the various Italian armies. In particular, line 645 encapsulates the goddesses' control of memory, essentialized in their ability to remember and to remind.[26] In this invocation, the narrator appears only in line 646 as the passive recipient of the story, a tale whose details, without the Muses' help, would be hopelessly shadowed by the intervening years.[27]

This and the epic's other three structurally insignificant invocations emphasize the Muse's ability to remember specific facts and, in particular, lengthy lists of people or things, whether that be the Trojan ships which turn into nymphs (9.77–9); the men Turnus kills in battle (9.525–8); or the Trojans' allies (10.163–5). These invocations, along with *Aeneid* 7.641–6, do not assign as active a role to the narrator as the epic's two programmatic invocations. Yet they also do not bestow the narrator's power of creating a song upon the Muse. The narrator, both at the epic's beginning and midpoint, claims this place for himself. The Muse provides details to him when he requests them, but the responsibility for his song lies with him, and, by implication, so too does the charge of memorializing the events it contains and causing them to be remembered in the future.

Mortal limits

Just as the narrator differentiates his command over memory from that of the Muse, he does the same in regard to his characters. In passages

[26] R. F. Thomas 1999, 182 (and see also 183) marks how "recalling the tradition . . . and . . . converting the recall into retelling" are crucial aspects of the poetic tradition. See Verg. *Ecl.* 7.19 for a similar statement of the Muses' ability. The epic's two longer invocations associate the ability to retell with the narrator.

[27] Jenkyns 1988, 472 argues otherwise: this invocation "softens the distinction between omniscience and ignorance."

that hinge upon a measure of perspectival play, the narrator showcases his comprehension of memory's inner workings at the same time as he exposes his characters' lack thereof. By demonstrating how various characters fall short of being remembered in the manner they wished, the narrator reveals the gap that exists between an individual's desire to be remembered in a certain manner and the memory which society holds of that individual. While his characters fail to achieve their memory-related goals, the narrator expertly traces the path a memory travels from the story an individual hopes will represent his life to the social memory a group shares of that person's existence. A brief example of this phenomenon comes in Mezentius' battle with Aeneas, but the epic's most fully developed illustration of the interplay between perspectives on memory stands in the description of Camilla's death at the hands of Arruns.

Two short passages, both describing battle trophies, show how Mezentius' commemorative hopes are never realized. As Mezentius prepares to fight Aeneas, he turns to his son Lausus and imagines the result of his victory (10.774–6):

> voveo praedonis corpore raptis
> indutum spoliis ipsum te, Lause, tropaeum
> Aeneae.
>
> I vow that you yourself, Lausus, clothed in spoils seized from the robber's body, will be my trophy over Aeneas.

Mezentius envisions Lausus as a trophy of his victory over a brigand.[28] A marker of Mezentius' deeds more than any action of Lausus' own, Lausus would stand as a living reminder of a protective and powerful father.[29] Yet Mezentius' desired trophy soon becomes unattainable. After Mezentius is wounded and Lausus dies while enabling him to escape alive, the narrator concentrates on how Lausus will be remembered for his pious valor. In doing so, he shifts the episode's mnemonic focal point away from Mezentius and displays his own capability to mold the memory of an event.[30]

[28] This sort of bold commemoration is not at all out of character for Mezentius. After killing the Trojans Palmus and Latagus, Mezentius gives their armor to his son to wear (10.700–1), a commemoration that prefigures his subsequent vow about how he will commemorate his battle with Aeneas. Later, when Mezentius is defeated by Aeneas, his body itself becomes a commemorative object, a shift that emphasizes the lack of control mortals have over how events are remembered.

[29] Scodel 2008, 133, writing on Aeschylus' *Oresteia*, touches upon how certain characters in the trilogy "try to control how their own time will be remembered." Mezentius engages in much the same behavior here.

[30] This passage is discussed in detail on pp. 145–6.

When Mezentius at last returns to battle, he himself is killed by Aeneas. Not only, of course, is it now impossible for Mezentius to memorialize this battle himself, but his arms are themselves turned into a memorial by Aeneas (11.5–11):

> ingentem quercum decisis undique ramis
> constituit tumulo fulgentiaque induit arma,
> Mezenti ducis exuvias, tibi magne tropaeum
> bellipotens; aptat rorantis sanguine cristas
> telaque trunca viri, et bis sex thoraca petitum
> perfossumque locis, clipeumque ex aere sinistrae
> subligat atque ensem collo suspendit eburnum.
>
> Aeneas sets a gigantic oak on a burial-mound, with its branches everywhere cut off, and he puts glittering arms on it, the spoils of prince Mezentius, a trophy for you, great god of war; he fastens the crested helmet, dripping with blood, and the man's broken missiles and his breastplate struck and pierced in twelve places, and he ties his brass shield on the left and hangs his ivory scabbard from the neck.

This memorial constructed by Mezentius' enemy marks a change in the erstwhile king's agency. Mezentius' passivity is emphasized by the excessive piercing of his breastplate.[31] With his armor set on a tree and stood up on a "burial-mound" (*tumulo*),[32] it is unlikely that Aeneas complied with Mezentius' final request that his body be placed in the same tomb as his son's (10.906). Instead of securing this joint burial or, as Mezentius initially hoped, having Aeneas' armor displayed on his son's body, Mezentius' commemoration is separated from Lausus. *Tropaeum* in 11.7 underlines Mezentius' shift from active agent to passive sufferer, as it recalls the same word in 10.775, where it stands in the same metrical seat; this allusion underlines just how wrong Mezentius was in his prediction of how his duel with Aeneas would be commemorated.

The narrator's description of Camilla's death and its surrounding events in *Aeneid* 11 further develops the motif of failure and frustration that

[31] Aeneas' dedication may also offer a critique of the method of commemoration Mezentius proposed. Horsfall 2003, ad 5–13 compares Aeneas' dedication of Mezentius' weapons to the gods with Mezentius' wish that Lausus wear Aeneas' arms, arguing that Aeneas' commemoration "is a statement of *pietas*, gratitude, and soldierly pride," while Mezentius' proposed commemoration was "irregular if not positively blasphemous."

[32] *Tumulo* could merely indicate a mound of raised earth (*OLD* 1), but in the context of Mezentius' death, it is better to understand it as indicating a burial-mound (*OLD* 2). See Horsfall 2000, ad 6 and Horsfall 2003, ad 6.

marks the relationship between a character's actual and imagined legacy. In his description of Camilla and Arruns, the narrator explores the distance between how these two would like to be remembered and how their lives are actually framed. Memory looms large in the movement toward Camilla's death.[33] Battling against Aeneas and his allies, Camilla takes a special interest in killing and stripping Chloreus, a Trojan warrior with exceptionally beautiful armor. Camilla chases him, the narrator says, (11.778–80)

> sive ut templis praefigeret arma
> Troia, captivo sive ut se ferret in auro
> venatrix . . .

> either so that she might affix his Trojan arms upon a temple or so that she might go about as a hunter in the gold taken from him . . .

Although the narrator does not use the word monument, he makes clear Camilla's desire to transform Chloreus' arms into a testament to her martial skill, either by showcasing them in a temple or on her own body. She wants to create a display that will foster a lasting and specific recognition of her accomplishments.

The Trojan Arruns also frames his motivation in terms of commemorative recognition. In a prayer to Apollo, he says (11.789–93):

> da, pater, hoc nostris aboleri dedecus armis,
> omnipotens. non exuvias pulsaeve tropaeum
> virginis aut spolia ulla peto, mihi cetera laudem
> facta ferent; haec dira meo dum vulnere pestis
> pulsa cadat, patrias remeabo inglorius urbes.

> Allow, all-powerful father, for this disgrace to be destroyed by my arms. It is not her arms or a trophy of the routed virgin or any spoils that I seek, other deeds will carry praise to me; provided that this dread pestilence falls, struck down by my wound, I will return, inglorious, to my fatherland.

Unlike Mezentius, who uses *tropaeum* to signify his wish for a monument to his victory, Arruns turns to the same word to deny any wish for his victory to result in praise.[34] Arruns is more interested in the abolition of memories.

[33] The theme of commemoration, in fact, is already delicately introduced in Diana's rendition of Camilla's back-story: "And her father named her Camilla after her mother Casmilla, with part of the name changed" (*matrisque vocavit* | *nomine Casmillae mutata parte Camillam*, 11.542–3).

[34] *Inglorius* contributes to this as well: see *TLL* 1555.60.

The narrator brings out a mnemonic aspect to Arruns' motivation with the verb *abolere*. This verb was used earlier in the *Aeneid* to designate the erasure of one person's memory of another.[35] Here, instead of desiring to secure fame from Camilla's defeat, Arruns wants to erase any remembrance of her deeds on the battlefield by ending her life.

The theme of memory is picked up again in Camilla's death. As Camilla feverishly chases Chloreus and his splendid arms, Arruns spots his opportunity. She stands no chance against his spear (11.801–4):

> nihil ipsa nec aurae
> nec sonitus memor aut venientis ab aethere teli,
> hasta sub exsertam donec perlata papillam
> haesit virgineumque alte bibit acta cruorem.

> Camilla herself is not at all mindful of the wind or of the sound or of the weapon flying through the air, until the spear, driven in deeply, clings to her protruding breast and drinks her virginal blood.

Camilla is caught unaware, and the narrator describes this lack of attention with the vocabulary of memory. *Memor* recalls Camilla's hunger for another sort of memory and makes clear the disastrous effects of that all-consuming desire. So focused on commemorating her battlefield prowess through winning Chloreus' armor, Camilla meets her death because she forgets her surroundings.[36] Her mental focus should, the narrator implies, be on the present, but instead she looks to the future.

In spite of the manner of her death, Camilla will not be forgotten. Diana had earlier vowed that Camilla would receive a proper burial (11.593–4) and dispatched the nymph Opis to complete this task. Now, with Camilla dead, Opis promises her that she will be remembered (11.845–7):[37]

[35] See 1.720 and pp. 99–100.

[36] A similar use of *immemor* occurs at 9.374, where Euryalus, who could not restrain himself from carrying off an enemy's helmet, is killed because of the light that helmet reflects. As he attempts to flee, "the helmet betrayed forgetful Euryalus in the barely luminous shade of night and reflected the light back from the rays of the moon" (*galea Euryalum sublustri noctis in umbra | prodidit immemorem radiisque aduersa refulsit*, 9.373–4). Much like Camilla and Arruns, Euryalus acts partly out of a desire to be remembered, a desire that, in the end is not achieved. On the role of memory in Euryalus' decision to act, see discussion of 9.194–5, 9.256, and 9.292–4 on p. 142.

[37] The narrator further highlights the theme of memory and foreshadows the commemoration Camilla will enjoy by mentioning that Opis stands atop an ancient king's "tomb" when she delivers this speech (*bustum*, 11.850) and when she spies Arruns in the distance (*tumulo*, 11.853). This recalls Diana's earlier promise that Camilla would be buried in a "tomb" (*tumulo*, 11.594). See Horsfall 2003, ad 103 on the various nouns used in *Aeneid* 10 and 11 to indicate a mound for the burial of a person's body or ashes.

> non tamen indecorem tua te regina reliquit
> extrema iam in morte, neque hoc sine nomine letum
> per gentis erit aut famam patieris inultae.

> Nevertheless, your queen did not leave you without honor at your time of death, nor will this death be unrenowned through the nations, nor will you suffer the reputation of one unavenged.

This is not the memory Camilla desired, but it nonetheless ensures that she will not be forgotten entirely.

Arruns fails in his hope to eradicate any memory of the virgin warrior. Yet, in a savage twist, Arruns, who had prayed to Apollo that he efface the memory of Camilla and that he not gain any fame from the deed, still has half of his prayer fulfilled. Opis' burial of Camilla guarantees Arruns' failure in obliterating Camilla's memory, but, as the narrator shows, he loses much more than any simple trophy for his deed. Shot dead by Opis' arrow, he is abandoned at his death: "His comrades leave him breathing out his last and groaning, having forgotten him in the unknown dust of the battlefield" (*illum exspirantem socii atque extrema gementem | obliti ignoto camporum in pulvere linquunt*, 11.865–6). With the detail "having forgotten" (*obliti*), the narrator points out how Arruns' prayer had unforeseen results, as his seemingly modest dismissal of recognition metastasizes into his own deserted anonymity. As Nicholas Horsfall points out, this is "a bitter fulfillment of [Arrun's] desire" to return home without fame.[38] Arruns had asked that he gain no glory for his deed, but he ends up deprived of any commemoration of his life.

Both Camilla and Arruns advance specific ideas about how they would like to be remembered in the future. Yet, much like Mezentius, neither receives precisely what he or she wanted and neither has control over the social memory that comes to define him or her. Unlike his story's characters, the narrator understands the process whereby the memory of a person arises. His renditions of these situations raise the question of just how social memories are shaped and who shapes them. As will be argued in a later section of this chapter, he takes up the question himself when he apostrophizes his characters.

Aetiological memories

The narrator elaborates on these themes of control and understanding in several of the poem's aetiological explanations of Roman customs and

[38] Horsfall 2003, ad 793. J. Miller 2009, 169 argues that Apollo does not grant the entirety of Arruns' prayer (11.789–93) because of the character's "ignoble" attributes.

place names. Here he highlights his own perspective on the formation and preservation of memory while also joining his audience with the song they hear. Two particular *aetia* vividly illustrate how he draws his audience into the time of the narrative. The first appears near the end of the Trojans' games in Sicily in *Aeneid* 5, and the second comes at the *Aeneid*'s midpoint, a location Vergil typically reserves for programmatic statements.

The narrator's description of the last part of the Trojans' games opens up a temporal play that links his audience with the events he narrates. As a coda to the commemoration of Anchises' death, a group of young Trojans executes a series of complex equestrian maneuvers. For the Trojan spectators, this performance reminds them of their ancestors: "The Trojans cheer the nervous youth with applause and rejoice in looking upon them, and they recognize their ancestor' faces" (*excipiunt plausu pavidos gaudentque tuentes | Dardanidae, veterumque agnoscunt ora parentum*, 5.575–6). The youths' actions make the viewers recall their progenitors, and they do so with pleasure. In a public setting, the Trojans share in a social memory that confirms societal continuity and vitality, as the audience views their youngest generation and is reminded of those who make up their heritage.

The characters and narrator alike are aware of such a custom's potential to ensure that a memory of previous generations endures. The narrator, though, goes one step further. Taking advantage of his temporal perspective, he dwells on the games' continuation in later times and links his audience back to this earlier occasion on Sicily.[39] Ascanius, the narrator says, brought the games over from Sicily to Alba Longa, where "he taught the ancient Latins to hold the games" (*priscos docuit celebrare Latinos*, 5.598), and Rome herself currently observes them: "Now the boys are called Troy, their band is called Trojan. Up to now, the contests are celebrated for Aeneas' sacred father" (*Troiaque nunc pueri, Troianum dicitur agmen. | hac celebrata tenus sancto certamina patri*, 5.602–3). Presently, a cultural institution in Rome, the Trojan games were preserved by the Trojans and Romans alike; in recounting the efforts that accomplished this, the narrator constructs a social memory the audience can hold of the games' past.[40]

[39] Feldherr 1995, 263–4 and Theodorakopoulos 2004 write on the links in these equestrian maneuvers between Trojan past and Trojan present as well as between Trojan past and Augustan present. Pavlovskis 1976 sees a merging between past, present, and future in the entire *lusus Troiae*. Associations between Rome's past and present may already be seen at 5.116–23, where the narrator points out the Roman families that take their name from various Trojan competitors and, in doing so, lays the ground for the more extended focus on temporal connections in the equestrian maneuvers.

[40] J. Assmann 2006 writes extensively about the concept of cultural memory and the various ways it may be created and maintained. Augustus strongly encouraged the games in Rome (Norden 1901; and Erskine 2001, 19–20).

By describing the continuous practice of this tradition, the narrator fashions a path from the here and now of the narrative time to the here and "now" (*nunc*, 5.602) of the narrating instance.[41] The transition between these times is first hinted at when the narrator terms the Latins of Alba Longa "ancient" (*priscos*, 5.598), a designation which signals a modern perspective,[42] and it is confirmed by the use of "now" (*nunc*, 5.602) to mark the Roman celebration. By referencing present-day Rome, the narrator brings his audience into the song's time-frame. With this maneuver, he creates a parallel between his Roman audience and the ancient Trojans who watched the games on Sicily: just as the Trojans rejoiced on Sicily to see their ancestors brought before them, now the Romans too remember their Trojan heritage when they watch the games at Rome.[43]

At the epic's midpoint, the narrator returns to these themes of originary connection and social memory with greater emphasis. At the halfway juncture of both the *Eclogues* and *Georgics*, the narrator speaks of his Muse and addresses a prominent character; Vergil's audience would arrive at the beginning of *Aeneid* 7 expecting a similar poetic reflection.[44] Instead though, the narrator apostrophizes a character who appears nowhere else in the epic (7.1–4):

> tu quoque litoribus nostris, Aeneia nutrix,
> aeternam moriens famam, Caieta, dedisti;
> et nunc servat honos sedem tuus, ossaque nomen
> Hesperia in magna, si qua est ea gloria, signat.
>
> You too Caieta, Aeneas' nurse, have given eternal fame by your death to our shores; even now the honors shown you preserve your resting-place, and your name marks out your bones in great Hesperia, if that is any glory.

The narrator draws attention to how Caieta and her eponymous city reinforce each other's fame. While the address of a heretofore unknown character may initially appear out of place at this programmatically significant juncture,[45] it proves to merit such a location. The narrator's apostrophe

[41] See p. 2 n. 124 for discussion of these terms.

[42] A similar shift in temporal perspective occurs when the narrator terms Carthage "an ancient city" (*urbs antiqua*, 1.12), a description that represents the narrator's perspective, not the narrative's (see Reed 2007, 129–40 for a consideration of the implications of this prolepsis). For similar shifts, see the designation of the Trojan War as "ancient" (*veteris*, 1.23) and Latium as "ancient" (*antiquo*, 7.38).

[43] Holt 1979/80, 119 notes the "dual perspective" of these equestrian ceremonies, split "between the Trojan audience within the epic and the Roman audience outside it."

[44] See p. 16 n. 128 on Vergil's "proems in the middle."

[45] The first two words of *Aeneid* 7, "you also" (*tu quoque*) would raise the audience's expectations even further that this passage would have a programmatic quality. Not only does "also" (*quoque*)

elucidates two linked goals of his song: to trace a path back from his Roman audience to their Trojan ancestors and to join his audience with him in commemorating their shared origins.

A good deal of this apostrophe's effect depends upon its curious relationship with the one other use of Caieta in the *Aeneid.* The name appears as a geographical marker at the end of *Aeneid* 6: "Then Aeneas proceeds on a straight route to the port of Caieta. The anchor is cast from the prow; the ships stand on the shore" (*tum se ad Caietae recto fert limite portum.* | *ancora de prora iacitur; stant litore puppes*, 6.900–1). Here the proper noun Caieta designates a location, but this seemingly straightforward detail is rendered anachronistic by the beginning of *Aeneid* 7. These verses reveal that when Aeneas sails to the so-called port of Caieta in *Aeneid* 6, his nurse still lives and the place should not yet bear her name.[46]

Certain factors make this prolepsis stand out.[47] First and foremost, the close juxtaposition of the geographical designation and the character after whom it is named highlights the passages' reversal of cause and effect.[48] This prolepsis receives further prominence from the structural break it straddles. A book division in the *Aeneid* is almost always joined by a corresponding narrative interruption, such as the death of a character. Here this practice is contravened.[49] Instead of beginning anew, *Aeneid* 7 opens with a death that returns to and explains the last lines of *Aeneid* 6. As mentioned above, this break between *Aeneid* 6 and 7 is no typical pause since it marks the epic's midpoint. Yet the narrator subverts the audience's expectations. He leaves the Muse unaddressed and offers no explicit meditation on his poetic practice. Instead he apostrophizes Aeneas' nurse, draws attention to his responsibility for the prolepsis,[50] and, in

hearken back to the start of the *Aeneid*, but, even more significantly, the two words together are a near repetition of the first two words of the programmatic opening of *Georgics* 4: "you also" (*te quoque*). R. F. Thomas 1988, 3.1–2 points out these connections.

46 See O'Hara 1996, 183 for further bibliography on this passage.

47 The epic's first prolepsis, for instance, lacks a similar emphasis. (See Syed 2005, 139 on this passage.) The narrator calls the shores to which Aeneas sails "Lavinian" (*Lavinia*, 1.2), but Lavinia is not mentioned until 6.764. Also, this prolepsis centered on Caieta is emphasized by its contrast with other descriptions of the origin of the name of a place, descriptions where there is a comparably straightforward relation of between and effect (see 6.234–5 and 6.376–81, two passages which show a simple movement from death to subsequent geographical commemoration). See Reed 2007, 128–47 for a discussion of the effect of prolepsis in the *Aeneid.*

48 It certainly does not escape Ovid's eyes. He delights in correcting Vergil: "Aeneas goes to the shores which do not yet have his nurse's name" (*litora adit nondum nutricis habentia nomen, Met.* 14.157).

49 Hinds 1998, 109; and Kyriakadis 1998, 21–44.

50 Kyriakadis 1998, 83 notes the poet's desire to make himself "emphatically noticed" here. An apostrophe is an excellent vehicle for making such a claim about one's poetic ability, as it draws just as much attention to its speaker as to its addressee (Culler 1977, 63). Behr 2005, 204 argues in general

doing so, hints that his treatment of Caieta reveals something of his artistic goals.

Just what it reveals can be found in the passages' reversal of cause and effect. Various interpretations are given for this reversal, ranging from its motivation of the audience to continue onwards[51] to its articulation of a narrative and poetic pivot from past to future.[52] These two passages, though, frustrate any simple transition from past to future or readerly movement from *Aeneid* 6 to 7. The description of Caieta's commemoration represents an event that ought to occur before the city gains its name; it directs the audience backward, even as Aeneas and his men venture forward. By contrasting these movements at a place of thematic importance, the narrator signals their link. If the *Aeneid*'s first proem encapsulates the epic's narrative drive from Troy to Rome, then *Aeneid* 7.1–4 reverses this journey.[53] Here, the narrator asserts that he will also trace the path from Rome to Troy, as he commemorates the Trojan origin of a Roman place name.

As part of this aetiological regression, the narrator joins his narrative audience with him in remembering an aspect of Rome's origins. Largely by means of his apostrophe, he enlarges his song's temporal breadth through connecting the here and now of the narrative to the here and now of the narrating instance.[54] Initiated by the first word of line 1, "you" (*tu*), and picked up by the vocatives "Aeneas' nurse" (*Aeneia nutrix*) and "Caieta" (*Caieta*), the narrator's apostrophe partly situates him and his song within the Trojans' present. Yet the narrator also terms the shores "ours" (*nostris*)[55]

that the *Aeneid*'s narrator "at crucial junctures . . . uses apostrophe to focalize our attention on his own voice."

51 Hinds 1998, 109. 52 Kyriakadis 1998, 90.

53 See Fowler 1997b, 261 and 2000, 217 on the linking of these two movements again at the poem's close.

54 G. Williams 1983, 187 advances a similar argument about the temporal effect of this apostrophe. Culler 1977 notes in general that "The narrator places [what is apostrophized] beyond the movement of temporality . . . Apostrophe resists narrative because its *now* is not a moment in a temporal sequence but a *now* of discourse, of writing . . ." (68, emphases original). This is an excellent point, but in reference to the *Aeneid*, it is more appropriate to talk not about the *now* of writing, but about the *now* of singing. (See Lowrie 2009, 1–2 on the narrator's emphasis on singing rather than writing as his mode of production.) This apostrophe, like others in the *Aeneid*, builds upon features of the epic which already connect its audience with its story, such as the narrator's tendency to create a "timeless now" through his extensive use of the present tense (Mack 1978, 87 and see 36 also). More generally, P. Hardie 1993, 2 notes a related temporal difference between Homeric and Vergilian epic: while the time of the narrative in Homer "is in a distant past, in an age, other than, and different from," the audience and narrator's own, the *Aeneid* strives "to forge a continuity, even identity, between the times of narrated events and narrating." See Behr 2005, 198 on the "importance of the present as a funnel through which all past events must pass" in Roman epic.

55 Jenkyns 1998, 463 observes that the Homeric narrator never engages in such a use of a first-person; R. F. Thomas 1986, 64 argues that this "parochial element . . . is a Hellenistic rather than an archaic or classical Greek feature."

and describes Caieta's action with a perfect verb, "you have given" (*dedisti*), words that characterize him as singing to an audience of present-day Romans. The two present verbs in lines 3 and 4 continue this trend, as does "now" (*nunc*), which marks out the name Caieta as surviving "to the present time."[56] As the poem crosses the literal divide between its first and second halves, the narrator showcases his ability to cross the metaphorical gap between his narrative and his audience; and, by drawing them into the expansive present of his song, he brings them closer to experiencing the events they hear.

One of the poem's most visible demonstrations of the narrator's engagement with memory and community, this passage also shows Aeneas' preoccupation with commemoration. While the narrative audience can look forward from Caieta's death with the heartening knowledge of her lasting fame, Aeneas can only offer her a grave (7.5–7):

> at pius exsequiis Aeneas rite solutis,
> aggere composito tumuli, postquam alta quierunt
> aequora, tendit iter velis portumque relinquit.

> But pious Aeneas, with Caieta's rites properly performed and her grave-mound heaped up, after the deep waters grew quiet, bends his course with the sails and leaves port.

The emphasis on the propriety of Aeneas' action (seen in *pius* and *rite*) indicates the religious and social necessity of commemoration for the Trojans.[57] The group cannot move on until this task is complete. If Aeneas' burial of Caieta satisfies the Trojans' need for commemoration, questions still remain for the poem's audience about just what associations will be attached to her death: the fame she gained through her geographical commemoration, or the pain that faces Aeneas as he loses yet another close companion?[58]

Commemorative apostrophes

In a series of apostrophes that punctuate the *Aeneid*'s second half, the narrator addresses characters who stand on the threshold of death. These apostrophes have been productively studied from a variety of perspectives,

[56] O'Hara 1996, 91.

[57] Horsfall 2000, ad 5 notes that *pius* is regularly linked with Aeneas' religious duties.

[58] While Caieta's death surely hurts Aeneas, Hardy 1991, 219 and Jenkyns 1998, 466 overplay its effect by claiming that it represents the loss of a final link with his Trojan past. Aeneas' memories still tie him to Troy (see, for instance, his speech to Ascanius at 12.432–40), and Horsfall 2000, ad 2 is right to term Caieta "simply another link with Troy."

such as markers of Roman identity[59] or judgments on the *Aeneid*'s teleological plot,[60] but their distinctive form and arresting emotional content can threaten to overshadow their consequential interaction with their context. Here, sometimes separated by only a few dozen verses, the epic's characters apostrophize the same characters as the narrator, and their commemorations, which prove to be starkly unlike his, have a significant impact on how his exclamations are understood.[61] This multitude of apostrophes demonstrates the deep-seated need of the *Aeneid*'s characters and narrator to frame and define the past, even as they create a superfluity of competing memories that reveals that any closure achieved by commemoration may prove illusory.

The characters and narrator's apostrophes create a striking juxtaposition. Having established the thematic importance of commemoration in his programmatic apostrophe of Caieta, the narrator commemorates a series of dead youths in the next three books. Here, he continues to manipulate time and perspective as he draws the audience in to share his commemoration. Through these apostrophes, he attempts to define the essence of the characters' existences and, at the same time, to transform his audience into a remembering community that shares his unique point of view. The narrator's apostrophes advance a view of these deaths through a specifically Roman temporal and cultural lens, while the characters speak from a more immediate and emotional vantage point with an eye toward understanding their losses within their present surroundings. The characters challenge these narratival apostrophes in a way that Aeneas' burial of Caieta did not, since they also avail themselves of the emotional intensity and focusing capability of apostrophe.[62]

These differing apostrophes lead to a superfluity of competing memories, an abundance of representations which confronts two distinct groups: the Trojans hear the majority of the apostrophes spoken by the epic's characters, while the *Aeneid*'s audience bears witness to every address made by the poem's characters and narrator. Ellen Oliensis draws out a commemorative

59 Reed 2007, 16–43.

60 Block 1982 finds that the narrator's apostrophes ask the audience to question their own response to various incidents, while Behr 2005 and 2007, 16–32 argues that his apostrophes either endorse or question the teleological movement of the *Aeneid*'s plot.

61 The term *apostrophe* typically refers to the narrator's direct address of one his characters (Behr 2007, 1 advances a definition of apostrophe along these lines), but I extend it here to include instances where a character addresses an absent person. Both represent a turning away from one's immediate task: the narrator from his description, the characters from interaction with one another.

62 The characters do not know their apostrophes challenge the narrator's, but this does not lessen their effect on the *Aeneid*'s audience. On contrasts between the knowledge possessed by the characters and the narrator of a literary work, see Oliensis 2009, 96.

tension created by any death: "Forgetting the dead is a culpable perfidy, tantamount to murder," but, at the same time, the underworld's Lethe River hints at a need to forget so that the living can continue on.[63] While some characters in the *Aeneid* are forgotten (Arruns) or threatened with such a fate (Aeneas by Dido), in these apostrophes the characters and narrator strive to remember the dead and to integrate that person into their own and their community's continuing existence. Each of the apostrophes under consideration here revolves around how a death is understood as part of the community's story, and each speaker aspires to have his commemoration become the community's standardized memory of that event, or, in other words, its oikotype. Shared social memories can bind a group together, yet, as the epic progresses, the characters' commemorations multiply and diverge to such an extent that they undermine the possibility that any social memory can become an oikotype for either Aeneas' community or the narrator's audience. Since the *Aeneid* commemorates a past that comprises its audience's origins, these clashes between various apostrophes are of special importance. Encountering a work that aspires to be their social memory, the audience faces a multitude of commemorations that challenges the very possibility of a standardized version of the past.

A few books after his address of Caieta, the narrator turns his attention to Nisus and Euryalus. Well before he apostrophizes them, though, the *Aeneid*'s characters have made it abundantly clear that the pair's actions will have a claim on the Trojans' memories. Nisus states that he acts out of a desire for "glory for the deed" (*facti* | *fama*, 9.194–5); Aletes, an older Trojan, promises the pair that Ascanius will "never be forgetful of such a service" (*meriti tanti non immemor umquam*, 9.256); and Ascanius, reminded of Aeneas' devotion to Anchises by Euryalus' dedication to his own mother (9.292–4),[64] vows that he will treat the boy's mother as his own (9.296–302). From every perspective, enshrinement within the community's memory stands as an inducement to perform a risky action, yet none of the characters' imagined futures matches the actual reactions to Nisus and Euryalus' deeds.[65]

Soon after Nisus and Euryalus' mission ends in their deaths, the narrator responds with an unexpectedly laudatory exclamation (9.446–9):

[63] Oliensis 2009, 29. [64] See S. J. Harrison 1991, ad 1.824 for this reading.

[65] These three interactions with memory enact a cyclical relationship between deeds and memory. Nisus acts because he hopes to be remembered; Aletes imagines how in the future Nisus and Euryalus' completed act will be remembered; and Ascanius' words show how a memory of the past (in this case a memory of Aeneas' piety) can incite others to act in the present (here, to encourage and reward those who behave with a similarly pious mind-set).

fortunati ambo! si quid mea carmina possunt,
nulla dies umquam memori vos eximet aevo,
dum domus Aeneae Capitoli immobile saxum
accolet imperiumque pater Romanus habebit.

Fortunate pair! If my songs have any power, then no day will ever remove you from a remembering age, not while Aeneas' house stands on the Capitoline's immovable rock and the Roman father holds sway.

The narrator memorializes Nisus and Euryalus within a larger community and time-frame, and he focuses as much on his own ability to offer a commemoration as he does on the pair themselves. This contrasts with the preceding lines (9.435–7), where he accentuates the pathos of Euryalus' death through likening the rolling of his head to the motion of a flower that droops in the rain or is cut by a plough. Now, though, the narrator shifts the perspective away from any specific image of slaughter. By doing so, he minimizes the trauma of their immediate deaths and characterizes them as fortunate for having been enshrined together in his song.[66]

There are three conditions that need to be met in order for the pair to be remembered: the poet's song must possess a certain amount of force; Aeneas must remain a central figure at the core of Rome; and a Roman leader must hold power.[67] These requirements intertwine the narrator's poetic capabilities with the longevity and cohesion of Roman society. His song will ensure that the pair will be remembered, but that memory needs a society, composed of his audience, to carry it on. His apostrophe, by bringing that pair into his audience's here and now, allows them to share this moment with Nisus and Euryalus and guarantee their memory.[68]

The epic's characters, though, have a far different view of Nisus and Euryalus, one closer in tone to the narrator's melancholic image of a flower than to his ringing apostrophe. For them, the pair's end is colored by the

[66] The narrator's commemoration of the two clashes with their dreadful end. For considerations of its tone, see Heinze 1993, 170; Otis 1964, 350; Johnson 1976, 62–3; G. Williams 1983, 205–7; Behr 2005, 204; and Reed 2007, 39, 169–70. Casali 2004, 351–4 finds contradiction and uncertainty within the narrator's apostrophe itself, pointing out that the house of Aeneas may not be immobile and that Nisus and Euryalus actually do more harm than good in their mission, succeeding only in undermining the Trojans' morale. These undertones are certainly there, but the strong praise on his apostrophe's surface still offers a stark contrast with the commemorations surrounding it.

[67] As Lowrie 2009, 166 notes, the narrator forgoes "universal claims for cultural particularity" by linking his power with the Roman Empire and not the Muse. For passages with similar imagery and concepts, see Hor. *C.* 3.30 and Ov. *Met.* 15.871–9.

[68] Block 1982, 19 notes how this apostrophe "shifts the emotional attention of the audience from its own to [the narrator's] response." This is certainly true, but the audience's emotional attention shifts again to Euryalus' mother shortly thereafter.

dread-inducing commemoration of Euryalus' mother.[69] After learning of her son's death, she rushes to the walls of the Trojan camp and sees his head impaled on a long pole.[70] She plaintively cries out: "Is this you I see, Euryalus?" (*hunc ego te, Euryale, aspicio?*, 9.481). The initial three words of her speech, all pronouns, reveal a shocked attempt to understand her relationship with her son in this new situation. Referred to both with a second-person pronoun ("you," [*te*]) and a third-person masculine pronoun ("this," [*hunc*]), Euryalus has been transformed into a terrible emblem of his death at the enemy's hands.[71]

The end of her speech elaborates on the pain this change causes (9.490–2):

> quo sequar? aut quae nunc artus avulsaque membra
> et funus lacerum tellus habet? hoc mihi de te,
> nate, refers? hoc sum terraque marique secuta?
>
> To where am I to follow? Or what land now holds your limbs and dismembered trunk and mangled corpse? Do you bring this back to me from you, son? Have I followed this on land and sea?

Euryalus' mother bemoans the fact that she cannot properly commemorate her son with a burial. She no longer designates his body with a masculine pronoun, such as she did at 481, but instead marks him out with the neuter pronoun *hoc* ("this," 9.491 and 9.492), which likely refers back to "corpse" (*funus*, 9.491).[72] Although she still addresses him as "son" (*nate*, 9.492), this tender word only points toward the cruel gap between his earlier existence and current state. His mangled corpse intrudes upon and even threatens to overwrite earlier memories of the child she faithfully followed over land and sea. Staring straight at Euryalus' severed head, she retrojects his death onto her recollections of their life together, while the narrator's apostrophe looks ahead to the future, where Nisus and Euryalus' remembrance is tied to Rome.

[69] Euryalus' mother is never named. Her child's existence defines her entire identity (see Fantham 1999, 224).

[70] She receives news of her son's death from "Rumor" (*Fama*) (9.473–5), the same *fama* that Nisus stated would suffice as his reward. The wordplay is biting, and this example fits well with the observation of Hedjuk 2009, 301 about the generally negative connotation of *fama* in the *Aeneid*.

[71] As Vernant 1991, 72 remarks, a mutilated corpse "can neither be celebrated nor forgotten," and Euryalus' mother struggles to reconcile what she sees now with her earlier memories of her son.

[72] *Hoc* in 492 could be a causal ablative, meaning "For this reason, I have followed [you] on land and sea." The verb *sequor*, though, generally has a direct object (see *OLD*), and the pronoun is more likely to be in the accusative. Conington 1884, ad 9.492 reaches the same conclusion.

Euryalus' mother's memorialization of her son inflames the Trojans with grief.[73] The entire army is on the verge of being overwhelmed by mourning when Ascanius and Ilioneus order that she be carried away. With this action, Ascanius fails to live up to his earlier promise that he would regard Euryalus' mother as his own.[74] For the Trojans, the youths' severed heads monumentalize an irrevocable and horrific death; for the audience the grisly display undercuts the narrator's heroic treatment of the pair.[75] The lament of Euryalus' mother ends this episode and exemplifies a strong alternative to the narrator's commemoration, but it offers no closure of its own, and doubts still remain about how the pair will be remembered by their community.[76]

In the next book, conflict again swirls around a character's commemoration. Here the battle concerns Lausus, an Etruscan who fights against the Trojans. Once more the narrator's memorialization differs from the characters', but this contrast, even more so than before, accentuates the rapid shifts that a memory undergoes according to the present circumstances of the one who remembers. Lausus' father Mezentius makes the first claim about what his son should signify as he prepares to fight against Aeneas. As already discussed above, Mezentius envisions his son as a "trophy" (*tropaeum*, 10.775), wearing the spoils Mezentius has stripped from Aeneas.[77] Mezentius believes that this living memorial will commemorate his action as a protective parent and martial champion.

The narrator knows, however, that the fight will not end with Mezentius commemorating a victory. Lausus will die in an attempt to save Mezentius, and the narrator commemorates the youth precisely when he bravely decides to come to his father's aid (10.789–93):

> ingemuit cari graviter genitoris amore,
> ut vidit, Lausus, lacrimaeque per ora volutae –
> hic mortis durae casum tuaque optima facta,
> si qua fidem tanto est operi latura vetustas,[78]
> non equidem nec te, iuvenis memorande, silebo.

[73] Wiltshire 1988, 51 notes how public and private overlap in the mother's reaction. Hardy 1991, 237–40; Fantham 1999, 225; and Casali 2004, 352–4 comment on how this lament undermines Aeneas' mission. For more on women and lament in the *Aeneid*, see Perkell 1997, passim and esp. 271 and Nugent 1992, 272–3.

[74] See 9.297–8: "For she will be a mother to me and only the name of Creusa will be missing" (*namque erit ista mihi genetrix nomenque Creusae | solum defuerit*).

[75] Contra Behr 2007, 21 who finds that "The narrator's externalized reflections orient our reading and reconstitute the movement of the plot toward a more unified meaning." This unified meaning is never achieved, as the apostrophe of Euryalus' mother ends this episode.

[76] Nugent 1992, 289.

[77] See p. 131.

[78] See S. J. Harrison 1991, ad loc. for the interpretation of this line.

> Lausus groaned deeply out of love for his dear father, when he saw [that Mezentius was wounded], and tears rolled down his cheeks – If in any way antiquity will lend credibility to such a deed, then I will be silent here neither about the misfortune of harsh death and your most excellent deeds nor about you, youth, so worthy to be remembered.

The narrator puts his temporal omniscience to good use, as he creates a memorial unencumbered by the bloody image of Lausus' death. At the same time as it acknowledges the harsh misfortune of this loss, the apostrophe devotes the majority of its energy to promising the youth that the narrator has a duty to commemorate his actions for the future.[79]

The commemoration itself is a stunning one. Voiced at the instant when Lausus makes a virtuous decision, it is a testament to his excellence as much as it is to the narrator's vision of his song as a bastion of memory, an art form that provides a worthy recompense for a heroic death. The phrase "youth so worthy to be remembered" (*iuvenis memorande*, 10.793) demonstrates that Lausus' valor makes the narrator responsible for creating a memorial.[80] This description of Lausus is encircled by the statement "I will not be silent" (*nec . . . silebo*, 10.793), an arrangement that embodies the close relationship between memory and song: memorable subjects form the basis of the narrator's song, and his song ensures that they remain remembered. The narrator extends this responsibility to remember to his audience. An array of temporal markers bring together the present of the narrative and the narrating-instance. The future status of the narrator's promise invokes a particular moment within the narrative, while his reference to the event's "antiquity" (*vetustas*, 10.792) represents his own point of view. Combined with his apostrophe, these markers create a continuous span of time into which the audience is invited as participants in the narrator's commemoration.

Not much later Lausus is apostrophized yet again, this time by the man who just killed him. Aeneas promises to return Lausus' body to his people for burial, but this promise is not enough for the Trojan. Lausus' actions have reminded Aeneas of his own piety toward Anchises,[81] and Aeneas searches for a way to honor the boy properly: "Unlucky, you will

[79] Behr 2007, 23 observes that Lausus' death is presented "as a justification of the glory of Rome and an encouragement to be selfless soldiers."

[80] P. Hardie 1993, 99 remarks on the tendency in epic for the poet and hero to be linked in the creation of fame, "the hero through the performance of memorable deeds, the poet through the commemoration of those deeds."

[81] See pp. 47–8.

nonetheless console yourself in your wretched death with this: you fall by the right hand of great Aeneas" (*hoc tamen infelix miseram solabere mortem: | Aeneae magni dextra cadis*, 10.829–30). The last line reads like an epitaph for Lausus' grave.[82] Aeneas imagines that the blow of death will be diminished for Lausus since he fell by the hand of so great a warrior.[83]

After Mezentius learns that Lausus died protecting him, the meaning of his son changes. Lausus' corpse now causes Mezentius to think only of his own wretched survival (10.846–9):

> tantane me tenuit vivendi, nate, voluptas,
> ut pro me hostili paterer succedere dextrae,
> quem genui? tuane haec genitor per vulnera servor
> morte tua vivens?
>
> Did so great a pleasure for living hold me, son, that I allowed you to battle the enemy in my place, you whom I begot? Am I, your father, saved by these wounds of yours? Do I live because of your death?

Mezentius does not use the vocabulary of memory, but Lausus' body clearly causes him to reflect upon his earlier decision to retreat. "Pleasure" (*voluptas*) has a particular bite, contrasting with the martial fortitude and paternal care Mezentius ought to have demonstrated. Mezentius' commemoration is the last in a line of apostrophes to Lausus, each contradicting previous memorials and each, in spite of its assertiveness, unable to secure a foothold in the community's understanding of the youth's death. Even the narrator's commemoration, far-sighted and broad in its glance toward the future, does not seem assured of permanence.

The splintering of commemorations intensifies later in the book when Pallas' death approaches. Here, the narrator makes his presence felt more so than before: in addition to contributing an apostrophe of his own, he chastises Turnus for his reaction to killing Pallas. Alongside the narrator, Pallas himself, Turnus, Aeneas, and Evander all consider the potential ramifications of the end of Pallas' life. The characters' various memorials stand against the backdrop of the narrator's commemorative force, and everyone

[82] Its concision and self-reference recall the inscription Aeneas places over the Greek arms he dedicates at Actium: "Aeneas [dedicates] these arms from the victorious Greeks" (*AENEAS HAEC DE DANAIS VICTORIBVS ARMA*, 3.288).

[83] Whether or not the victory enhances Aeneas' claimed martial superiority is debatable at the least. Glory does not naturally attach itself to a victory over a young and overmatched opponent who is valiantly protecting his father, and the reference to Aeneas' "cruel anger" (*saevae . . . irae*, 10.813) darkens his actions and reminds the reader of his later treatment of Turnus in *Aeneid* 12 (see there *saevi . . . doloris*, 12.945 and *ira | terribilis*, 12.946–47).

who apostrophizes Pallas, the narrator included, fails in his attempt to crystallize the meaning of the boy's death.

Pallas is the first to imagine his death. About to enter battle with Turnus, he says, "I will be praised either for already carrying off the supreme spoils or for a distinguished death: my father is equal to either fate" (*aut spoliis ego iam raptis laudabor opimis | aut leto insigni: sorti pater aequus utrique est*, 10.449–50). These divergent outcomes, Pallas asserts, will impact his father in the same way. His statement's structure, though, belies this idea: Pallas lingers over his victory for an entire line but hastens past defeat in two words. His attempt to preemptively define the meaning of his battle demonstrates Pallas' need to secure a positive commemoration for himself. Focalizing the outcome through his father, he shows his belief that the public glory of a valiant defeat would trump any private feelings of loss.[84] In Pallas' mind, his closest relation's memory will reflect the valor he earns on the battlefield.[85]

The focus on Evander persists following Pallas' death. After killing the youth, Turnus stands over his body and calls out to Pallas' Arcadian followers (10.491–5):

> "Arcades, haec" inquit "memores mea dicta referte
> Evandro: qualem meruit, Pallanta remitto.
> quisquis honos tumuli, quidquid solamen humandi est,
> largior. haud illi stabunt Aeneia parvo
> hospitia."

> "Arcadians, remember these words of mine," he says, "and bring them back to Evander: I send Pallas back to him in the state that he deserved. Whatever honor there is in a grave, whatever solace there is in burying him, I bestow. His welcome to Aeneas will cost him no small price."

As Aeneas does with Lausus, Turnus returns the body of a young foe to his people for burial. Unlike Aeneas' commemoration though, Turnus' is designed to produce regret and dismay.[86] Pallas' grave will not signify the youth's martial excellence, but rather the terrible toll of an alliance with Aeneas.[87] Driven to ensure that his painful message is delivered, Turnus

[84] As S. J. Harrison 1991, ad 10.449 remarks, the idea of glory coming in either victory or defeat is seen also at Enn. *Ann.* 382–3, Skutsch 1985. Vergil complicates this model by having Pallas focalize the battle's results through his father.

[85] O'Sullivan 2009, 454 notes that the *Aeneid* concentrates on parents' reaction to their children's deaths rather than on the circumstances of the deaths themselves.

[86] See S. J. Harrison 1991, ad 10.491–500 for a thorough comparison of Aeneas and Turnus' behavior.

[87] See Otis 1964, 356 on Turnus' motivation for Evander to see the battle's result.

places a premium on its accurate reporting, and the cue of *memores* hints at the role recollection will play in Evander's reaction to Pallas' death.[88]

Having used the context of commemoration to get a bitter message through to Evander, Turnus secures a monument for himself by stripping Pallas of his sword-belt. Engraved on the baldric is a representation of the Danaids' murder of their husbands, but this elaborate decoration means nothing to Turnus.[89] For him, the belt stands solely as a marker of his victory.[90] The narrator forcefully indicts Turnus' decision to strip Pallas (10.500):

> . . . quo nunc Turnus ovat spolio gaudetque potitus.
> nescia mens hominum fati sortisque futurae
> et servare modum rebus sublata secundis!
> Turno tempus erit magno cum optaverit emptum
> intactum Pallanta et cum spolia ista diemque
> oderit.

> . . . Turnus now triumphs in the spoils and rejoices at their acquisition. How ignorant of fate and of their future lot are the minds of men, and how they fail to observe the mean when they are lifted high by good fortune! A time will come for Turnus when he will wish that Pallas could be bought back untouched and when he will hate these spoils and this day.

This scene is modeled on Hector's stripping of Achilles' armor from Patroclus, but in the *Iliad*, Zeus, not the narrator, condemns Hector.[91] Here the *Aeneid*'s narrator speaks. Picking up on Turnus' taunting commercial metaphor, he asserts that the Rutulian's overconfident mode of commemoration sets in motion events that will bring him misfortune. By changing the speaker, Vergil aggrandizes the narrator's role and highlights the narrator's interest in ensuring that his audience understands the impropriety of Turnus' action.[92]

A few lines later, the narrator himself addresses Pallas. While his earlier apostrophes generally stress the glory attached to the dead and push the grief inspired by their loss to the side, he now couples glory with grief (10.507–9):

88 See 2.547–50, 6.377, and 11.176–81 for similar emphases on remembering a message; the latter passage is discussed below.

89 For a consideration of the significance of the sword-belt's design along with bibliography on that topic, see Conte 1986, 185–95; S. J. Harrison 1991, ad 497–9; and Putnam 1998, 240 n. 1.

90 Lowrie 2009, 162.

91 The scene comes at *Il.* 17.201–8. See Knauer 1964, 417 and S. J. Harrison 1991, ad 501–5.

92 As S. J. Harrison 1991, ad 501–5 notes, Turnus is not "blamed for the act of spoliation itself, normal in heroic warfare, but for ostentatiously putting on the spoils, a token of fatal over-confidence."

o dolor atque decus magnum rediture parenti,
haec te prima dies bello dedit, haec eadem aufert,
cum tamen ingentis Rutulorum linquis acervos!

O, you, about to return to your father as a great grief and a great glory, this first day gave you to war, this same day takes you away, when, nevertheless, you leave great heaps of Rutulians!

The first four words of the narrator's apostrophe, *o dolor atque decus*, distill the potential meanings of Pallas' death. The subsequent lines expand upon these possibilities, fixing upon the terrible brevity of Pallas' single day of combat and the tangible evidence of his success. With Pallas' death once again focalized through Evander, the narrator imagines the pride and sadness the father will feel over the loss of his son.

These two perspectives on Pallas' death play out in Aeneas' words and deeds. When Aeneas first learns that Pallas has been killed, images of the past come to him unbidden (10.515–7):

Pallas, Evander, in ipsis
omnia sunt oculis, mensae quas advena primas
tunc adiit, dextraeque datae.

Pallas, Evander, everything comes before his very eyes, their tables, the first to which he came then as a stranger, the right hands given in agreement.

A stream of pictures appear before Aeneas' eyes, comprising selective details from his visit to Pallanteum: his encounter with Pallas and Evander, his partaking in a feast of Hercules, and his treaty with the Arcadians. This final climactic visualization presents the very gesture with which Evander formalized their alliance: "Therefore also my right hand, which you seek, is joined in treaty" (*ergo et quam petitis iuncta est mihi foedere dextra*, 8.169). Its appearance here reveals Aeneas' deep feeling of responsibility for Pallas, a responsibility which he has not successfully discharged. While the narrator does not say what emotions these memories provoke in Aeneas, his subsequent behavior (a boundless and indiscriminate slaughter, whose victims include priests and youths captured alive for sacrifice) makes his rage clearer than any description.[93]

On the next day, as Aeneas prepares to return Pallas' body to Evander, he addresses Pallas and laments the fact that the boy will never see

[93] For considerations of Aeneas' behavior, see Lee 1979, 85–8; S. J. Harrison 1991, ad 517–20; and J. Miller 2009, 160–4.

Aeneas' reign.[94] As his speech becomes more contemplative, Aeneas shifts his address from Pallas to Evander (11.55–8):

> . . . at non, Evandre, pudendis
> vulneribus pulsum aspicies, nec sospite dirum
> optabis nato funus pater. ei mihi quantum
> praesidium, Ausonia, et quantum tu perdis, Iule!

> . . . Yet, Evander, you will not look upon a body beaten back with shameful wounds, and you will not wish for a dread funeral with your son alive. Alas me, how great a bulwark you lost, Ausonia, and you, Iulus.

Horsfall notes that at the end of his speech, Aeneas turns to address Evander as if the Arcadian had just asked him if Pallas had died well.[95] Aeneas gives a different answer now than he did with his actions in *Aeneid* 10, as he comforts himself by imagining that Evander's viewing of his son's body will lead to an appreciation of Pallas' bravery.

Aeneas provides a model of commemoration for an audience larger than Evander in these lines. His address of Ausonia and Iulus imagines a future community ruled over by his son. Within this expansive context, Aeneas strives to define the standardized memory of Pallas. Pallas' defeat remains a loss, but it is also an act of glorious heroism that shatters neither the group's spirits nor its bond.[96] The commemoration Aeneas offers is not far from the reaction Pallas implied he would receive from his father because of a "distinguished death" (*leto insigni*, 10.450), and it is also not terribly different from the tone of the narrator's apostrophe of Nisus and Euryalus. Euryalus' mother, though, showed that that apostrophe was an unrealistic representation of how people react to immediate death. Evander has already indicated to Aeneas that he would rather die than learn of Pallas' death in battle (8.578–83), and, now, as his son's body journeys home to him, the audience is left to wait to see if his subsequent reaction will confirm his earlier feelings.

[94] See Lyne 1987, 178–9 on Aeneas' sensitivity here; as Feeney 1983, 215 points out, this is the only time Aeneas directly addresses Pallas.

[95] Horsfall 2003, ad 55. Reed 2007, 183 also comments on Aeneas' "understandable obsession with Evander's reaction."

[96] Two exclamations Aeneas makes over his father's death mirror the change that occurs in his reaction to Pallas' death from *Aeneid* 10 to *Aeneid* 11. Aeneas despairingly laments Anchises' passing right after it occurs at 3.708–15, but, later, when Aeneas commemorates that death's one-year anniversary on Sicily, he says that he will always regard the day as both "bitter" (*acerbum*, 5.49) and "honored" (*honoratum*, 5.50).

When Evander does eventually view his son's body, his words match the bitterness of Euryalus' mother's and forgo the expansive perspective of Aeneas'.[97] Evander's grief has the potential to indict any celebratory view of Pallas' death even more forcefully than the words of Euryalus' mother, for Evander speaks as one who is an elite member of society and who himself sent Pallas off to war. Furthermore, Evander turns his grief into a call for action, telling the Trojans that Pallas' corpse represents a debt Aeneas owes him (11.176–81):

> vadite et haec memores regi mandata referte:
> quod vitam moror invisam Pallante perempto
> dextera causa tua est, Turnum gnatoque patrique
> quam debere vides. meritis vacat hic tibi solus
> fortunaeque locus. non vitae gaudia quaero,
> nec fas, sed gnato manis perferre sub imos.

> Go, remember these orders and bring them to your king: your right hand is the reason why I drag out this wretched life even though Pallas is dead, that hand which, you see, owes Turnus to son and father. This opportunity alone is left for your worth and fortune. I do not seek this joy for my own life – that would be wrong – but so that I may bear this to my son under the lowest shades.

Evander's request to deliver a specific message mimics Turnus' orders to the Arcadians, and, like Turnus, his emphasis on memorization hints at the role recollection will play in Aeneas' retrospective understanding of Pallas' death. One assertion in particular has the potential to strongly affect Aeneas. Evander makes brutally clear why he suffers a wretched life: "Your right hand is the reason" (*dextera causa tua est*, 11.178).[98] The phrase bites Aeneas in two ways. Most obviously, "right hand" (*dextera*) refers to Aeneas' fighting skills, which ought to have kept Pallas safe before and which ought to kill Turnus now.[99] Yet the right hand also ratifies a treaty (8.169) and serves as a marker of hospitality (11.165), and Aeneas had just seen an image of his hand joined with Evander's. According to Evander, Aeneas ought to feel doubly responsible for Pallas' death: his right hand

[97] See Fantham 1999, 225 for a comparison of the effects of Evander's speech with that of Euryalus' mother.

[98] The "interwoven order" of the first three words gives them a "strong emphasis" (Horsfall 2003, ad 178).

[99] As 8.567 and 12.436 show, both Evander and Aeneas view the right hand as a weapon in war.

initiated Pallas' entry into war and then failed to protect him once battle began.[100]

Moreover, if Evander's words cause Aeneas to think back on the origins of their alliance, then this reflection may prompt the bitter realization of how he has failed in comparison with his father. When Aeneas seeks Evander's help in *Aeneid* 8, Evander tells Aeneas about Anchises' long-ago visit. Evander wanted to speak with Anchises, who, as Evander recollects, treated him kindly. The benefits of that meeting, as Evander says, extend all the way down to Pallas (8.166–8):

> ille mihi insignem pharetram Lyciasque sagittas
> discedens chlamydemque auro dedit intertextam,
> frenaque bina meus quae nunc habet aurea Pallas.

> As Anchises was leaving, he gave me a distinguished quiver and Lycian arrows and a cloak interwoven with gold, and two golden bridles which my Pallas now possesses.

Evander takes care to explain the connection that arose first between himself and Anchises and, then, because of Anchises' gifts, between Anchises and Pallas. Pallas, like Evander once did with Anchises, wishes to talk with the older stranger who visits his town,[101] but the repercussions of those two meetings between Trojan and Arcadian could not be more different.[102] Aeneas does not bestow gifts that are passed down from one generation to the next, but rather sees his young charge die. Anchises' departing presents to Evander clinch their bond and remain as symbols of his beneficent influence all the way down to the present time. Aeneas' relationship with Pallas leads to Pallas' death and, because Pallas is Evander's only son, to the end of Evander's line.

When Evander instructs the Trojans to repeat his words to Aeneas, he crafts a message to communicate that his son's loss is a "grief" (*dolor*), not a "glory" (*decus*). While the final repercussions of Pallas' death will be explored in Chapter 5, in Evander's mind Aeneas is obligated to take Turnus' life, and it is likely that the memories associated with Evander's words drive Aeneas in that direction. For now, it is enough to say that when

100 Additional connections between Aeneas' right hand and Pallas and Evander only further underscore Aeneas' earlier responsibility for the youth's life and his current need to avenge him. At 8.124, Pallas grasps Aeneas' "right hand" (*dextram*) immediately after meeting him; and at 8.558 Evander grasps Aeneas' "right hand" (*dextram*) as he sends Pallas and Aeneas off to battle.

101 See 10.160–2, where Pallas sits by Aeneas' side and asks him about the landmarks that presently surround them as well as Aeneas' earlier journeys.

102 In one sense, of course, this comparison is unfair since Anchises did not take Evander into war.

Aeneas at last gains the opportunity to kill Turnus, Evander's interpretation of Pallas' death has become the Trojan's oikotype. At this point in the text, *dolor* ("grief") does become overriding, a shift that shows the potential of apostrophe to concretize interpretations of events and construct a definitive memory of the past, one which comes to influence the poem's main character, its plot, and its audience's perspective.

Yet at this point in the *Aeneid*'s narrative, Evander's orders for revenge are only one of several conflicting commemorations that arise from Pallas' death, an enormously influential and productive locus of memory. The youth's body becomes a site open to manipulation. Turnus sets up his death as a marker of the high price of Evander's alliance with Aeneas, and he takes Pallas' baldric as spoils in a gesture that eerily echoes Pallas' own wish for "the supreme spoils" (*spoliis . . . opimis*, 10.449).[103] Here, the boy, in his own contemplation of his life's end, failed to anticipate his father's grief. Aeneas rages over Pallas' death at the end of *Aeneid* 10, but near the opening of *Aeneid* 11, he can already contemplate Evander's admiration of his son's end. When anger and revenge, not admiration, take center stage in Evander's reaction, this only adds to the multitude of reactions surrounding Pallas' death. If the narrator's apostrophe treats Pallas' death as a source of glory and grief, the characters cannot reconcile the contradictory nature of this view as they face down the tangible evidence of their own regrets. The narrative audience, having heard the story of Pallas' death and entered into the expansive present of the narrator's song, is left with no single model to guide their remembrance.

Audience, community, and memory

At the narrator's prompting, the Muse reminds him of certain events. Whether it is more precise to label the Muses' memory as learned or with a different word that reflects their divinity, it is not natural memory.[104] There is no indication that the Muses themselves have lived through the events they remember.[105] Similarly, the narrator himself exists apart from

103 For the significance of Pallas' designation of these spoils as *opimis*, see S. J. Harrison 1991, ad 449–50.

104 Learned memory depends upon active memorization; it is also referred to as artificial memory (Small 1997, 113). Natural memory is "memory from experience of past events"; it is also called "episodic or autobiographical memory" (Small 1997, 113). For more on the distinction between natural and learned memory, see J. Assmann 2006, 2.

105 The *Aeneid* never makes clear how the Muses learn of the events they relate. Compare this with the *Iliad*, which links the Muses' knowledge of events with their omnipresence: "Sing to me now you Muses, holding Olympian houses, for you goddesses are everywhere and know all things" (ἔσπετε νῦν μοι Μοῦσαι Ὀλύμπια δώματ' ἔχουσαι / ὑμεῖς γὰρ θεαί ἐστε πάρεστέ τε ἴστέ τε πάντα, Hom. *Il.* 2.484–5).

the events of his story, singing a song that is a learned memory with the perspective and insight of foreknowledge.

In one way, though, the narrator transforms his learned memory into natural memory. Occupying a space between the Muse's divine connection with past events and his audience's temporal remove, he bridges the gap between himself and the story he tells through his apostrophes. An apostrophe leaves only the present moment, and it is a moment that the narrator, the character addressed, and the audience inhabit together. By creating this shared present, the narrator blurs the boundaries between events he could have experienced and those he could not: Caieta, for example, died several centuries before the narrator's time, but he centers an apostrophe on her passing and reacts to it as if it were an event he experienced. Her death is enshrined in his song and, by extension, in the memory of the audience he invokes. In creating a moment that both he and his audience can inhabit together, the narrator brings himself and his audience closer to experiencing the events of his story and retaining them as a natural memory.

The status of the narrator's song as a social memory for his audience encourages their formation as a remembering community. Since the *Aeneid* tells the story of their origins, this content makes for a personal connection between audience and song. When the audience is presented with the opportunity to experience and remember the Trojans' journey, the narrator offers them the chance to make a personal connection with their society's story. Eviatar Zerubavel uses the term "sociobiographical memory" to describe memories that come from the "fusion of our own personal biography with the history of the groups or communities to which we belong."[106] This term aptly describes the sort of memory the narrator's song prompts. The Muse could never take part in this slippage between individual and group: she can neither hold this story as a social memory nor share in its events as something her community experienced. The narrator, though, can fashion a community from his song's audience and attempt to dictate the meaning of significant elements of its past. Alan Kirk observes that "A community *marks* certain elements of its past as being of constitutive significance," and this is precisely the process the narrator strives

[106] Zerubavel 1996, 290. On the same page he argues that "being social presupposes the ability to experience events that had happened to groups and communities to which we belong long before we joined them as if they were part of our own past." See also Freeman 95–123, where he considers "the process by which sources beyond the perimeter of the individual become woven into the fabric of memory, resulting in . . . 'the narrative unconscious'" (p. 96) and see Shils 1981, 51, who writes how memory, in addition to one's own experiences, also comes "from the memories of others older than himself with whom he associates."

to influence.[107] When he apostrophizes dead characters, he emphasizes these elements more so than others in his song, a strong signal that they ought to be remembered and, just as importantly, remembered in a specific way. The narrator's version of the past in these apostrophes situates death within an expansive frame and emphasizes its glory to a greater extent than the characters' apostrophes.

Yet the memories with which the audience is left and the reactions those memories prompt are far from set in stone. Vergil undermines the narrator's commemorations by including the often contradictory reactions of characters, which add to the poem's narrative complexity.[108] "The strength of apostrophe," Francesca D'Alessandro Behr argues, "resides in the emotional intensity which the trope contributes to the text."[109] The vital point to consider is that it is not only the narrator's apostrophes that enjoy this emotional intensity; it resides in the words of Euryalus' mother as well, along with those of Mezentius, Aeneas, Turnus, and Evander.[110] Significantly, in all of the cases discussed above, the characters' commemorations follow and, frequently, oppose the narrator's. He never has the last word.[111] Aeneas, as described in Chapter 1, strives to form an oikotype that minimizes the Trojans' earlier suffering and presents their past as worthy of preservation. He appears to generally enjoy success in doing so, as the Trojans never dispute the oikotype he advances. It is a different story for the narrator.[112] Each of his commemorations of a supposedly worthy death is followed by a variety of reactions driven by the blow of immediate devastation and the specter of lasting loss.

Alessandro Barchiesi, writing about the different perspectives mortals and immortals bring to events in the *Aeneid*, notes that "The representation

[107] Kirk 2005, 5 (emphasis original).

[108] This view of the *Aeneid*'s apostrophes builds on and contributes to a view of the epic as a piece of literature that contains a multiplicity of perspectives, sometimes shifting and sometimes conflicting. Lyne 1987 and Reed 2007 are two recent examples of scholarship that point out the epic's multiplicity of perspectives. On polyphony and dialogism in general, see Bakhtin 1981 and 1984.

[109] Behr 2007, 1.

[110] For another view, see Syed 2005, 53. She argues that while the "reader is guided by the narrator wherever his voice manifests itself . . . the reader is not always invited to share the fictional character's emotional response."

[111] Contra Behr 2007, 30: "In the apostrophes to the Nisus and Euryalus, to Pallas, and to Lausus . . . the Roman cause is prioritized and narrative closure achieved . . . the polyphony created by the empathetic rendering of each character's point of view is quickly corrected."

[112] This comparison between the *Aeneid*'s narrator and Aeneas is encouraged not only by the fact that each narrates lengthy tales of earlier events, but the verb *canere* is used to describe the action of each in doing so (1.1 and 4.14). Gasti 2006, 116 points out ways that Aeneas and the narrator are alike in their use of "the basic poetic mechanism of memory."

of suffering within a story of humans and gods compels one to a bifocal vision."[113] The import of this point can be extracted to the differences between the apostrophes of the *Aeneid*'s narrator and characters. Vergil presents the audience with representations of multiple reactions to human suffering, offering the audience an opportunity to appreciate the various ways of commemorating a character. Each audience member must decide how to remember any one of these deaths, and each makes this decision as an individual who is also part of the *Aeneid*'s remembering community. In consideration of the contrast between the narrator's apostrophes and the richness of the characters' commemorations, the project of establishing an oikotype becomes more challenging and complex.

The basic differences between the characters and narrator's interactions with memory call into question whether the audience will commemorate the past the way the narrator does. The narrator takes evident delight in memory's working and is keen to charge his audience to remember his song. Memory's impact is decidedly darker in the epic's action. While Aeneas does use memory to move forward and foster happiness (such as in his speech to his men on the shores of Carthage or in his "recollection" of the tables prophecy), these instances are rarely straightforward (the narrator reveals that Aeneas doubts what he says to his men at Carthage, and Aeneas' memory of Anchises' tables prophecy is fabricated).[114] A good portion of the characters' experiences with memory involves feelings of grief, regret, and suffering.

Vergil exploits these differences in the characters and narrator's apostrophes to show that no one commemoration may be dominant for a group. Faced with all these apostrophes, it is possible for the audience to remember and commemorate these characters in their own individual ways. Perspective matters, personal relationships matter, and, ultimately, the remembering individual's own life, in all its facets, matters. As these issues of remembrance arise, the audience is drawn in to a problem central to the *Aeneid*. This theme is the challenge of being part of a group that survives traumatic events, only to face the daunting task of remembering them. The importance of this challenge is signaled with clarity and force when the narrator introduces Caieta only to have her die. Building on this programmatic commemoration, Vergil paradoxically questions the possibility of the communal possession of a standardized version of the past even as he writes the version of Rome's past that will soon become a

[113] Barchiesi 1999, 329.

[114] For discussion of Aeneas' speech on Carthage's shore, see pp. 79–82; for the tables prophecy, see pp. 28–31 and 40–6.

classic. The pull between public and private, communal and individual, impacts every memory, and the *Aeneid* ponders whether a community can be formed of individuals who react so differently to events composing a social memory. So long as characters can promote and even tolerate the existence of different social memories, such as initially occurs in the process surrounding Pallas' death, the community's memory can shift in its content and even grow to accommodate new perspectives. Yet once an oikotype is formed, or, rather, once a community's leader decides that an oikotype has been formed, tolerance vanishes. The *Aeneid*'s final book, where the epic's narrator, characters, and audience, all must confront the possibility of memory's failure, faces this issue directly and complicates it further by calling into question the extent anyone, Aeneas included, can control what and how something is remembered.

CHAPTER FIVE

Imperatives of memory
Foundation and fury in Aeneid *12*

A glint of metal, a moment of recognition, and a furious slaughter: the essential elements of the *Aeneid*'s ending are so captivating that they threaten to obscure just how close Turnus comes to saving his life. His plea for mercy, partly based on an appeal to Aeneas' memory of his father, causes Aeneas to hesitate, and a peaceful dénouement is within reach not just for these characters but for the epic song in which they appear. Of course this is not the way the *Aeneid* ends. Once Aeneas sees Pallas' baldric on Turnus' shoulder, that "monument of savage grief" (*saevi monimenta doloris*, 12.945) reminds him of how it came to be there, and his reaction is immediate and deadly. Aeneas buries his sword in Turnus' chest, simultaneously bringing an end to his enemy's life and to the epic's narrative. Turnus appeals to memory in an effort to save his life, but, instead, a savage grief provoked by memory ends it. This contrast between the effects of an invocation of a past relationship and the consequences of a martial commemoration demonstrates the imperative force of memory in the *Aeneid*, the active and often uncontrolled influence it exerts over characters' minds and actions.

The sheer weight of the *Aeneid*'s final act, one of the most controversial deeds in all of Latin literature, tends to distance it from its immediate context. For a long period of time, the scene could stand as the final proof to an argument either that the epic celebrates the necessity and glory of Empire or that Vergil's poem exposes the personal pain and sacrifice Empire demands.[1] Under this rubric, it is all too easy for memory to be reduced to a predetermined cog in the evaluation of Aeneas' action. If we regard Aeneas' slaughter of Turnus as the justified capstone to the résumé of a leader who willingly serves a larger cause, memory's importance is minimized. It becomes a mere trigger for his killing of Turnus, a mental

[1] Putnam 1995, 28 notes the influence of the ending on the interpretation of the entire poem. Tarrant 2004, 116–8 outlines the two critical positions on this scene.

action whose sole significance lies in the fact that it prompts the Trojan to perform a deed he is fated to accomplish.[2] On the other hand, if the savage anger and sacrificial overtones of Aeneas' behavior take center stage and his references to Pallas evoke his numerous losses in the pursuit of a collective goal, then memory becomes a purely negative phenomenon, a process that brings Aeneas searing emotional pain, not the salutary release from the past forgetting may offer.

Yet just as scholars have come to recognize that the epic as a whole resists any "straightforward . . . pro- or anti-Augustan interpretation," so too is it necessary to re-evaluate memory's place in the *Aeneid*'s final lines.[3] This chapter argues that such a re-evaluation offers a fresh perspective on the poem's ending as well as issues central to memory's function in the epic as a whole. In this scene, Aeneas loses control over his interactions with memory as the past and future fold together. Up to this point, Aeneas has leveraged memory as a means to influence the Trojans' identity and emotions, reframing the Trojans' history as a necessary part of their future success. Now, though, the narrator depicts Aeneas' loss of control not as a failure, but rather as the unavoidable intrusion of the past into the present. As Rome is born out of an action dictated by memory, we are left questioning not whether Aeneas was right to kill Turnus, but rather what memory's centrality to this killing means for Rome's foundation, Aeneas' hopes for the future, and, as we shall see, even the narrator's relationship to his song.

An examination of *Aeneid* 12 shows that the characters' interactions with memory are anything but a straightforward process dictated by a larger scheme. Three scenes preceding Aeneas' killing of Turnus explore what role memory will play in Rome's origins: when Aeneas addresses Ascanius; when the narrator speaks out about his commemoration of the events of Aeneas' story; and when Juno and Jupiter reach an agreement about Troy's future. These passages largely revolve around Troy: Aeneas orders his son to remember and imitate the Trojan past; the narrator finds pain in commemorating Rome's Trojan roots; and Jupiter and Juno agree that the Romans will forget Troy altogether. These scenes draw out memory's

[2] Quint 1993 advances certain aspects of this claim. He sees Aeneas, in general, as a "lackluster, depersonalized hero" (83) and writes that in the poem's final scene "Once again, we cannot tell whether Aeneas has a will of his own" (95). Hershkowitz 1991, 76 claims that Aeneas is dehumanized "with his acceptance of his role as a tool of Roman destiny," and Oliensis 2009, 132–3, comes close to accepting such a portrait of Aeneas as well, although she somewhat distances herself from it.

[3] Tarrant 2004, 118. See also Conte 2007, 157–8, who argues that "in Virgil contradiction does not ask to be resolved, but only accepted for what it is, as double and irreducibly double." On the evaluation of this final scene, see Tarrant 2012, 16–30.

transitional potential. Throughout the *Aeneid* memory acts as a hinge that facilitates and frustrates transitions, both between different times and between different groups of people. With Aeneas' foundation of a new city hovering just over the horizon, the Trojans face an epochal transition between past and future, and the characters and narrator strive with a particular intensity to make meaning out of the shift from one civilization to another.

The issues of trauma, progress, and identity raised by these scenes come to a head in Aeneas' last action. Throughout the epic, and in this book with particular urgency, Aeneas turns to memory in his attempt to cross the divide between Troy and Rome as well as between himself and the Trojans. A linchpin of his leadership, recollection and commemoration have become central to Aeneas' thoughts and emotions. He is as susceptible to being influenced by memory and its attendant emotional spurs as he is adroit in managing them. In Aeneas' final deed, the weight of all the different memories that press upon him is so great that the boundaries between past and future and individual and society fade away. At the time when Aeneas may be seen as acting on behalf of either a purely personal feeling or the Roman fate that drives him, his slaughter of Turnus springs from the interaction of a private grief and a collective need; and at the moment when he is compelled to make a choice between past and future, his deed stands just as much as a model to be remembered as a testament to the power of earlier times.

A message between generations

Aeneas addresses his son a little less than halfway through *Aeneid* 12. The instructions he gives to Ascanius represent the only example of direct speech between the two in the epic, and Aeneas' words make memory and, specifically, the remembrance of Troy central to his relationship with his son.[4] By delaying this one speech until *Aeneid* 12 and setting it within Aeneas' dramatic return to battle after being wounded, the narrator heightens its impact.[5] It stands as a programmatic marker of Aeneas and Ascanius'

[4] Lyne 1987, 192 argues that the narrator's inclusion of only this single speech indicates that Aeneas has but "rare contact" with his son, yet this does not take into account the likelihood of unnarrated conversations between the pair. It is likely that Aeneas and his son have spoken many times over the course of events described in the *Aeneid*, especially given that Ascanius' importance to Aeneas is clear throughout the epic (see, for example, Aeneas' attention to him as Troy falls (2.563, 2.723–4) and the weight of his son's welfare in his decision to leave Carthage (4.274–6, 4.354–5)).

[5] Kristol 1990, 5 also notes how the speech's singularity and late appearance emphasize its importance.

relationship, an embodiment of all Aeneas must have said to Ascanius in the past and all the hopes he holds for him in the future (12.432–40):

> postquam habilis lateri clipeus loricaque tergo est,
> Ascanium fusis circum complectitur armis
> summaque per galeam delibans oscula fatur:
> "disce, puer, virtutem ex me verumque laborem,
> fortunam[6] ex aliis. nunc te mea dextera bello
> defensum dabit et magna inter praemia ducet.
> tu facito, mox cum matura adoleverit aetas,
> sis memor et te animo repetentem exempla tuorum
> et pater Aeneas et avunculus excitet Hector."

> After Aeneas fits his shield to his side and his corselet to his back, he wraps his arms around Ascanius and hugs him, and, lightly kissing him through his helmet, he speaks: "Learn, boy, valor and true labor from me, fortune from others. Now my right hand will defend you in war and lead you among great prizes. Since you will soon become a man, take care to remember and let both your father Aeneas and your uncle Hector rouse you as you seek examples of your people with your mind."

In his six-line speech, Aeneas portrays recollection as a morally beneficial process, necessary for his son's success. Still a "boy" (*puer*, 12.435), Ascanius should draw upon memories of Aeneas and Hector to complete his transition to manhood.[7] By remembering earlier actions, he will be inspired to perform heroic deeds himself when he becomes an adult.[8]

[6] The connotations of *fortunam* are a matter of some dispute. Quint 1993, 94 and Keith 2000, 8 claim that it represents an external force outside of Aeneas' control, while Gotoff 1985, 39 believes it represents the good fortune which Aeneas does not enjoy. Kristol 1990, in a monograph on the meanings of *labor* and *fortuna* in the *Aeneid*, thinks it best to take this instance of *fortuna* as representing an "external force . . . which may visit the individual with good or bad luck . . . in a capricious manner" (168 and see 166–7), yet she is careful to note that no one meaning of *fortuna* is predominant in the epic (176) and that this particular "statement [at 12.436] is ambiguous" (254). It seems most reasonable to understand both meanings of *fortuna* in this passage: Aeneas certainly recognizes that his losses are many (bad fortune) and some of them occurred because of circumstances out of his control (luck).

[7] Servius ad 12.439 notes, Aeneas' command "remember" (*sis memor*) should be understood as meaning remember "my deeds" (*meorum factorum*). This is likely the initial meaning of Aeneas' injunction, but once Aeneas specifies in the next line that both he and Hector ought to serve as examples for Ascanius, the object of Ascanius' memory expands to include Hector's deeds alongside Aeneas'. E. Henry 1989, 3 also notes that Aeneas' words show that his son will "need a living awareness of the past" as he becomes a man.

[8] This order keys into a strong Roman tradition of using the memory of earlier deeds to guide future behavior (for examples, see Ennius *Ann.* 156 Skutsch 1985, Cic. *De Rep.* 5.1.1, and Polybius 6.53.3, 6.54.3).

An allusion at the end of Aeneas' speech reveals the care he takes in shaping his words. The final line is a close echo of something Andromache said to Aeneas at Buthrotum. Shortly after seeing him, Hector's widow asks Aeneas about his son: "Do both his father Aeneas and his uncle Hector at all rouse Ascanius to ancient valor and manly courage?" (*ecquid in antiquam virtutem animosque virilis | et pater Aeneas et avunculus excitat Hector?*, 3.342–3). Andromache's question reveals a belief that past memories can encourage future generations to perform virtuous actions. Inscribed within its original context, it stands alongside her tearful prayers to an empty grave, a question that seeks to know whether the past will be repeated in the future. Aeneas strips this remark of its stultifying associations and adds to it a measure of dynamism and progress. He sets the past examples as part of an active process of recollection that should accompany and aid Ascanius' maturation. Instead of concentrating the results of this activity on a return to "ancient virtue" (*antiquam virtutem*), Aeneas makes it integral to the transition to valorous manhood. By carefully selecting one aspect of Andromache's beliefs and transposing it into a speech that looks both backward and forward, Aeneas honors Andromache's devotion to Troy while eschewing her paralyzing immersion in earlier days.

Aeneas' choice of models for his son to imitate asserts his commitment to ensuring that Troy and its people be remembered in a productive and honorable way.[9] As a father, Aeneas is a natural example for Ascanius to follow. The selection of Hector, though, is more surprising. While Ascanius might remember Hector's defense of Troy from his earliest years, in the *Aeneid* that warrior is known only in death.[10] For the poem's audience as well as Ascanius, Hector has been largely left to the past; the battleground has shifted from Troy to Italy and Aeneas is the Trojans' undisputed leader. Yet this pairing asserts Hector's equality with Aeneas. Hector and, by extension, the city that fell along with him are endowed with the same vital relevance to Trojan society as Aeneas himself.[11] Aeneas wants Ascanius to

[9] Troy remains a central and constant part of Aeneas' identity, contra Jenkyns 1998, 413, who argues that Aeneas' Trojan identity fades. While Trojan qualities are just one aspect of the nascent Roman identity the epic suggests, Aeneas struggles to be sure that they endure and are passed down. On the complexity of the Roman and Italian identity, the *Aeneid* constructs, see Toll 1991, 4 and Reed 2007, passim and esp. 202.

[10] See 2.268–9, where Hector appears to Aeneas in a dream with his death wounds still fresh; and 3.303–5 and 3.311–12, where Andromache, Hector's widow, prays at his grave and wonders if she is in the underworld with Hector.

[11] Hector's death is linked almost immediately with Troy's destruction via metaphor in *Iliad* 22. Here, as Achilles drags his corpse around the city, the whole city mourns "as if all of majestic Troy were completely burning with fire" (ὡς εἰ ἅπασα | Ἴλιος ὀφρυόεσσα πυρὶ σμύχοιτο κατ' ἄκρης, *Il.* 22.410–1).

remain a Trojan, even as he will build a new society, and he orders him to extend his memory back to include Troy and the deeds Hector performed there.[12]

Two other allusions in this passage, one to Homer's *Iliad*, the other to Sophocles' *Ajax*, further highlight Aeneas' belief in memory's ability to provide generational continuity. Aeneas' inclusion of Hector as an example strengthens the connection of these verses with an Iliadic scene portraying a similar father–son interaction. This link draws out the distinctive qualities of Aeneas' orders and suggests that he is enacting a new paradigm of father–son interaction centered on the successful use of memory. This passage's Homeric counterpart comes when Hector addresses Astyanax before going out to battle in *Iliad* 6.[13] Hector tells his infant son how he hopes that "Sometime someone may say the man [Astyanax] coming from war is much better than his father" (ποτέ τις εἴποι πατρός γ᾽ ὅδε πολλὸν ἀμείνων | ἐκ πολέμου ἀνιόντα, *Il.* 6.479–80). Hector imagines an anonymous individual who sees Astyanax returning from war and compares him with his father. The anticipation of such a comparison reveals Hector's yearning for continuity and growth between the generations.

The scene's frame undercuts Hector's optimistic message.[14] Before he even addresses Astyanax, there is already a hint that the connection between father and son is not secure. When Hector first sees Astyanax, he tries to hold him in his arms. His helmet, however, terrifies the boy, who shrinks from his father's embrace, screaming. The scene's conclusion is even darker.[15] As soon as Hector leaves for battle, Andromache proceeds to her quarters. She cries as she goes on her way, and she finds her handmaidens in a similar state (*Il.* 6.500–2):

αἳ μὲν ἔτι ζωὸν γόον Ἕκτορα ᾧ ἐνὶ οἴκῳ·
οὐ γάρ μιν ἔτ᾽ ἔφαντο ὑπότροπον ἐκ πολέμοιο
ἵξεσθαι προφυγόντα μένος καὶ χεῖρας Ἀχαιῶν.

[12] The mention of Hector's name would invoke all his deeds. A person's name, as Maya Lin writes, is a generous memory prompt: it "bring[s] back everything someone could remember about a person" (quoted in Tatum 2003, 4).

[13] The links between these passages go beyond the simple fact that in each a father speaks to his son and that Aeneas names Hector at 12.440. The scenes' frames are also similar: Aeneas kisses his son before he speaks and Hector does the same, and both warriors head off to battle immediately after their speeches. Also, just like in the *Aeneid*, this is the first time in the *Iliad* that Hector speaks to his son. MacKay 1957, 16 offers a much different reading of this passage's allusions to the *Iliad* and *Ajax*. He argues that Vergil "intended the apparent incongruity" between Aeneas' success and Hector and Ajax's failures to reveal Aeneas' character to be "that of a man who had outlived the sense of personal achievement, almost the sense of personality."

[14] Arthur 1981, 34 notes how the mood of Hector's speech contrasts with the despair that surrounds it.

[15] See Kirk 1990, ad 6.500 on how this passage's syntax highlights "its pathos and paradox."

> They wept over Hector in his house, even though he was still alive. For they thought he would never return from war alive, having fled the force and hands of the Achaeans.

The servants prematurely mourn a living man, behaving as if they were already burdened with Hector's death.[16] Their lamentation bookends the terror that grips Astyanax when he sees his father in arms. The young boy's fright betokens a gap between the generations, and recollection – here linked with mourning and death – fails to bridge it.

In contrast, the context surrounding Aeneas' speech reinforces his connection with Ascanius. Before Aeneas' wound is miraculously healed by Venus, Aeneas and a group of warriors stand about in frustration and worry (12.398–400):

> stabat acerba fremens ingentem nixus in hastam
> Aeneas magno iuvenum et maerentis Iuli
> concursu, lacrimis immobilis.

> Aeneas was standing, bitterly shouting and leaning on his giant spear, surrounded by a great crowd of warriors and weeping Iulus, but he was unmoved by the tears.

Iulus mourns his father, yet Aeneas stands untouched by his son's mourning. The mood changes dramatically when the enemy arrow leaves Aeneas' leg seemingly of its own accord and this miraculous healing is attributed to the gods. The narrator neither specifies Ascanius' mood here nor when Aeneas later kisses him through his helmet,[17] but, once Aeneas runs off to battle, no sign of mourning appears that could move the scene away from its mood of purposeful haste and optimism.[18] Instead, the mourning that comes to a decisive end when Aeneas is healed mirrors and reverses the mourning that follows Hector's speech, suggesting that Aeneas and Ascanius' fortune will be different than Hector and Astyanax's. This positive context enables Aeneas' words to exercise their full impact, and it leaves his interaction with his son as a new paradigm of a father–son relationship that overwrites Hector's relationship with Astyanax.

[16] Hector, too, often imagines how others will view him when he is dead (Martin 1989, 130–45 and esp. 136; Martin terms this phenomenon "eulogistic dramatization" (137)). Redfield 1994, 180 offers general remarks about mourning which aptly describe the handmaidens' behavior in this passage: mourning "celebrates the departed, not for what he did, but for how much he will be missed. The living person is thus dismissed, and a new social figure, the absent one, is created."

[17] This kiss may be light, impeded by Aeneas' helmet, but it is nonetheless a kiss. See *TLL* 441.20–4 for parallels.

[18] Contra Lyne 1987, 192 and C. Lloyd 1995, 19, who argue that the Vergilian passage is gloomy and stark.

This passage's allusion to Sophocles' tragedy offers another contrasting example of generational instruction that underlines the active moral function Aeneas attributes to recollection. 12.435–6 recalls Ajax's words to his son at Soph. *Ajax* 550–1, a passage that shows a break between the generations.[19] Ajax, after having resolved to commit suicide, speaks to his infant son: "Oh son, may you be more fortunate than your father, but like him in all other things. Indeed, then you would not be base" (ὦ παῖ, γένοιο πατρὸς εὐτυχέστερος | τὰ δ᾽ ἄλλ᾽ ὁμοῖος· καὶ γένοι᾽ ἂν οὐ κακός, *Aj*. 550–1). The optative mood of Ajax's verb, "May you be" (γένοιο, *Ajax* 550), makes no claim that his desire will be accomplished, and he does not give his son any advice that explains how to behave. This contrasts with Aeneas' imperative, "Learn!" (*disce*, 12.435), as well as with the explicit mnemonic instructions that follow it.

Aeneas' instructions actually find a somewhat similar model in a passage preceding Ajax's advice by a mere thirty lines. Here Ajax's wife Tecmessa pleads with him to reconsider his decision to commit suicide (*Aj*. 520–4):

> ἀλλ᾽ ἴσχε κἀμοῦ μνῆστιν: ἀνδρί τοι χρεὼν
> μνήμην προσεῖναι, τερπνὸν εἴ τί που πάθοι.
> χάρις χάριν γάρ ἐστιν ἡ τίκτους᾽ ἀεί:
> ὅτου δ᾽ ἀπορρεῖ μνῆστις εὖ πεπονθότος,
> οὐκ ἂν γένοιτ᾽ ἔθ᾽ οὗτος εὐγενὴς ἀνήρ.
>
> Come, remember me, too. Memory ought to be present for a man, if he experiences something pleasant. For one kindness always begets another: but whoever allows the memory of a good deed to escape him, no longer would he be a noble man.

According to Tecmessa, a man ought to act upon his memories of good experiences. This ethical function is similar to the role Aeneas assigns to memory. Aeneas, like Ajax, views his fortune dimly, but this does not dissuade him from attempting to instruct his son, and this attempt, at the very least, gives Ascanius a chance to succeed in his transition to manhood, while Ajax offers his son no mechanism to aid him.

Looking to the future, yet rooted in the past and communicating an active potential for success, Aeneas' instructions offer more than the possibility of bridging the gap between two generations. Repeated *ad infinitum* in a process where the son who is instructed to remember eventually

[19] See Lyne 1987, 8, 152–3, 191 ff., 205–6; Hardy 1991, 120–1; and MacKay 1957, 15–6 on this speech in *Ajax* and its relation to the *Aeneid*. A fragment of Accius' *Ajax* recorded by Macrobius (*Saturnalia* 6.1.58) could be a bridge between Vergil and Sophocles; see Tarrant 2012, ad 435–6 on the connection.

becomes the father, the method Aeneas enjoins has the potential to preserve Trojan identity far beyond the present of the narrating-instance.[20] Even as Aeneas' words acknowledge his inevitable death through their imagination of the passage of time,[21] they also secure him a measure of immortality by ensuring that he will be remembered perpetually. They do the same for Troy. Although his enemies taunt him with a repetition of his disastrous past,[22] Aeneas believes that Troy still has something to offer and his injunction to Ascanius signals that he ought to possess a similar commitment: Troy is not dead now and Ascanius should act in a way in the future to make sure that it never perishes.[23] Moreover, from the audience's perspective, the narrator marks the goal of Aeneas' speech and the mechanism inscribed therein as constitutive elements of their society by choosing this father–son communication between as the sole example to include in his song. The past can and should impact the future, and memory can and should govern that interaction.

The Muse's absence

Shortly after Aeneas addresses his son and hastens off to battle, the narrator speaks out in *propria persona* to a degree rarely found in the *Aeneid*. As Seymour Chatman writes, "Commentary, since it is gratuitous, conveys the overt narrator's voice more distinctly than any feature short of explicit self-mention."[24] Here the narrator both comments on his song and mentions himself. The question is what precisely does his voice communicate and why does he choose to communicate it at this moment? His words' content and formal characteristics reveal his dissatisfaction with the Muse and disclose the angry bitterness his commemoration of the Trojans' story brings him.

The narrator's remarks follow his description of a war that has reached a bloody but static peak. Aeneas, infuriated by his inability to track Turnus down, unleashes his rage upon whatever enemies come before him, and

[20] This preservation of identity across the generations is not at all alien to Roman culture; as Oliensis 2009, 58 points out, the Roman practice of nomenclature, which hands down the father's name to his son, yields a long series of identical names and betokens the reproduction of identity as well.

[21] Tarrant 2012, ad 435–40 points out other aspects of this passage that give it the "character of a farewell," hinting at the possibility that Aeneas' death is near.

[22] See p. 38, n. 33.

[23] See Anderson 1957 for an opposing argument about Aeneas' relation to Troy and its remembrance. He claims that Turnus "has done the utmost to keep Ilium alive, both in his misguided words and his actions" and it is Aeneas who "effaces the only reminder left of the ruinous career of Troy" (30).

[24] Chatman 1978, 228.

Turnus, kept away from Aeneas by his divine sister Juturna, does the same.[25] The narrator speaks out in the midst of describing these battles (12.500–4):

> quis mihi nunc tot acerba deus, quis carmine caedes
> diversas obitumque ducum, quos aequore toto
> inque vicem nunc Turnus agit, nunc Troius heros,
> expediat? tanton placuit concurrere motu,
> Iuppiter, aeterna gentis in pace futuras?
>
> What god now could explain to me so many pitiless events, what god could describe in song the different killings and the deaths of leaders, whom now Turnus, now the Trojan hero drive in turns on the whole field? Was it pleasing, Jupiter, that nations destined for eternal peace come together in such upheaval?

Beginning with a question about a divinity, the narrator raises the expectation that he will invoke a Muse. Just as he does in the epic's six prior invocations, the narrator disengages from telling Aeneas' story to talk about his production of the narrative and to seek information via a question.[26] And, just as the narrator establishes his presence with a first-person pronoun or verb in all but two of these invocations, he does with the pronoun "to me" (*mihi*) here.[27]

Yet this passage does not turn into an invocation. No Muse is addressed. Adding this unexpected absence, the narrator's two questions are similarly unique. Unlike the queries in the epic's invocations, these do not seek factual information about Aeneas' story. Rather, the narrator first asks what god could tell him about these events and then focuses on the emotions they provoked in Jupiter. In yet another departure from the typical form of an invocation, the narrator offers no indication that he anticipates an answer. He addresses Jupiter with a vocative, but the god is an actor in the drama itself and should not be expected to reply. By giving this passage the initial appearance of an invocation, the narrator draws attention to the Muse's absence and the role of his own voice. Up to this point, the narrator has called on the Muse for memories of specific events or people while claiming for himself the role of the creator of memory via his song. Now,

25 This ineffective but deadly fighting recalls Juno's earlier words when she realized that she could not stop the Trojans from finding success in the end: "Well, it is permitted to draw out such matters and add delays to them and to destroy the people of both kings" (*at trahere atque moras tantis licet addere rebus, | at licet amborum populos exscindere regum*, 7.315–6).

26 The *Aeneid*'s six invocations come at 1.8–11; 7.37–44; 7.641–6; 9.77–9; 9.525–8; and 10.163–5 (see pp. 125–30 for more on these).

27 The only two invocations without a first person verb or pronoun are 9.77–9 or 10.163–5.

when the Muse's presence is very much expected, her absence begs for an explanation.

An explanation comes partly in the verb of the narrator's first question. *Expediare* often indicates who will narrate a particular story,[28] but it can also denote the process of explaining an obscure or incomprehensible matter.[29] The two meanings easily coexist: after all, a narrative of a sequence of events often explains, explicitly or implicitly, why they occurred.[30] Here, the meanings are intertwined. The narrator's question focuses on the violence marking the Trojans and Latins' battle, and his insistent repetition of grim phrases evokes the excessiveness of this slaughter: "so many pitiless events" (*tot acerba*); "different killings" (*caedes diversas*); "the deaths of leaders" (*obitum ducum*). The narrator, as a member of the community tracing its origins back to the Trojans, looks on these events from a vantage point different from that of an impartial observer. No god could sufficiently explain this violence to him, since no immortal's point of view could correspond with his own. Any reminder that a Muse could afford of these events would come from a different and, therefore, insufficient perspective.

The narrator's second question further elucidates the reason that he turns away from the Muse. Here, he focuses on the emotions, or rather lack thereof, which Jupiter experienced in this unification: "Was it pleasing, Jupiter, that nations destined for eternal peace come together in such upheaval?" (*tanton placuit concurrere motu, | Iuppiter, aeterna gentis in pace futuras?* 12.503–4). The question's sarcastic edge betrays the narrator's displeasure.[31] It recalls the theological query he posed at the end of the epic's proem: "Does a wrath so great exist in the hearts of the gods on high?" (*tantaene animis caelestibus irae?* 1.11).[32] Like his question to Jupiter, this query concerns the intersection between mortal suffering and divine responsibility. The key difference is that in *Aeneid* 1 the narrator

[28] See *TLL* 1611.52–1612.35.

[29] See *TLL* 1613.5–6 and, for this specific example, 1613.18–9. The narrator uses the verb with himself as the subject at 7.40.

[30] *OLD* 4 ("to give an account of, explain, expound") shows the overlap. Purcell 2003, 17, writing on the perception and differentiation of "history as record" and "history as explanation," claims that scholars ought not to posit a strong difference between the two, as "Record always explains; explanation always reveals." This overlap between a record and an explanation could apply here to the story of the *Aeneid*'s narrator as well.

[31] Tarrant 2012, ad 503 notes that Vergil "reserves [tantus] for anguished or indignant questions."

[32] Along with their subject matter and speaker, "so great" (*tantus*) begins each question. Hejduk 2009, 322 also argues that the two questions are bound together by their identical metrical structure, formal parallelism, and expressions of and "unique authorial intrusions." Behr 2005, 212 likewise sees a link between these questions.

had invoked the Muse just a few lines earlier, thus giving the impression that she would provide a satisfactory answer.[33] So far no reply has appeared, but the narrator's story offers a resounding "Yes" through its exposition of Juno's anger, Jupiter's diffidence toward it, and the ceaseless progression of grief and loss that haunts the Trojans.[34] Now, the narrator's comments in *Aeneid* 12 pointedly imply that the gods were concerned neither with explaining nor justifying the devastating loss of life tied to Rome's founding.

These two questions in *Aeneid* 12, through their similarity to Aeneas' metanarratival comments in *Aeneid* 2 and 3, hint at the grief the narrator experiences in remembering these bloody details of his story. Having earlier displayed a certain mnemonic sprezzatura in his aetiological explanations, invocations of the Muse, and apostrophes of the dead, and having showcased his belief that he could make even the most dreadful losses palatable by including them in his song, the narrator now acknowledges the challenges he faces in remembering and representing his society's past. Perhaps the most intriguing aspect of the narrator's pain is that it stems from the remembrance of events he himself did not experience. The potential for the narrator to be affected by his learned memories, in the same way as Aeneas is impacted by his natural memories, only further blurs any boundaries between the narrator and the Trojans. Only those who are part of a community can experience the sorrow prompted by narrating a shared and difficult past, and the narrator comes closer and closer to being a part of the community formed by the Trojans and his Roman audience, so often linked to their ancestors.[35] The narrator never associates the Muse with this community, and thus, by implication, he claims that she can neither know nor explain the pain that accompanies its formation.

The Muse's absence may even betoken that this pain will reach the *Aeneid*'s audience. In the *Theogony*, Hesiod tells of the emotional benefits that accompany the Muse's song (*Th.* 98–103):

[33] This interpretation of 1.11 goes against Wright's (1997, 174) reading that this question shows that a "permanent disposition toward anger is a divine characteristic." The adjective "such" (*tantae*) reveals the passion to be an extraordinary one. If divinities were permanently disposed to anger, then this question would lose much of its force.

[34] Hejduk 2009, 322 argues persuasively that the answer to the question posed to Jupiter is "yes."

[35] Behr 2007, 27 argues that the narrator is confused and that these five verses manifest "his limitations and inability to understand what happens in the plot." This question does not show the narrator's confusion, but rather his surprise and indignation that the gods cruelly allow such bloodshed to (needlessly) occur. Behr goes on to write that the narrator "seems unwilling either to understand or endorse this story" (28); the second option that Behr advances here seems closer to the truth: the narrator understands what happened but is disturbed by what it reveals.

εἰ γάρ τις καὶ πένθος ἔχων νεοκηδέι θυμῷ
ἄζηται[36] κραδίην ἀκαχήμενος, αὐτὰρ ἀοιδὸς
Μουσάων θεράπων κλεῖα προτέρων ἀνθρώπων
ὑμνήσει μάκαράς τε θεοὺς οἳ Ὄλυμπον ἔχουσιν,
αἶψ' ὅ γε δυσφροσυνέων ἐπιλήθεται οὐδέ τι κηδέων
μέμνηται· ταχέως δὲ παρέτραπε δῶρα θεάων.

Though a man, even one feeling sorrow from a fresh-grieving spirit, be dried out with mourning in his heart, if then a singer, servant of the Muses, sings of the glorious deeds of men of old and the blessed gods who hold Olympus, then he swiftly forgets his cares and does not remember his troubles but is quickly diverted by the goddesses' gifts.

According to Hesiod, a servant of the Muse offers his audience a song that turns them away from distress. At this point in the *Aeneid* there is no Muse and, by implication, no song with the capability of making the narrator's audience forget their grief. In the Muse's absence the narrator fashions a song which reflects and incorporates his own pain. Even though his song, like the one imagined by Hesiod, tells of the great deeds of heroes and the majesty of divinities, these topics are the source of grief, not an escape from it. Not only will his song offer his audience no respite from remembering their personal troubles, its description of battles between nations destined to live in peace may even remind them of their sorrows from recent civil wars, accentuating that anguish by setting its origins in their society's beginning.

The weight of oblivion

Not too long after the narrator resumes describing the events of his story, he sings of how Jupiter and Juno come to an agreement about how the Trojans' quest will end.[37] This scene strips the mnemonic opposition between Aeneas and Juno down to its barest elements and, at least from a divine perspective, provides a resolution. As seen first in *Aeneid* 1 and then time and again over the course of the epic, Juno and Aeneas are set against one another in their aims: the goddess desires to destroy any memory of the Trojans, while Aeneas tries to ensure that both he and his city are

[36] For the meaning of this word, see M. L. West 1966, ad loc.

[37] The interpretation of this scene, typically referred to as "the reconciliation of Juno," has come under scrutiny. Johnson 1976, 123–7 and Feeney 1984 point out how Juno does not at all capitulate to Jupiter's will, but rather walks away satisfied with what she has achieved.

remembered. Now, as Juno finally accedes to Jupiter's plan for Aeneas' victory, she strikes a bargain in order to achieve her mnemonic goal.

Jupiter addresses Juno near the end of *Aeneid* 12 out of a specific concern. Having recognized the tenacity with which his wife opposes the Trojans, he worries that their fated victory will leave her filled with indignant rancor. He tells her (12.800–2):

> desine iam tandem precibusque inflectere nostris,
> ne te tantus edit tacitam dolor et mihi curae
> saepe tuo dulci tristes ex ore recursent.
>
> At last, stop already and bend to our prayers, lest so great a resentment eat away at you in silence and bitter cares come to me incessantly from your sweet lips.

In language reminiscent of the narrator's description of Juno's memory-inspired wrath in *Aeneid* 1,[38] Jupiter predicts that a Trojan victory, unless his wife agrees to it beforehand, will leave her bitter and resentful. It is not that Jupiter cannot accomplish his goals without Juno's cooperation, but that the aftermath will be far more pleasant for him if he secures her agreement.

Juno leverages her husband's worry in a brilliant response. She acknowledges that his will is supreme and then, by listing all the anti-Trojan tactics she has refrained from attempting, audaciously implies that she has respected his superiority all along.[39] Her magnanimous preamble behind her, the goddess exploits Jupiter's fear to the fullest extent. When she at last promises that she will no longer fight, she includes one all-important caveat: "And now, indeed, I yield and leave the battle, although hating it" (*et nunc cedo equidem pugnasque exosa relinquo*, 12.818). The specification of her attitude as "hating" (*exosa*) stands as a threat. It keys into Jupiter's concern over her emotional state: Juno's departure will be bitter, and she will punish Jupiter for it later.

Now that Juno has confirmed Jupiter's worry, she offers him a simple way to ensure that it does not come to fruition. She makes a request about

[38] "Grief" (*dolor*) occurs at 1.25 and 12.801, and the description of an action caused by an inner state at 12.801–2 recalls 1.29–36.

[39] Juno's sudden new respect for Jupiter "must somehow puzzle us," as the goddess who has fought the Trojans for so long against her husband's command now appears to capitulate (Johnson 1976, 125). Yet perhaps her change is not so great. Even though Juno seems to acknowledge the finality of Jupiter's word, she still tries to punish the Trojans as much as she can. Her acceptance of her husband's will signals a recalibration of her strategy, not an abandonment of her aim (Johnson 1976, 126–7).

the Roman race, with the implication being that she will depart peacefully if it is granted (12.819–28):

> illud te, nulla fati quod lege tenetur,
> pro Latio obtestor, pro maiestate tuorum:
> cum iam conubiis pacem felicibus (esto)
> component, cum iam leges et foedera iungent,
> ne vetus indigenas nomen mutare Latinos
> neu Troas fieri iubeas Teucrosque vocari
> aut vocem mutare viros aut vertere vestem.
> sit Latium, sint Albani per saecula reges,
> sit Romana potens Itala virtute propago:
> occidit, occideritque sinas cum nomine Troia.
>
> On behalf of Latium, on behalf of the dignity of your people, Saturn's descendants,[40] I beg of you this matter which is held by no law of fate: when the Trojans and Latins will already make peace with a happy marriage (let it be), when they will compose laws and strike treaties, do not order the native Latins to change their ancient name nor to become Trojans and be called Trojans, and do not order the men to change their language or their dress. Let Latium be, let the Alban kings rule through the ages, let the Roman race be powerful in Italian valor: Troy has fallen, let her remain fallen along with her name.

By this point in the epic, Aeneas has frustrated Juno by surviving her wrath. He refuses to let his past be forgotten and even draws strength from his history, such as when he orders Ascanius to remember himself and Hector and when he finds hope in the commemoration of the Trojan War in Juno's Carthaginian temple.[41] With full knowledge of the purpose to which Aeneas puts his interaction with memory, Juno sets out to trump him; she plots an opposing course that will erase any memory of him and Troy. Juno's anger is long-lasting, and she is willing to let Aeneas win the day so long as he loses the commemoration he has struggled to attain.

[40] *Tuorum* must refer to the followers of Latinus, who claims descent from Saturn, Jupiter's father (see Conington 1884, ad 12.819–20).

[41] Johnson 1976, 104 and Lyne 1987, 210 both argue that this passage in *Aeneid* 1 reveals a deep need on the part of Aeneas to believe that his wishes are fulfilled since reality is simply too harsh to face. This is certainly true, yet, Aeneas' behavior also proves productive for him (he secures help from Dido). Even as Juno could delight in just how mistaken Aeneas is in his interpretation of these images, she must experience a certain measure of frustration in that he can find safety by misreading a commemoration honoring Troy's destruction.

Juno's words imply that Rome and Troy cannot co-exist, even that Rome cannot exist if it contains any Trojan characteristics.[42] With the Trojans' name, language, and dress gone, so too is the prospect for the continuation of any rituals that may carry on their social memory. As Egbert Bakker notes, writing about memory in general, "The act of remembering will perform and make present the thing remembered."[43] The Roman people will know nothing of their Trojan past, and in this new community Troy will neither be remembered nor made present.[44] This is a fitting punishment for Juno to propose: the goddess has manipulated her own memories to stoke her anger, and she moves to satisfy her wrath by ensuring that Troy will be forgotten.

Juno specifically targets Aeneas for oblivion. Silence is the most potent weapon of all for this purpose, and Aeneas' absence in Juno's speech reflects the depth of her fury. Without even mentioning Aeneas' name, Juno finds an ingenious way to assert that any commemoration of his role in Rome's origins must be forfeit.[45] She does so with a seemingly innocuous epithet that describes the Latins: "native" (*indigenas*, 12.823). As part of Jupiter's earlier effort to convince Juno to retire from battle, he said: "You yourself know Aeneas is the country's native god" (*indigetem Aenean scis ipsa*, 12.794).[46] The exact meaning of *indiges* was in dispute even among the Romans, but they sometimes used the adjective to indicate a "native god."[47] Its context here supports this interpretation, as Jupiter is trying to convince Juno that Aeneas' victory is inevitable, and a reference to Aeneas' future status as the country's indigenous divinity bolsters this claim. Now Juno effectively denies her husband's point by appropriating *indigena*, a

42 See Ceauşescu 1976, 88 on this point and the possible relevance of these verses to Octavian's battle against Antony. See also Edwards 1996, 63–8 on the relationship between Rome and Troy in Roman literature and culture. She argues that this scene, along with certain passages from Horace, would lead readers "to link the revival of Troy with disaster for Rome itself" (65) and might key into Roman anxiety that Troy could "displace Rome . . . [and] reclaim its own identity" (64).

43 Bakker 2008, 67

44 Toll 1997, 41 writes on the importance of a people's "beliefs about their origins and histories" to their communal existence. For discussion of memory sanctions in the Late Republic, which have some similarities with Juno's request, see Flower 2006, 67–111.

45 See Kepple 1976, 358 for other hints in the epic that Aeneas might die unremembered.

46 See Tarrant 2012, ad loc. for the emphasis given to *indigetem* and the word's implications.

47 See Servius ad 12.794: "Some claim that the country's gods ought to be called *indigetes*" (*alii patrios deos indigetes dici debere tradunt*). For this and other explanations of the adjective, see Maltby 1991, *Indigites dei*. Ernout and Meillet 1932, *indiges, -getis* argue that the Romans used the adjective to indicate national gods as opposed to newly established gods. For further examples of the use of *indiges* with the meaning "native god," see *TLL* volume 7, 1177.57–84, and, in particular, Livy 1.2.6 where that specific meaning is applied to Aeneas: "Aeneas was buried there over the Numicus river, whatever it is lawful and right to call him: they call him native Jupiter" (*situs est, quemcumque eum dici ius fasque est super Numicum flumen: Iovem indigetem appellant*).

word closely related to *indiges* in meaning and etymology, to describe the Latins. They, not Aeneas, are indigenous to Italy, and, as such, they ought to supply the Romans' identifying characteristics.[48]

With Aeneas absent and without any institutional markers to carry on a memory of the Trojans, Juno seeks nothing less than a cultural oblivion. The ferocity that motivates this request is on display in the final line of her speech. Her repetition of the verb "die" (*occidit, occiderit*) leaves no doubt as to her wishes, and the climactic placement of "Troy" (*Troia*) affirms what is at the core of her wrath.[49] In spite of Troy's physical destruction, the Trojans have been keeping the city alive by commemorating it in spirit. This has only exacerbated Juno's anger, and now she wants to ensure the complete annihilation of both the city and its name. Troy is the final word of her speech and the final word she speaks in the *Aeneid*, and it brings the epic back to the memories that motivated her anger in *Aeneid* 1 and reaffirms that they still motivate it now in *Aeneid* 12.[50]

The narrator's subsequent description of Jupiter underlines what is at stake in this negotiation. Before relating Jupiter's response to Juno, the narrator labels him "the inventor of men and things" (*hominum rerumque repertor*, 12.829). Most obviously, the word "inventor" (*repertor*) implies that Jupiter and Juno are discussing the origination of Rome. In addition, the noun hints at the boundaries that Rome's foundation will break. The only other appearance of *repertor* in Vergil's poetry comes in *Aeneid* 7. Here the narrator terms Asclepius "the inventor of such a medicine and art" (*repertorem medicinae talis et artis*, 7.772) on account of Asclepius' having discovered how to bring the dead Hippolytus back to life. According to what Anchises told Aeneas in *Aeneid* 6, the boundary between death and life can only be crossed by forgetting, yet any mention of Lethe is absent in the narrator's description of how the dead, reanimated by Asclepius, returned to life: "Then the all powerful father, angry that some

48 Contrast this prescription with Venus' thoughts of another Troy (10.60–2), and see Feeney 1991, 145.

49 For other evidence of Juno's passion in this speech, see the alliteration in 12.823–5 (Jenkyns 1998, 411).

50 In an analysis of the epic's invocations, A. Hardie 2007 argues that Juno, who initially fosters discord, "will yield ultimately to reconciliation" (587) and that "the concordant aspect of [Juno's] character . . . will ultimately bring concord and peace to Italy" (578) (and see 581). Hardie makes several incisive points about Vergil's treatment of the Muses and Juno's links with those goddesses, yet he addresses neither Juno's drive to postpone the Trojans' rule by bringing suffering to the Trojans and Italians nor the "reconciliation" between Jupiter and Juno in *Aeneid* 12. Even if Juno somehow fosters concord in Italy (which, according to the *Aeneid*'s depiction of the goddess, is questionable) her request that the Trojans be forgotten and Jupiter's subsequent reaction to it show that her rage has not at all subsided. For a consideration of the persistence of Juno's anger throughout the epic, see Tarrant 2012, 5.

mortal rose from the infernal shadows to the light of life . . . " (*tum pater omnipotens aliquem indignatus ab umbris | mortalem infernis ad lumina surgere vitae* . . . , 7.770–1). Oblivion, emphasized so strongly in Anchises' description of the reincarnation of souls, does not attend Asclepius' act of reanimation. Asclepius paid for his audacity with death by Jupiter's thunderbolt.[51] Associated with the violation of a boundary that ought to be divinely controlled and crossed only through forgetting, "inventor" (*repertor*) now refers to Jupiter. It shows that the invention of Rome will violate a similar boundary and require a similar sort of oblivion. Before Jupiter even begins his reply, the narrator's choice of this epithet hints that Jupiter understands Juno's request and will agree to it.

The opening lines of Jupiter's speech show that he recognizes Juno's motivation. In Jupiter's eyes, the anger behind Juno's request stands as evidence of her true nature and identity: "You are the sister of Jupiter and another child of Saturn, [for][52] you roll such waves of anger under your chest" (*es germana Iovis Saturnique altera proles, | irarum tantos volvis sub pectore fluctus*, 12.830–1). Jupiter recognizes the gravity of the punishment Juno desires and the wrath that motivates such a desire, and, as Richard Tarrant remarks, "he seems almost to admire the intensity of her anger."[53] The vehemence of her rage confirms her identity as well as the continuing connection between her anger and memory. The words "such waves of anger" (*irarum tantos . . . fluctus*, 12.831) bring to mind a question from the *Aeneid*'s proem, "Does such an anger exist for heavenly souls?" (*tantaene animis caelestibus irae*? 1.11), along with a phrase associated with this question: "on account of the unforgetting anger of savage Juno" (*saevae memorem Iunonis ob iram*, 1.4). Likewise, the words "under your chest" (*sub pectore*, 12.831) agree with the narrator's earlier depiction of Juno's memories and anger as something in her "thoughts" (*animo*, 1.26) and "stored away in the depths of her mind" (*manet alta mente repostum*, 1.26). These links raise the possibility that Jupiter's metaphorical use of "waves" (*fluctus*, 12.831) alludes to the actual waves of the sea storm that Juno caused in

[51] See Hejduk 2009, 311 on Jupiter's anger and concern over the breaking of boundaries in this case and others.

[52] There is no conjunction marking the relationship between lines 830 and 831, but the independent meaning of each line along with their context dictates that their relationship must be causal. See Conington 1884, ad loc.

[53] Tarrant 2012, ad loc. See also Johnson 1976, 126 and Wright 1997, 174 on Jupiter's recognition of Juno's true self. Lyne 1987, 97 notes that Juno's "vast anger is proof to him of her pre-eminent status as his sister . . . it is the deduction which he draws from her anger." Jupiter's remark also confirms what can be learned from the *Aeneid*'s narrative: the answer to the narrator's question in the proem (*Aen* 1.11) is "yes."

Aeneid 1. Taken with Jupiter's remarks about Juno's identity, the echoes imply that her memory and rage are tied as closely together now as they were at the epic's beginning. For her, there is neither forgetting nor forgiveness, and this is just as Jupiter expects. She possesses the sort of personality he admires and rewards.[54]

The rest of Jupiter's reply confirms Juno will have the oblivion she seeks.[55] He quickly promises her that the Ausonians will retain their name, language, and customs;[56] he will provide the religion.[57] Jupiter's prescription for the Trojans is stark: "Mixed in body alone, the Trojans will subside" (*commixti corpore tantum | subsident Teucri*, 12.835–6).[58] One of Jupiter's primary roles in Roman society was to ensure the community's survival while overseeing its "religious and social development,"[59] and his verdict carries an extraordinary amount of weight. Over time, the Trojan culture, having contributed no distinguishing characteristic to the new city, will

[54] Quint 1993, 76 argues that Jupiter's agreement to Juno's requests "indicates a policy of forget and forgive." It is hard to see either of these actions. Although Juno accepts Jupiter's will, nowhere does she state that she forgives the Trojans (and she does not even say that she will forget their perceived wrongs). The only act of forgetting here is the forgetting that Juno imposes upon the Trojan race, and the cruel totality of this punishment indicates all too well that Juno has not stopped manipulating her rage-inducing memories.

[55] Feeney 1984, 182–3 is right to note that this conversation ends with a "great victory" for Juno. See also Feeney 1991, 146–9 on this passage, and Mackie 1990, 84 on Juno's "joy." Horsfall 1989, 22 diminishes the importance of Juno's request and Jupiter's acceptance by noting that Vergil has "very little room for maneuver" in this scene, since the "resolution of [Jupiter and Juno's] negotiations is to a large extent predetermined by the known facts of history and ethnography." (D. West 1974, 24–5 makes a similar point.) To an extent this is true, as the contents of the *Aeneid* must not clash too greatly with historical expectations, yet Vergil certainly contravenes them when he wishes (e.g., in the chronologically impossible meeting of Aeneas and Dido) and, even when he does not, he still has a good amount of choice in deciding how to reach an end of the *Aeneid* that could result in Rome. He certainly could have chosen not to include this scene or to portray this reconciliation as coming about in a different way altogether.

[56] From an historical perspective, this agreement can appear to be part of an effort by Vergil to bring the Italians and Romans closer together. Toll 1997, 51 writes that the gods' pact, which sets the origins of Roman values in Italian peoples, is "an effective and salient part of the poem's strategy for getting the Roman-born to be more accommodating and respectful of their new fellow citizens." Yet Aeneas' desire to perpetuate memories of Troy and a Trojan identity via Ascanius hints that this melding will not necessarily be painless or desired. (For an argument similar to Toll's, but more closely focused on Roman religion, see Orlin 2007, 78.)

[57] This is against the claim put forth time and again in other passages in the *Aeneid* that the Trojan religion will endure (see Lyne, 1987, 81–2 for a discussion and list of the relevant passages). This picture of complete oblivion also contradicts the narrator's depiction of the continuation of the *lusus Troiae* and the narrator's own recently elaborated stance.

[58] Orlin 2007, 73 argues that *subsident* means either (or both) that the Trojans will settle in Italy or "sink down into oblivion." There is no reason to choose between the alternatives; both are appropriate for the passage.

[59] Rea 2007, 52.

become lost in the swirl of other traditions. In Juno's proposal, the Trojans' martial victory must come at the expense of their mnemonic defeat.

An agreement has been struck by the gods, allowing the foundation of Rome's ancestral city but denying the continuity of identity and the centrality of memory, two values central to Aeneas' order to his son. Aeneas' enjoinment implies that Ascanius, building upon his father's deeds and foundation, will continue to move toward Rome's founding by recollecting the past. Yet, as Maurizio Bettini notes, Jupiter and Juno's reconciliation leaves it to the Trojans "to agree to amnesia."[60] Aeneas' contest with the gods' vision of Rome's founding is of course not an equal one, and, in fact, Aeneas has little reason to suspect that the immortals oppose his plans.[61] The narrative audience, however, witnesses all and recognizes that Aeneas might have an ally in this unfair fight.[62] As the narrator reveals to his audience at 12.500–4, he is committed to remembering this story from the perspective of their community, a community he implies to be Trojan and Roman alike.

Imperatives of memory

These clashing goals about memory, Troy, and Rome stand as the backdrop to Aeneas' final battle with Turnus.[63] At last arrayed against one another in single combat, Turnus attacks Aeneas first, but his effort is ineffective and Aeneas soon wounds him with his spear. The injury is not fatal, though, and Turnus retains enough strength to address Aeneas from the ground (12.930–8):[64]

60 Bettini 1997, 31.

61 See Commager 1981, 112–3; Feeney 1991, 182; and P. Hardie 1997, 148 on the gap between human and divine.

62 Armstrong 2002, 326 notes that the *Aeneid*, by its canonical status, ensures that Juno's desire for Troy's oblivion "is never fulfilled."

63 The role Aeneas' memory plays in his decision to attack Latinus' city (pointed out by Berlin 1998) adds to this backdrop. When Aeneas looks on Latinum, currently untouched by war, "straightaway the image of a greater fight incites him" (*continuo pugnae accendit maioris imago*, 12.560). Prompted by his viewing of Latinum, Aeneas remembers the greater fight that brought down Troy. That memory of Troy's destruction sets his purpose to destroy Latinum, and he soon urges his men on to do just that. Berlin also notes how *maioris*, by recalling Vergil's allusion to the *Iliad* with *maius opus* (7.45) links "the construction of memory to the poet's reconstruction of both the mythical-historical and the literary past" (36). This association foreshadows the further links, offered by allusions to the *Iliad* and *Odyssey* in the *Aeneid*'s final scene, between memory's construction in the *Aeneid* and the poet's engagement with the mythic and literary past.

64 Tarrant 2004, 104 points out that the close contact between Aeneas and Turnus throughout *Aeneid* 12 enacts a "process of mutual definition." Their interchange here sharpens our understanding of Aeneas' interactions with memory.

ille humilis supplex oculos dextramque precantem
protendens "equidem merui nec deprecor" inquit;
"utere sorte tua. miseri te si qua parentis[65]
tangere cura potest, oro (fuit et tibi talis
Anchises genitor) Dauni miserere senectae
et me, seu corpus spoliatum lumine mavis,
redde meis. vicisti et victum tendere palmas
Ausonii videre; tua est Lavinia coniunx,
ulterius ne tende odiis."

Turnus, humble, suppliant, looks around and, extending his right hand in prayer, speaks: "Indeed, I deserved it, and I don't beg relief. Use your chance. If a wretched parent's grief can still touch you, I beg (for Anchises was also such a father to you), that you take pity on Daunus' old age and return me or, if you prefer, my corpse, robbed of light, to my people. You have conquered, and the Ausonians have seen me, conquered, hold up my hands; Lavinia is your wife, go no further in your hatred."

Turnus yields to Aeneas and acknowledges his defeat. He stakes his life, or at least his burial, largely upon an appeal to memory.[66] He invokes two distinct mnemonic perspectives, as he implores Aeneas to recall specific memories of his past and to imagine how the future will remember their battle.

Turnus looks to the past by likening his father to Aeneas' in lines 932–4. While Aeneas has heard battlefield pleas before that implore him to think of Anchises, those did not explicitly draw a likeness between Aeneas' father and his foe's. In *Aeneid* 10, for instance, Magus begs Aeneas to let him live for the sake of his own son and father "by your father's shade and your hopes for growing Iulus" (*per patrios manis et spes surgentis Iuli*, 10.524),[67] Magus subsequently offers Aeneas a sizable amount of gold and silver, but Aeneas rejects his plea altogether, going out of his way to declare the intergenerational support for his decision to kill him: "Anchises' shade decides this, Iulus decides this" (*hoc patris Anchisae manes, hoc sentit Iulus*,

[65] The noun *parentis*, dependent on *cura*, could be either a subjective or objective genitive (meaning either "a parent's grief" or "thought for a parent," respectively). In the end both constructions tend toward a similar meaning, as "thought for a parent" indicates concern about Daunus' potentially grief-filled reaction to Turnus' death.

[66] Quint 1989, 48 writes that clemency would be possible in this scene if Aeneas forgets the past; this is surely true, but it also necessary to note that Turnus tries to secure clemency through remembering, not forgetting. Not only, as Turnus presents it, is Aeneas' clemency dependent upon his memory of various people and things, but, as is argued below, Turnus implies that Aeneas can afford to spare his life since people have seen and will remember the outcome of their battle.

[67] Smith 2005, 155 remarks how Magus builds his appeal on the past and future.

10.534).[68] While Magus, like Turnus, appeals to Aeneas' father, he does not concentrate Aeneas' attention on any perceived similarity between his father and Aeneas', and Magus further shifts the focus away from any potential likeness by focusing on the large amount of gold he can offer as a ransom. Turnus, meanwhile, eschews any mention of a ransom and instead invokes the similarity between Daunus and Anchises. His request that Aeneas pity Daunus depends upon Aeneas' performance of two mental actions; first, Aeneas must remember his attachment to Anchises and, second, he must acknowledge a similarity in both his and Turnus' relationships with their respective fathers. Compelled to remember Anchises and, specifically, the mutual devotion that defined their relationship, Aeneas ought to be deeply affected; his tie with his father is apparent in Aeneas' helpless and angry reaction to his father's death (3.709) as well as in Anchises' joyful recognition of his son in the underworld (6.687–94). Now, if Aeneas follows Turnus' line of reasoning and sees a similarity between their fathers, he will choose to spare Daunus' son.

Concerns about remembrance mark the last books of the Homeric epics as well. Through a present allusion to the *Iliad* and a later one to the *Odyssey*, the narrator brings up moments when recollection leads both to reconciliation and revenge, thus raising the possibility for either to occur here. Turnus' request at the end of the *Aeneid* recalls a similar plea from *Iliad* 24.[69] There, Priam makes his way to Achilles' tent in order to seek the return of Hector's body. Priam gives Achilles the following order: "Remember your father, god-like Achilles, of such an age as I am, on the baneful threshold of old age" (μνῆσαι πατρὸς σοῖο θεοῖς ἐπιείκελ' Ἀχιλλεῦ, | τηλίκου ὥς περ ἐγών, ὀλοῷ ἐπὶ γήραος οὐδῷ, *Il.* 24.486–7). Like Turnus, Priam begs Achilles to think of his father and to recognize the similarity between that parent and another. Priam's rhetoric moves Achilles. When Achilles cries for both Patroclus and his own father, it is as if he weeps for Priam as well.[70] Having gained Achilles' pity, Priam also secures Hector's body for burial.

The Homeric intertext suggests to the *Aeneid*'s audience that Turnus' appeal to paternal memory should be similarly effective in this context, and it is likely that Aeneas either knows of the role memory played in

[68] Note also how Aeneas moves the focus of Magus' attempt to appeal to memory by selecting the verb *memorare* to describe Magus' mentioning of gold and silver: "Spare for your sons the many talents of silver and gold which you mention" (*argenti atque auri memoras quae multa talenta* | *gnatis parce tuis*, 10.531–2). For the mnemonic implications of *memorare*, see pp. 11–13.

[69] Barchiesi 1984, 111–9 analyzes the extensive connections between these two scenes.

[70] MacLeod 1982, ad 509–11 points out how both Priam and Achilles "have to indulge their own grief if they are to feel for the other's." Achilles' grief for Patroclus is his own, but his tears for his father are also tears for Priam.

Priam's request or at least shares the beliefs about memory that underlay that request. Aeneas' reaction to a section of the pictures of the Trojan War on Juno's temple at Carthage establishes a base line for his knowledge (1.483–7):

> ter circum Iliacos raptaverat Hectora muros,
> exanimumque auro corpus vendebat Achilles.
> tum vero ingentem gemitum dat pectore ab imo,
> ut spolia, ut currus, utque ipsum corpus amici,
> tendentemque manus Priamum conspexit inermis.
>
> Achilles had dragged Hector around Troy's walls three times and was selling his lifeless corpse for gold. Then Aeneas gives forth a great sigh from the depths of his heart, when he saw the spoils, the chariot, the very corpse of his friend, and Priam, stretching out his defenseless hands.

These lines show that Aeneas recognizes the story of Priam's ransoming of his son and responds to it with feeling,[71] but they do not reveal whether or not he is aware of the role memory played in that action.[72] Priam could have explained to the Trojans how he secured Hector's body, and, if he did so, then his memory-based plea would have become part of the Trojans' social memory and stand as a paradigm for an appeal for mercy based on the remembrance of one's father. Yet even if Aeneas never learned the role memory played in Priam's securing of Hector's body, Aeneas may still have a view of memory's power much like that which appears in *Iliad* 24. Priam's use of memory as a tool of persuasion hints at a belief that an appeal to memory should work across cultural and battlefield divides, an assumption Achilles confirms when he agrees to Priam's request. In all likelihood, Aeneas, so recently a member of Priam's society, shares this same belief, and he therefore ought to be predisposed to respond favorably to Turnus' plea.

One other memory of Aeneas' should help Turnus as well. The Rutulian's posture in defeat, combined with his mention of Anchises, ought to prompt

[71] Given that these pictures are viewed from Aeneas' perspective, it is difficult to ascertain just how much of this story is represented on the temple and how much of it filled in from his memory. See Roller 2004, 10 on how even "nonnarative monumental forms" either refer to or require "a narrative that accounts for that occasion." See Putnam 1998, 33 on the centrality of Aeneas' reaction to these verses.

[72] To complicate the matter further, the setting of Hector's mutilation around the city walls and not around Patroclus' tomb indicates that Vergil is following a post-Homeric source; neither can the source itself be pinpointed with certainty nor can the role memory plays in that source's story (on the source, see Conington 1884, ad 1.483). Aeneas also refers to Priam's ransoming of Hector's body in his narration of Priam's words to Neoptolemus at 2.541–3; here, Priam contrasts Neoptolemus' current impieties with Achilles' respect for proper behavior in his return of Hector's body.

Aeneas to remember a set of instructions he received from his father.[73] Anchises delivered these orders in the underworld (6.851–3):

> tu regere imperio populos, Romane, memento
> (hae tibi erunt artes), pacique imponere morem,
> parcere subiectis et debellare superbos.
>
> Remember, Roman, these will be your arts: to rule over nations rightly, and to impose a custom on peace, and to spare the subjected and subdue the proud.

Turnus shows himself to be a conquered foe in word and deed. Fallen to the ground because of his wound, he acknowledges Aeneas' control over his life. Anchises' injunction should predispose Aeneas to spare Turnus not just because of its specific content, but also because its very form emphasizes the importance of memory. The imperative "remember" (*memento*, 6.851), governing four other verbs, hints at the need to rule by remembering the past.[74] In his speech so far, Turnus has done nothing but cause Aeneas to do just that, and if Aeneas does recall Anchises' orders, he ought to spare Turnus.

Aeneas' established pattern of behavior also weighs in Turnus' favor. As argued in Chapter 1, Aeneas forges onwards in Italy by acting on his memories. He finds aspects of the present similar to what he remembers from the past, and then guides his actions based on those likenesses. By keying into various memories, Turnus presents Aeneas with similarities between past and present and invites him to act accordingly. A decision to spare Turnus' life or body would be consistent with Aeneas' typical memory-based mode of behavior. More so than ever, Aeneas should be primed to act in this way. After all, he has just told Ascanius about the importance of using memory as a guide for future behavior.

These prompts to look toward the past represent only half of Turnus' strategy, as he urges Aeneas to look toward the future as well. A glance back at two earlier scenes shows just how much stock Turnus sets on how he will be remembered in the future and just how much he knowingly offers to lose in his request at the end of *Aeneid* 12. In *Aeneid* 10, after Turnus realizes that he has been fooled into following a false image of Aeneas away from the main battle, he bemoans his plight and asks the winds to bring him to an anonymous death:

[73] Putnam 1966, 193 finds a connection between Turnus' words and Anchises' orders, and argues that, in the epic's final verses, Aeneas "loses sight of what his father defined as Rome's grand mission."

[74] Smith 2005, 89.

> "in rupes, in saxa (volens vos Turnus adoro)
> ferte ratem saevisque vadis immittite syrtis,
> quo nec me Rutuli nec conscia fama sequatur."
> haec memorans animo nunc huc, nunc fluctuat illuc. 10.677–80

> "I, Turnus, willingly entreat you: carry my ship into the cliffs, into the rocks and smash it on the sandbank's cruel shallows, where neither the Rutulians nor fame, knowing what I have done, may follow me." Speaking these things, he wavers now here, now there in his mind.

At the end of a twelve-verse monologue in which Turnus wonders why he deserved to be led astray from battle, he begs to be dashed to death in a place where the infamy of his deed may not follow. The narrator's use of *memorans* in 680 to denote that Turnus is speaking brings out the latent mnemonic undertones of Turnus' request. In the final line of his speech, Turnus moves from his concern over the "rebukes of his comrades . . . [to] the general shame of ill-fame,"[75] a transition which hints at his worry about the potential for a social memory of his cowardice to first arise among his compatriots and to then spread and solidify. Embarrassed at what he has done, Turnus cannot stomach the thought that others will remember these cowardly actions in the future. Shortly thereafter, as *Aeneid* 12 begins, it becomes clear that this worry over his future reputation still weighs on him. As the prospect of single-combat with Aeneas looms, he begs Latinus, "May you allow me to barter death for glory" (*letum . . . sinas pro laude pacisci*, 12.49), and, at the close of his speech just a few lines later, Turnus alludes to his previous ignominy by referencing Aeneas' earlier escape. For Turnus, his single-combat with Aeneas is an opportunity to repair his reputation and improve his standing in the social memory of the future.

These thoughts of how he and Aeneas will be remembered must stand at the forefront of Turnus' mind as he looks up at the Trojan. Given how concerned Turnus is that he will not be remembered with praise, his words to Aeneas are astounding: "You have conquered, and the Ausonians have seen me, conquered, hold up my hands" (*vicisti et victum tendere palmas | Ausonii videre*, 12.936–7). They are a bald admittance of his society's knowledge of his defeat. Turnus asserts that he is ready to live with that defeat's social memory guaranteed, a particularly remarkable sentiment given that Turnus had asked to exchange death for praise at the beginning of *Aeneid* 12. As Turnus' words move from Aeneas' action to its effect, they verify the

[75] S. Harrison 1991, ad 679,

same result from three different perspectives: Aeneas, Turnus, and the spectators all register Aeneas' victory.[76] The repetition of the verb "to conquer" (*vicisti, victum*) in active and passive forms illustrates that Aeneas' victory is identical from his point of view as well as Turnus'. And, in an emphatic enjambment, Turnus points out that the Ausonians, too, have seen Turnus' defeat and his acceptance of it.[77] Aeneas' victory over Turnus has completed its journey from being achieved to being remembered. By showing that no ambiguity exists between these two poles, Turnus implies that a standardized memory of Aeneas' victory can already be established and, therefore, that there is no need for his own body to stand as a monument to Aeneas' supremacy. Willing to forgo the praise he believed death would bring him, Turnus now offers Aeneas the chance to secure praise for himself via the complete array of witnesses for his victory.

Turnus' pleas fail. Although Aeneas initially checks his right hand, his mercy does not last (12.940–7):

> et iam iamque magis cunctantem flectere sermo
> coeperat, infelix umero cum apparuit alto
> balteus et notis fulserunt cingula bullis
> Pallantis pueri, victum quem vulnere Turnus
> straverat atque umeris inimicum insigne gerebat.
> ille, oculis postquam saevi monimenta doloris
> exuviasque hausit, furiis accensus et ira
> terribilis . . .
>
> And, as Aeneas hesitated, Turnus' words had already begun to move him more and more, until the ill-fated baldric appeared high on Turnus' shoulder and gleamed with its known studs, the baldric of the boy Pallas, conquered in battle, whom Turnus had laid low with a wound and whose fatal emblem he was wearing on his shoulders. After Aeneas drunk in the monument of savage grief and the spoils with his eyes, he burned with fury and was terrible in his wrath . . .

The speed and power of Aeneas' memory drive these lines forward. Aeneas at first bends to Turnus' request, but his consideration soon ends: *infelix*, fronted so far from *balteus*, casts a pall over the line and undermines

[76] P. Hardie 1997, 147 notes that the active and passive verbs "present the perfected reality of victory, duly witnessed."

[77] 12.221–33 and 12.928 corroborate his claim. Juturna's comments at 12.234–7, where she goads the Rutulians into action by contrasting the living fame Turnus will earn by his death with the desultory servitude that marks their future, indicate that the Rutulians envisage the result of this battle as becoming an important social memory.

any expectation that Turnus will live. Soon Aeneas recognizes the belt, a recognition underlined by the hyperbaton between *notis* and *bullis*.[78]

The enjambment in line 943 designates "the boy Pallas" as the belt's one-time owner, a realization that floods Aeneas' mind much like his earlier memories did when he learned Pallas had been killed. As the participle *victum* shows, Pallas' defeat is what defines him from Aeneas' perspective. Granted additional importance due to its position outside of its relative clause, *victum* recalls and undermines Turnus' characterization of himself with that very same word only a handful of lines earlier: "The Ausonians have seen me, conquered" (*victum . . . | Ausonii videre*, 12.936–937). There Turnus had claimed that his death was unnecessary since his defeat had been witnessed. Now, though, Aeneas sees that the same standard of commemoration did not satisfy Turnus. It was not enough for people to see Turnus' victory; Turnus had to take a material marker of his superiority as well.

The narrative's perspective shifts with the pronoun "that one" (*ille*) at the beginning of line 945. After having described the process of seeing the baldric, recognizing it, and remembering its history from Aeneas' point of view, the narrator takes a step back to reveal how it impacts the Trojan. "Monument" (*monimenta*, 12.945) makes memory's role explicit in Aeneas' reaction, as well as its relationship to the emotions that flood over him.[79] Pallas' belt not only signifies the boy's death but also evokes the emotions associated with it. The narrator leaves the precise relationship between memory and emotion suggestively vague: the description "monument of savage grief" (*saevi monimenta doloris*, 12.945) implies that the belt reminds Aeneas of his emotions at the time of Pallas' death and that Aeneas still experiences similar feelings of grief and anger over this loss even now.[80]

Grief, anger, and guilt drive Aeneas. He claims to act on Pallas' behalf (12.947–52):

[78] The baldric itself was designed as a monument to the Danaids' slaughter of their husbands on their wedding night. For a reading of this ekphrasis and its relation to the final scene, along with further bibliography, see Spence 1991; Barchiesi 1997, 279; S. J. Harrison 1998; and Putnam 1998, 189–207.

[79] Berlin 1998, 38–9 also notes that this word shows memory's importance to the end of *Aeneid*. See Maltby 1991, *monumentum* for the word's various links with memory. Contra Gross 2003/04, 153, who argues that Aeneas' "past vanishes" when he kills Turnus.

[80] The narrator's description of the belt is quite suggestive; the possibilities noted above do not cover every way that it could act as a reminder. Fowler 2000, 213, for instance, finds that the baldric is "a monument of savage grief" in at least four ways: it is a monument of Pallas' pain at his death; of Aeneas' present pain; of the pain Aeneas will now inflict upon Turnus; and of a scene filled with pain. Tarrant 2004, 127 raises yet another possibility, noting that the characterization of the belt might "also describe the *Aeneid* itself and its memorializing of cruel grief."

"tune hinc spoliis indute meorum
eripiare mihi? Pallas te hoc vulnere, Pallas
immolat et poenam scelerato ex sanguine sumit."
hoc dicens ferrum adverso sub pectore condit
fervidus; ast illi solvuntur frigore membra
vitaque cum gemitu fugit indignata sub umbras.

"Are you to escape from me, clad in the spoils of one of mine? Pallas sacrifices you with this wound, Pallas exacts punishment from your accursed blood." Saying this Aeneas buries his sword into his enemy's chest, raging; and then Turnus' limbs go slack with cold and his soul, indignant, flees with a groan to the shades.

The epic ends on a note of rage and indignation, emotions which Aeneas feels toward a wide range of targets: Turnus and himself, as well as his own fate, which has forced him to suffer through so many losses.[81] This last act is marked by a troubling and "uncharacteristic brutal intensity," a passion highlighted all the more by the fact that Aeneas was prepared to respond to Turnus' request "with restraint and humanity."[82] Christopher Gill points toward "the extreme pressure of this situation" as the factor responsible for this change,[83] and this analysis has much to recommend it, as it neither demonizes nor exonerates Aeneas, but rather tries to account for his behavior by pointing toward the extraordinary demands which weigh upon him. From this perspective, it remains to consider what exerts such pressure on Aeneas; or, in other words, why and how he comes to enact vengeance in this particular manner.

The *Aeneid* comes to this close because Aeneas' memory of Pallas is so forceful.[84] The tone of Aeneas' question to Turnus is incredulous. As a leader, any reminder of a fallen comrade would move him to contemplate revenge, but this token of Pallas, a young man for whom he was personally responsible, is particularly galling.[85] In a general comment about monuments, Don Fowler writes that "What people are seen as using the monuments for is what matters, not some mystic notion of inherent meaning."[86] It is irrelevant to Aeneas that the baldric Turnus wears was designed to commemorate the Danaids' slaughter of their husbands. The mnemonic

[81] Bews 1987, 96 notes that Aeneas' anger "must be partly self-directed." Also see Johnson 2005, xlv on the possible targets of Aeneas' anger.

[82] Gill 2006, 459. [83] Gill 2006, 459.

[84] Currie 1962/63, 26 and Putnam 1966, 193 and 1984, 240 argue that Aeneas' anger is irrational. Yet while Aeneas' anger does come about quickly, that does not necessarily make it irrational from Aeneas' point of view. The Trojan might regard this deed as prompted by Turnus' past actions and his own promises to Evander.

[85] 8.514–7 and 11.45–8 establish Aeneas' responsibility for Pallas. [86] Fowler 2000, 210.

significance of Pallas' death has been foreshadowed for quite some time: in a series of passages in *Aeneid* 10 and 11, Pallas, Turnus, Aeneas, Evander, and even the epic's narrator all consider how Pallas' death will be commemorated. Now, as Aeneas sees Pallas' sword-belt on Turnus' shoulder, he might not even notice the belt's original commemorative purpose. What matters to him is that Turnus wears it as a celebration of his slaughter of Pallas,[87] and he will not tolerate Turnus' plea for mercy while clothed in such a monument.

If Aeneas recognizes that Pallas' sword-belt has an effect upon him, then what does this imply about all the other memories that Turnus' speech prompts? It is not the case that Turnus' efforts are ineffectual. After all, Aeneas does hesitate. Also, it is not as simple as claiming that a natural memory (Aeneas' memory of Pallas death) overpowers a learned memory (the instructions Anchises ordered Aeneas to remember). Aeneas' natural memories of his father should have aided Turnus as well, along with the recognition that no physical monument is necessary to ensure that his victory be remembered. Yet based upon Aeneas' actions, Pallas' baldric trumps Turnus' mnemonic arguments. Part of this is due to its late and surprising appearance, an appearance that indicts Turnus' request for mercy as hypocritical.[88] Another factor is at play here as well: the baldric reminds Aeneas of an especially recent and painful event for which he was responsible and which still provokes raw emotions. Aeneas never truly forgot Pallas' death, but, as he shifted his focus to securing a fight with Turnus, that loss no longer held the center of his attention.[89] When it is forced out into the forefront of his mind, it provokes a deadly reaction.

A passage in *Aeneid* 6 offers a better understanding of how and with what effect the memory of a devastating incident can suddenly and completely occupy a character's mind. In this earlier scene, Aeneas views a set of carvings Daedalus fashioned on the doors of Apollo's temple. In the midst of describing the various representations, the narrator comes to the space Daedalus had set aside for depicting his flight from Crete. Here, the narrator's tone and perspective change dramatically, as he reveals the sudden and uncontrollable effect memory had on Daedalus (6.30–3):[90]

87 Aeneas interprets the baldric as a spoil of war, not within the context of its images (Lowrie 2009, 157, 162–3).

88 E. Henry 1989, 20 perceptively notes how, when Aeneas sees it, Pallas' baldric "is so powerful a reminder of what he has seen and known in the past, and of the true meaning of what is happening in his present experience."

89 Stahl 1990, 198 makes a similar argument.

90 Fitzgerald 1984, 54 argues for an earlier tonal shift at 6.28, but the shift in 6.30 is of a greater magnitude. The earlier part of the narrator's description focuses on the emotions of the characters

> tu quoque magnam
> partem opere in tanto, sineret dolor, Icare, haberes.
> bis conatus erat casus effingere in auro,
> bis patriae cecidere manus.
>
> Also you, Icarus, would have a great part in such a work, if grief were to allow it. Twice he had tried to fashion your fall in gold, twice your father's hands fell.

While Aeneas only sees an empty panel on the temple doors, a lacuna in Daedalus' story, the *Aeneid*'s narrator tells his audience why this space stands unadorned.[91] In his apostrophe to Icarus, the narrator brings out the causal relationship between Daedalus' paternal grief and artistic failure. The narrator's apostrophe of Icarus,[92] the mention of "grief" (*dolor*, 6.31), and the insistence that Daedalus twice tried and twice failed to depict his son's death are all a testament to the painful emotions that held him back.[93]

When Daedalus decided to carve his Cretan story onto the doors of Apollo's temple, he could not have forgotten the tragedy that marred his escape. His memory of Icarus' death must have remained with him, yet set back far enough in his mind so that the idea of representing it seemed possible. When it came time to actually fashion this panel, however, Daedalus needed to consciously remember that loss; forced into a full awareness of its details, grief did not allow him to proceed. A comparison of this scene with the end of *Aeneid* 12 brings out a set of striking similarities

depicted on the carvings, but now he describes the emotions of Daedalus at the moment of failed artistic creation.

91 Lowrie 2009, 160 points out how the audience, but not Aeneas, sees this failed attempt at commemoration. Aeneas and his men arrive at the temple and surely notice its images, but the narrator specifies that they do not have time to look at every one of the scenes since the Sibyl interrupts their viewing (see 6.33–7). Moreover even if Aeneas is able to look at the temple doors, all he would see here is a blank panel, not the story that explains why it is in this state.

92 Note how the second-person pronoun "you" (*tu*) and the identity of this second-person addressee both appear at the bucolic diaeresis, an emphatic position.

93 O'Sullivan 2009, 471 observes that Daedalus tries "to externalize his grief by transferring his son's death onto another medium, by looking at his death with the objective eye of an artist, and not of a grieving father." Daedalus' memories simply will not allow this, though. Persistent and powerful, they prevent him from leaving his paternal identity behind. Ironically, because of his own memory Daedalus fails in his attempt to commemorate his son and hence secure his son's memory in other peoples' minds. The narrator, though, still commemorates Icarus by remembering Daedalus' vain efforts. Fitzgerald 1984, 62 sees this scene as showing artistic creation as a first step towards coming "to terms with the tragic past," an act that then allows the subject to incorporate the past back into his life by engaging in an action "that repeats the past as it looks towards the future." Although Aeneas does not engage in artistic creation like Daedalus does, some of his actions do repeat the past in a different way, the second step that Fitzgerald describes. For the argument that art fails here, see Pöschl 1975.

between Daedalus and Aeneas.[94] Like Daedalus, Aeneas brought a young man on a dangerous endeavor, and, just as Icarus perished, so too did Pallas. And now, like Daedalus with Icarus, Aeneas is suddenly reminded of Pallas' death, and, like Daedalus, he is struck by grief (*dolor*). Daedalus felt grief because he was forced to remember his son when it came time to commemorate him (*dolor*, 6.31), just as Aeneas feels grief when the baldric compels him to remember Pallas (*doloris*, 12.945).

The power of a memory of a dreadful incident stands at the center of both men's interactions with the past. The narrator's description of Daedalus' repeated efforts to commemorate his son reveals the loss of control memory can bring, and the implication now is that Aeneas experiences a similar loss. Aeneas' memory overpowers his consideration of Turnus' request, just as Daedalus' memory of Icarus stopped him from carving a planned scene. In both cases, recollection proves imperative, a mental process that forces the one who remembers to stop what he is currently doing. Unlike Daedalus, though, who was about to carve another event and whose memory causes inaction, Aeneas, who was waiting and considering Turnus' plea, is driven to act.[95]

The rage that arises from Aeneas' memory begs the question of whether he has become similar to Juno, the enemy who has hounded him since the epic's opening verses.[96] Both of them, mortal and goddess alike, strike out in angry violence because of their memories. At the epic's opening, Juno attacks the Trojan fleet since she remembers earlier wrongs suffered at their hands. Now Aeneas presents his killing of Turnus not as a legitimate act of war, but rather as a vengeful sacrifice he must perform.[97] Specific words link Juno and Aeneas as well: the phrase "savage grief" occurs only at 1.25 (*saevi . . . dolores*) and 12.945 (*saevi doloris*), and in both instances it describes the emotions that memory prompts. These similarities point to a shared trait between Aeneas and Juno: they react to memory with strong emotions and it is these emotions which in turn prompt a violent response.

Yet these likenesses threaten to obscure a significant difference. Even though Aeneas reacts in a Juno-esque manner to his memory of Pallas, his

94 Scholars have long drawn attention to various parallels between Aeneas and Daedalus (see Zarker 1967; Rutledge 1967 and 1971–72; Pöschl 1970, 150; DuBois 1982, 35–41; Paschalis 1986, 40; Putnam 1998, 75 ff.; Syed 2005, 81–3; and J. Miller 2009, 137), but only a few have examined Aeneas and Daedalus with an eye towards Aeneas' behavior at the epic's end (e.g., Putnam 1998, 95).

95 Putnam 1998, 95 makes this same point.

96 Knox 1997, 233 writes that circumstances have brought Aeneas "to the point where he most resembles his most bitter foe." Putnam 1998, 72 and 90; Tarrant 2004, 120; and A. Hardie 2007, 572 note this as well.

97 Lowrie 2009, 163.

behavior is fundamentally unlike the goddess' in one crucial way.[98] Juno actively fosters her memories of past wrongs and uses them to stoke her anger. This creates a cycle, as her wrath causes her thoughts to return to offending memories, which, in turn, spur on her rage. Aeneas, though, does not purposely dwell on Pallas' death. Indeed, before Pallas' baldric appears, he is ready to grant Turnus' appeal and seems to have allowed his memory of Pallas' death at Turnus' hands to float out of his consciousness. There exists the possibility that, if Evander had not ordered Aeneas to regard his son's body as a marker of a debt that must be paid, the baldric might not have occasioned that very deed. After all, Aeneas moves from his bloody rage in *Aeneid* 10 towards a calmer perception of Pallas' death in *Aeneid* 11, one that regards it more as a glorious passing than a grievous loss.[99] Evander's orders, though, prompt Aeneas' view of Pallas' death to shift once more between the beginning of *Aeneid* 11 and the end of *Aeneid* 12.[100]

Aeneas' rage is an overpowering emotion that leads to a brutal and unsettling end to the epic.[101] The savagery and loss that mark the poem's closing lines have led scholars to assert that Aeneas would have been better off forgetting Pallas.[102] If this had occurred, the argument goes, Aeneas could have shown mercy to Turnus.[103] The very premise of this assertion,

98 Tarrant 2004, 120 argues for another difference between the two, namely that while Juno's anger shows no signs of dissipating, Aeneas' will fade after Turnus' death. Yet it is difficult to know whether Aeneas' anger will be assuaged by killing Turnus. Even if it is, would this be much different from what might happen with Juno, especially seeing how pleased she is to have gained Jupiter's assent to the Trojans' oblivion in their earlier conversation? For a consideration of how Maffeo Vegio addresses some of these questions in his fifteenth-century continuation of the *Aeneid*, see Rogerson 2012.

99 For a discussion of these scenes in *Aeneid* 10 and 11, see pp. 150–1.

100 Stahl 1990, 209 also points out the potential impact of Evander's orders upon Aeneas, and Servius considers it too: "Aeneas avenges Pallas' death out of consideration for Evander" (*Evandri intuitu Pallantis ulciscitur mortem*, ad 12.940).

101 Much has been written about anger in the *Aeneid* in general and in this moment in particular. For their views and bibliography, see Galinsky 1988; Putnam 1990; Gill 1997b, 239–40 and 2006, 435–6, 439, 459; and Wright 1997.

102 Quint 1993, 64 writes that the reconciliation of Juno and Jupiter, along with the souls' oblivion in the underworld, implies that the need for war-survivors "to forget the tragic memories of their past is as deep-seated as life itself, part of the basic process of the psyche." But this is exactly what does not occur; instead, the act of remembering is depicted as a fundamental human trait.

103 Quint 1993, 78 argues that even though Aeneas chooses *pietas* over *clementia* in the *Aeneid*'s final scene, *clementia* is still on view in the reconciliation of Jupiter and Juno. According to Quint, *clementia* overcomes the past by forgetting, while *pietas* overcomes the past by undoing it and offers the possibility of mastering it. Quint argues that the *Aeneid* "discloses the contradictions in the [Augustan] regime's ideology: its promise to pardon and to avenge at the same time." I would agree with Quint that the *Aeneid* and especially *Aeneid* 12 challenge certain ways in which Augustus presented his interactions with the past, but, as argued above, I do not see *clementia* in Juno's reconciliation with Jupiter. If anything, the scene only demonstrates how the goddess is still committed to obliterating any memory of the Trojans' due to her own memory-based rage.

namely that Aeneas has a choice between remembering and forgetting, is questionable; the oversimplified demand that Aeneas forget Pallas sidesteps the more basic question of whether Aeneas is capable of or would even desire to do this.[104] The interaction between Aeneas and the baldric is complex, particularly in regard to agency. Fowler implies that Aeneas had a choice even after he saw the baldric: "What matters is what Aeneas does with [the baldric]: the monuments mean what the audience wants them to mean."[105] The audience does at least partly determine a monument's meaning, but this formulation gives too little credit to the content of the monument and the context in which it is seen.

It is of fundamental significance that Aeneas notices this specific monument at this specific moment on this specific location. As argued above, when Aeneas sees Pallas' belt on Turnus' shoulder, just as when Daedalus arrives at the panel reserved for his depiction of Icarus' fall, he has no choice but to remember. The narrator confirms this by terming the baldric "a monument" (*monimenta*, 12.945), and Aeneas' mnemonic interactions with the baldric dominate him. This sort of remembrance is not far from what modern researchers call a "flashbulb memory," a term that describes a particularly vivid and emotional recollection generally prompted by an object associated with a negative event.[106] For Aeneas, his recollection of the youth is instantaneous and occurs without any conscious effort. There is no indication that the Trojan could forget Pallas's death if he tried, and his reaction is directly in accord with the *Aeneid*'s consistent portrait of remembering and responding to memory as expected human actions.

A comparison with the end of the *Odyssey* adds weight to the idea that it is natural to expect characters to remember and then to react to their memories. Just as the end of the *Iliad*, alluded to earlier by Turnus' speech, offers one paradigm for how a character may respond to memories, the end of the *Odyssey* likewise offers another potential paradigm for human reaction to past memories. Unlike the *Iliad* though, whose last book shows memory prompting reconciliation, memory naturally leads to revenge in

Galinsky 1996, 89 writes that Aeneas' final deed displays *pietas* while illustrating the limits of *clementia*. Most 2001, like Quint, argues that Aeneas must choose between *pietas* and *clementia*. He claims that while the Trojan's choice of *pietas* may be appropriate for the bloody heroic age, *clementia* is necessary for the Augustan age (165–9).

104 On the question of Aeneas and self-control, see Gill 1997, 213 and 2006, 435–6, 439, 459.

105 Fowler 2000, 217.

106 For much further discussion and bibliography of flashbulb memories, see Conway 1995; Fivush et al. 2009, 167; and Luminet and Curci 2009. See Scodel 2002, 105 on Eurycleia's recognition of Odysseus' scar, a bodily mark which inspires a flashbulb memory of its own.

the *Odyssey*.[107] Similarities link the closing scene of *Odyssey* 24 with the final moments of *Aeneid* 12: revenge plays a role in both passages and both passages describe fights that revolve around marriage – a marriage with Penelope in the *Odyssey*, with Lavinia in the *Aeneid*. Given these associations, the similarity between the role memory plays in each is noteworthy. As Homer's epic comes to a close, the kin of Penelope's dead suitors are eager to avenge their relatives. With news of their deaths spreading throughout Ithaca, Zeus and Athena look to prevent a cycle of killings.[108] Zeus says to his daughter: "And let us make [the suitors' relatives] forget the slaughter of their sons and brothers" (ἡμεῖς δ' αὖ παίδων τε κασιγνήτων τε φόνοιο | ἔκλησιν θέωμεν, *Od.* 24.484–5).[109] Zeus's order reveals an assumption that the suitors' fathers and brothers will refrain from fighting only if they forget how their relatives died. He does not even raise the possibility that the Ithacans will forgive Odysseus or forget his actions on their own. When the *Odyssey* finds its peaceful resolution, the success of Athena and Zeus' enforced forgetting is apparent.

This Homeric scene characterizes forgetting as unnatural, a process initiated only through divine intervention. This is similar to the *Aeneid*, where forgetting is also divinely enforced. In *Aeneid* 6, a god calls the shades down to Lethe for a draught of oblivion, and, in *Aeneid* 12, Juno and Jupiter plan to cast the Trojans and Troy into oblivion. David Quint argues that Juno and Jupiter's agreement is similar in intent to that of Zeus and Athena. Hearkening back to his argument about the epic's first half, Quint writes "The Odyssean *Aeneid* [*Aeneid* 1–6] saw the Trojans escaping their past by a process of forgetting, and here this new intrusion of Odyssean elements into Vergil's second *Iliad* [*Aeneid* 7–12] also indicates a policy of forget and forgive."[110] Quint is right to consider these divine conversations side by side, but the sort of forgetting Juno and Jupiter propose is nothing like the *Odyssey*'s oblivion. The Odyssean gods foster peace by making a specific group of people (the suitors' relatives) forget a specific act (Odysseus'

[107] Galinsky 1988, Fowler 1997b, 262 and Putnam 1998, 92 compare the ends of the *Aeneid* and *Odyssey* with a focus on the role anger plays. Knauer 1964a, 430 notes the general parallel and marks specific correspondences between the reconciliation of Juno and Jupiter in the *Aeneid* and the conversation between Athena and Zeus in the *Odyssey*.

[108] The ancients recognized the baneful effects that could come from nourishing painful memories. In classical Athens, there was a "sanction against certain types of or uses of memory" (Flower 2006, 23), and the expression "to bear no malice for past injuries" (οὐ μνησικακεῖν) signified an agreement to neither remember evils from the past nor use memory for harm's sake.

[109] Stanford 1962, ad loc. likens the meaning of the Greek ἔκλησις to the Latin *oblivio*. This is the word's only occurrence in classical Greek literature. For further consideration of ἔκλησις, see Russo et al. 1992, ad loc.

[110] Quint 1989, 45.

slaughter of the suitors), while Juno strives to sate her memory-based anger by effacing the memories of an entire civilization. Juno neither forgets nor forgives. And, as far as Aeneas is concerned, with no god compelling him to forget, it is unsurprising not only that he remembers Pallas' death in the epic's last scene, but also that he acts upon his memories and continues the cycle of vengeance.[111] Aeneas' memory precludes forgiveness, just as Zeus and Athena presumed would be the case with the suitors' relatives.

Memory and foundation

Aeneas, who attempts to preserve Trojan identity through recollection and commemoration, loses control over his interactions with memory in the epic's final scene. The end of the *Aeneid* portrays the remembrance of and reaction to the past as an expected process, but this does not make the epic's final lines any less unsettling. Instead of describing a hero who grants mercy to his foe, such as in the *Iliad*, or a feud that ends in reconciliation, such as in the *Odyssey*, the *Aeneid*'s narrator leaves his audience with the vision of Aeneas, driven on by the past, slaying his already subdued enemy.

What makes this ending all the more disquieting is that the narrator links Aeneas' memory-based revenge with Rome's foundation. Eleven books earlier, at the end of the *Aeneid*'s proem, the narrator exclaimed: "How great a labor it was to found the Roman race!" (*tantae molis erat Romanam condere gentem! Aen.* 1.33). At the epic's close the narrator uses the same verb, *condere*, to describe Aeneas' sword-thrust into Turnus' chest. By selecting this verb once again, the narrator associates Rome's foundation with an act motivated by a personal memory. This characterization associates a deed borne out of an all too human interaction with memory with the beginning of a city divinely arranged to come about through forgetting. Even as he is metaphorically founding a city that will flourish on a cosmic scale, Aeneas remains an individual human being with particular memories that motivate his actions. The narrator's depiction of this foundational killing sets memory as a central, yet problematic, aspect of Roman identity. Aeneas begins Roman civilization with an act dictated by his own personal memories, in contravention of the oblivion Juno and Jupiter had agreed would follow Rome's origins. The narrator implies that Aeneas' action will not allow this oblivion to occur, since it places a private memory of the past, a memory that can be suppressed neither by the gods nor by Aeneas, as central to Rome's origins.

[111] See Dyson 2001, *passim* and esp. 210–35 on revenge-cycles in the *Aeneid*.

The narrator's choice of *condere* to describe both Aeneas' sword-thrust and Rome's foundation has another implication. One persuasive interpretation claims that this verbal repetition associates Rome's founding with civil war, "since both Aeneas and Turnus are Rome's ancestors."[112] This association recalls the narrator's recent anguished question to Jupiter, which reveals that he is passing on a memory imbued with his own pain, a commemoration of death and slaughter for which he cannot find a sufficient explanation and whose meaning he struggles to accept. Yet the narrator has no choice but to remember and commemorate these deaths; after all he has committed himself to telling Aeneas' story and, furthermore, he has shown himself to be part of a larger remembering community linked with Aeneas.

At the end of *Aeneid* 12 the narrator must remember another act of civil strife associated with Rome's foundation, and, along with his audience, he surely experiences emotions similar to those he felt before, yet now these emotions are explicitly centered on Aeneas. While the narrator takes his memories of past suffering and turns them into song, an artistic creation of the sort that Daedalus could not accomplish, Aeneas only transmutes his painful memories into more anguish, for Turnus as well as for himself. Memories of earlier events, hurtful, unavoidable, and personal, remain with Aeneas and the narrator at the epic's end, and they become intertwined with a transition between one society and another, a transition that takes on the bloody overtones of a civil war. Juno and Jupiter would have this transition occur as a clean break from the past, founded on forgetting. Rome's beginnings, tinged with civil discord, come about through remembering the past and still stand to be remembered in the future.

Aeneas' last action and the narrator's arresting depiction of it show that the past cannot always be reconstructed to fit the needs of the present. Aeneas may try to do so in the last verses he speaks in the epic, substituting Pallas for himself as Turnus' killer: "Pallas sacrifices you with this wound, Pallas exacts punishment from your accursed blood" (*Pallas te hoc vulnere, Pallas | immolat et poenam scelerato ex sanguine sumit*, 12.948–9).[113]

[112] James 1995 details how over the course of the *Aeneid condere* shifts from being used to mean "bury the body" to "bury the sword." Vergil is the first to give the word this meaning, and James argues that its use here emphasizes that Rome was founded with the sword by those fighting in a "form of civil conflict" (636). (Quint 1993, 80 also makes the claim that this final scene is "unmistakably one of civil war," and Quint 2010 claims that the theme of civil war is already strong in the poem's first half.)

[113] There is certainly something to be said for P. Hardie's view (1993) that Aeneas is "caught up in a logic of sacrificial substitution" (34) and is alienated from himself both in loss of emotional control and through his use of Pallas' name (33). Yet this loss of control and self-alienation are brought upon Aeneas by the most personal of factors, his memory of and relationship with Pallas.

Distancing himself from this deed and attributing it to Pallas, Aeneas wants to overwrite the memory of Pallas' death prompted by the "monument" (*monimenta*, 12.945) he sees on Turnus' shoulder. As part of his attempt to do so, he verbally commemorates Pallas' slaughter of Turnus, an impossible event which can never be reconciled with what actually occurred in the past. Having struggled throughout the entire epic to reconstruct a memory of the past that will help him bear the present, Aeneas now is faced with a recollection that can be reshaped by nothing less than a complete break with the past's reality. The break is an ineffective one: Aeneas cannot actually bring the boy back. His extraordinary anger at seeing the baldric only verifies that there is nothing he can do to change his own memory of Pallas' death. He, not Pallas, will be remembered as Turnus' killer by all who witness this act. Sometimes there is only a truth so bitter, whether it be Pallas' death in battle or Rome's birth in civil war, that its content cannot be reshaped and its impact cannot be tempered.

Conclusion

Aeneas' memory of Pallas is the last recollection of the epic's action, a complex and multilayered process that inspires fury and regret. A nearly opposite response, one of amazement and satisfaction, is prompted by the first act of remembrance Aeneas describes in his narrative to Dido in *Aeneid* 2 and 3. At the very beginning of his tale, Aeneas relates how the Trojans reacted when they thought the Greeks had sailed away. The particular mix of emotions evoked by these lines has long attracted the notice of the poem's audience (2.25–30):[1]

> nos abiisse rati et vento petiisse Mycenas.
> ergo omnis longo solvit se Teucria luctu;
> panduntur portae, iuvat ire et Dorica castra
> desertosque videre locos litusque relictum:
> hic Dolopum manus, hic saevus tendebat Achilles;
> classibus hic locus, hic acie certare solebant.

> We thought they had left and sought Mycenae with the wind. And all Troy loosens itself from its long grief; the gates are opened, it is pleasing to go even to the Greek camps and to look upon the deserted places and the shore they left behind: here was the Dolopes' camp, here savage Achilles made his home, here was the place for their fleet, here they were accustomed to fight in battle.

Aeneas' description, peppered with the deictic adverb *hic* four times over, calls attention to how this location evokes an entirely different time and situation for the Trojans. Quintilian discusses how a person may be impacted by returning to a particular place: "For when we return to a place after an absence, we not only see the place itself but we remember whatever things we did there, and the people return to us, and even our quiet thoughts come back to our mind" (*nam cum in loca aliqua post tempus reversi sumus,*

[1] See Austin 1964, ix.

non ipsa agnoscimus tantum sed etiam quae in iis fecerimus reminiscimur, personaeque subeunt, nonnumquam tacitae quoque cogitationes in mentem revertuntur, *Inst.* 11.2.17). This vivid experience, though, is not available to everyone. A short quotation from Rammikar, a fifteenth-century Mayan philosopher, captures how it is only for the right person that a place conveys more than its present characteristics: "The young man sees the vacant field; the old man sees the cottage that was once on the land."[2] All too familiar with the people and structures that once existed on this shore, the Trojans are reminded of the Greeks and their battlements when they look upon this presently desolate strip of beach.

Relief and pleasure greet the Trojans as they safely revisit places of earlier terror. The beaches are deserted instead of swarming with enemies, and the Trojans benefit psychologically from seeing the tangible evidence that the war has been survived.[3] There are certain aspects of the process of remembering that heighten this reaction. Rammikar focuses on the memories of a single old man, but here people remember together as a group. Each individual has his own recollections of particular enemies he faced or incidents he survived, but those memories all occur from the same general perspective and represent roughly similar experiences. For the Trojans as a group, a more general social memory may arise out of the threats this beach held. Their very existence threatened by the Greek invasion, they realize that their society has survived, and this social element of their experience heightens the emotions each feels. This process also fosters the construction of a successful narrative told from their perspective. A formidable enemy occupied their shores and laid siege to their city, but the Trojans prevailed and can now lay claim to the title not only of survivors, but, more importantly, of victors. By experiencing their memories together and reacting to them in the same way, the Trojans affirm their shared identity.

Out of all its extraordinary qualities, what is most remarkable about this scene is that it is the *Aeneid*'s sole representation of the Trojans reminiscing with pleasure about their earlier suffering.[4] Aeneas imagined just this sort

[2] Quoted in Hoppál 1981, 288 from Port, 1962, 126.

[3] Beyond signifying that something is enjoyable (*OLD* 5), the verb *iuvare* can also indicate that something is medically or otherwise beneficial (*OLD* 3).

[4] A potential example of non-Trojans remembering their earlier troubles with pleasure comes in the Arcadians' viewing of the dead body of Cacus. As Evander tells Aeneas, after the monster had been killed by Hercules, the Arcadians "cannot satisfy their souls' desire to look upon [Cacus]" (*nequeunt expleri corda tuendo*, 8.265), a description that hints at their amazement in viewing the dead body of a creature which they remembered terrifying them many times before. (See Austin 1971, ad 713 for a construction similar to that of *expleri corda*, and see *OLD* 2 for *corda* as designating the center of the process of memory.) Unlike the Trojans' act of recollection on the beach, this recollection is not subsequently undermined.

of recollection in *Aeneid* 1. Here, standing upon Carthage's shores, having barely survived the sea storm, he tries to rally the Trojans by telling them that "Perhaps one day it will be pleasing to remember even these things" (*forsan et haec olim meminisse iuvabit*, 1.203). The connection between these words and Aeneas' present description of the Trojans' recollection goes beyond general similarity. Aeneas' use of the word *iuvare* to describe the beneficial effect of such remembering (1.203, 2.27) links the two passages together. Yet in *Aeneid* 1, Aeneas' words are almost immediately undermined when the narrator reveals how the Trojan leader doubts what he says (1.208–9), and, surely enough, the rest of the epic proves Aeneas' misgivings correct. Rarely does remembering bring the Trojans pure happiness, and, when it does, the circumstances complicate that mnemonic interaction. Apart from the passage under discussion in *Aeneid* 2, Aeneas' recollection of his father's tables prophecy in *Aeneid* 7 is the one other example of memory that prompts unadulterated joy. Yet there Aeneas' "memory" is not at all straightforward, and it cannot be claimed that the Trojans are remembering past traumas with pleasure. After all, the prophecy at the heart of Aeneas' memory, attributed to his father Anchises, was actually spoken by Celaeno.

It is just as easy to be overly hasty in evaluating the pleasure exhibited by the Trojans' reactions in *Aeneid* 2. For the Trojans themselves it could not remain uncomplicated for long, as they discover the Greeks' treachery that night. From the perspective of Aeneas' present audience, this emotion has been compromised from the moment Aeneas describes it. Aeneas' retelling of this event is part of a well-known larger story of the Trojans' defeat, one in which, his audience knows, the Greeks do not actually sail away. Moreover, as if to truly foreclose any possibility that his audience may share even for a moment the happiness he describes the Trojans enjoying, Aeneas prefaces this six line passage with the statement that the Greeks were only hiding on the far side of Tenedos (2.24). The Trojans' pleasure appears naïve in retrospect, and Aeneas' memory of the Trojans' recollections on the deserted beach, a memory of a memory, must fill him now with feelings of disillusionment and regret. Perhaps, at some point after Troy's destruction and before his arrival in Carthage, Aeneas reflects on the doomed innocence of the Trojans' shoreline recollections and this prompts him in *Aeneid* 1 to doubt his own promise to his men that they will find happiness in reminiscing about earlier troubles.

Above and beyond standing as an explanation for Aeneas' wariness toward promising his men a pleasant memory of earlier troubles, the manner in which 2.25–30 are transformed from Aeneas' apparently straightforward recollection of an earlier memory into his troubled remembrance of the Trojans' foolish reaction to their past emblematizes memory's multilayered role in the *Aeneid*. Here we see memory's varied emotional impact, its role within a larger social setting, and it close relationship with a group's identity and narrative. While no single act of memory in the epic offers a complete picture of recollection or commemoration in the *Aeneid*, the characters and narrator's interactions with memory function in a consistent manner and, as outlined further below, share several core traits.

This book's central argument is that memory acts as a social and narrative mechanism for integrating a traumatic past with an uncertain future for both the narrator and Trojans alike. This process of moving forward is often painful, but it is never depicted as anything less than necessary. Indeed, the Trojans and the narrator make remembrance and commemoration fundamentally consistent aspects of their existence. For Aeneas and the Trojans, the narrative aspect of memory is apparent in how they turn to remembering and commemorating the past in an attempt to construct a coherent version of their lives, one that incorporates their past traumas as relevant events within a longer and more successful story. This occurs in Aeneas' speech to his men in *Aeneid* 1, for instance, and also in Anchises' quick move, after his earlier memory was proven wrong, to remember Cassandra's suddenly correct prophecy in *Aeneid* 3. From a social perspective, Aeneas' interaction with memory and with the Trojans takes on two different roles. He tries to dictate how the Trojans will remember the past (such as in his eulogy of Pallas in *Aeneid* 11), and, with a future goal in mind, he attempts to influence how the generations to come will remember himself, his followers, and Troy (such as in his speech to Ascanius in *Aeneid* 12).

The narrator also turns to memory as a social and narrative process. He characterizes his own narrative as an act of commemoration, as is common for epic singers to do, but he distinguishes himself from earlier poets by asserting his primacy vis-à-vis the Muses as the creator of memory. From a social point of view, he continually charges his audience with remembering a story that forms their origins, in the process blurring the boundaries between natural and learned, social and individual memory. Like Aeneas, the narrator too comes to feel the grief that remembering traumatic events can bring, but, also like Aeneas, that does not stop him from setting remembrance as an essential aspect of his and his audience's experience of his song.

As part of the narrator and characters' engagement with memory a set of core properties comes to be consistently associated with recollection and commemoration in the *Aeneid.* These properties are not apparent in every instance where the narrator or a character interacts with memory, but they do stand as the predominant characteristics of remembering and commemorating the past. These four properties both facilitate and challenge the narrator and characters' engagement with memory: (1) as the characters and narrator create and recreate the past, their recollections display nuance and fluidity; (2) remembrance has the potential to collapse borders between different times as well as between individuals and groups; (3) the act of remembering creates a host of emotions; and (4) both the process and contents of memory, along with the emotions to which they give rise, are difficult for the narrator and characters to control.

In its status as a representation, memory in the *Aeneid* shows a remarkable amount of mutability. This is in direct contrast with an argument that the epic's characters use the "art of memory" to recall earlier events without bias, in the manner of retrieving a photograph.[5] Aeneas and his followers do not reproduce their past, but present a version of it that, consciously or not, they have in some way reconstructed. A number of factors, including a character's own aims and personal identity, along with his status within a larger group and that group's overall composition, influence this reconstruction. This trait is seen in commemorations for the future as well, particularly in those instances where multiple characters, along with the narrator, offer different commemorations of a person, each projecting his own version of what is significant and how it ought to be remembered.

Memory also enables the characters and narrator to cross boundaries that otherwise might remain impermeable. The boundaries that memory collapses are both temporal (past/present, present/future) and social (individual/group). By remembering the past and commemorating it for the future, the characters and narrator make the gap between these time-periods seem insignificant. A similar statement holds true for the impact an individual's particular version of the past can have on a group, or the influence a group exerts on an individual's construction and vocalization of a recollection. The plot of the *Aeneid* concentrates on the transition between past and future and the evolution of the Trojans from a group of survivors that gathers around Aeneas to a nascent community that stands as Rome's origin. Vergil places memory at the heart of these various transitions.

A third property the *Aeneid* repeatedly associates with recollection is that it creates moments of emotion. These emotions range in tenor and

[5] Scarth 2008.

intensity, but they are rarely, if ever, absent. A remembrance draws upon the emotion attached to the original event while joining that emotion with a new feeling that arises from the process of recollecting the past in one's present circumstances. The famous actions of the epic's opening and closing lines, where memory gives rise to "violent grief" for Juno and Aeneas alike, demonstrate this most vividly, but memory's force is felt as well even when the emotion is not so destructive or emphatic. Aeneas' behavior toward Lausus, for instance, displays respect and admiration after the boy's corpse causes him to remember his own filial piety. Characters sometimes successfully manipulate memory to foster certain emotions, but, just as often, they prove unable to anticipate or control the emotions memory provokes in themselves or others.

Lastly, there is one other marker of memory's role in the *Aeneid* of particular consequence: the challenge of successfully manipulating the processes of remembering and commemoration. A wholesale commitment to memory, which involves both confronting the past and trying to create the future's memory of the present, changes a person in a fundamental way: having made memory a central part of his life, he predisposes himself to interact with it and opens himself to all its influences. While Aeneas sometimes successfully harnesses memory for his own purposes, no person in the *Aeneid*, not even the epic's narrator, exercises complete control over memory, either in its meaning or in its impact. Aeneas opens himself to memory's energy because of his extensive engagement with it. For example, in *Aeneid* 12, just a few hundred lines after calmly instructing his son to remember himself and Hector as a guide for future actions, Pallas' baldric brings an unbidden memory of the boy's death to Aeneas' mind and drives him to kill Turnus, an action that is the opposite of what he was considering a few lines earlier. This is not the only example of failure somehow marring an intergenerational charge to remember. Turnus' posture and words in defeat should remind Aeneas of Anchises' orders in the underworld, but Aeneas does not act upon his father's earlier injunction in *Aeneid* 12, and thus loses an opportunity to provide an example for Ascanius of the sort of father–son memory he himself had so recently enjoined. Just as neither Anchises nor Aeneas can entirely control what their sons will remember, the narrator too finds difficulty in trying to mold the memories of others. He feels pain at commemorating events that, he believes, perhaps ought not to have occurred, and more generally, the multiple apostrophes of characters that contradict his commemorations show that he cannot simply dictate what meaning and memories his audience will take from these characters' deaths.

Yet even when Aeneas and the narrator struggle to control the meaning of past memories and commemorations for the future, memory nonetheless stands as a mechanism for each of them to move forward and to integrate the past with the future. Aeneas' killing of Turnus is prompted by a memory he did not voluntarily recall, but, all the same, it still acts as the conclusion to the story of his relationship with Pallas and becomes an example, albeit perhaps not the one he intended, to be remembered by his son, as well as by the crowd that watches and even by the *Aeneid*'s audience. The same is true when the narrator remembers events that are painful for him to recollect. He continues to commemorate those deeds via his narrative, and he continues to link those deeds to his audience's origins.

Vergil's depiction of memory in the *Aeneid* as a complex and challenging phenomenon, important to the life of the individual and of the society alike, has extraordinary relevance for Augustan society. The Romans considered a relationship with the past to be vital to personal and group success, and the *Aeneid* was written in an era when concern was rising over the viability of Rome's link with its past. At the same time, Augustus, in his effort to establish and strengthen his position, used monuments, inscriptions, and public ceremonies to promote a particular memory of the Republic and to link his rule with a version of the past that minimized his role in the recent violence and civil strife. In several different ways, the *Aeneid* shows that people's interactions with memory are more complex and less liable to control than Augustus' efforts at mnemonic fashioning would hope. The temple of Mars Ultor, for instance, with its lines of statues of Roman heroes and Julian ancestors, would seem to prompt a coherent and controlled recollection of the past. As part of his creation of this narrative of continuity with the Republic's glorious past, Augustus omitted any indication that he had originally vowed this temple at the Battle of Philippi, an episode in Rome's civil wars. The *Aeneid* demonstrates, though, in Aeneas' reaction to the ekphrasis on Juno's temple in *Aeneid* 1, how someone's personal memories can move the meaning of a monument away from its intended message.[6] Someone with a personal memory of Philippi, for instance, may have a very different reaction to the temple of Mars Ultor than someone who looks at the temple a hundred years later.[7]

[6] For an alternative reading of the relationship between the *Aeneid* and this temple of Mars Ultor, see Galinsky 1996, 211, who argues that the justified vengeance of Aeneas' killing of Turnus, which has both personal and public aspects, is similar to this "monument to both Augustus' private and public revenge, respectively, on the murderers of his adoptive father and on the Parthians."

[7] On the possibility of "subversive 'counter-memories'," see Alcock 2002, 16.

Above and beyond the pitfalls the narrator exposes in any attempt at controlling memory, the *Aeneid* time and again shows that it is not in human nature to forget painful aspects of the past. Traumatic experiences are remembered, and, what is more, no pleasure attends the recollection of them even when they have been overcome. Vergil, however, does not just write about trauma in general. Rather, his epic's closing battles allude intensely to the recent civil wars that had plagued Rome. The *Aeneid*'s narrator openly speaks of the pain of remembering the battles between the Latins and Trojans, but he persists in commemorating them all the same. By emphasizing the need to remember such wars, Vergil hints that the past does not vanish for the community that comes out of a civil war. The internecine battles are remembered in a process that is not necessarily pleasant, but rather involves a search for a proper way to weave the meaning of the lives of the dead into the community's identity. Jennifer Rea argues that conflicting memories in Augustan Rome "brought the society together . . . [giving Romans] something to focus on as they created a new cultural narrative for themselves."[8] Yet this is not the case in the *Aeneid*, as conflicting commemorations create opposed narratives. Larger groups such as the Trojans do not necessarily splinter, but various members possess competing memories, rather than one uniform standardized version of the past.

This process of remembering prior suffering is presented as an essential and unavoidable part of individual and communal life. Vergil does not offer his audience an easy formula that would facilitate a successful transition from a bloody past to a peaceful future. Instead, he writes an epic where the characters and narrator remain committed to experiencing and renegotiating, time and again, their memories of the past and their hopes for commemoration in the future. Part of this process, for both Aeneas and the narrator, involves forming communities that will do this as well, even when those communities' mnemonic interactions lie beyond their control. Both the *Aeneid*'s narrator and protagonist must incorporate painful memories into their own lives as well as into the fabric of a meaningful community.

[8] Rea 2007, 83. She claims that a recognition of the "mobility and mutability [of memory] allowed for opposing viewpoints" to either be reconciled or approached from varying perspectives, thus enabling the society to overcome previous battles and secure a peaceful life (70). In this vein, "various members of the Roman community . . . reflect on the past and create new public memories" after crises that help them to "cope with memories of the conflict" that foment divisions and spur competition "for control of the past" (139). While I differ from Rea in her conclusions, I agree with her assertion that Vergil engages his audience and asks "them to consider how to handle the challenges of restoring the city of Rome after civil war. His entire epic is a thoughtful articulation of the power that memory of the past has to shape the human experience" (13–4).

This task is brought home most forcibly by the *Aeneid*'s final act. So long as characters can promote and even tolerate the existence of different social memories, such as initially occurs in the process surrounding Pallas' death, the community's memory can shift in its content and even grow to accommodate new perspectives. Yet once an oikotype is formed, or, rather, once a community's leader decides that an oikotype has been formed, tolerance vanishes. The *Aeneid*'s final battle ends with the validation of one view of Pallas' death and the dismissal of another. The same could be said of the narrative constructed by the Temple of Mars Ultor, which offers a teleological view of Rome's development that renders civil war not just invisible but even unthinkable.

Yet, as the *Aeneid* shows, whatever calm such enforced closure may provide proves evanescent. There is always a new social memory battle on the horizon: even as Aeneas' killing of Turnus strives to establish the correct memory of Pallas, it gives rise to a more daunting commemorative challenge. With Turnus dead, each member of Aeneas' inchoate community, composed of recently opposed races, must figure out how to remember Turnus' death in a way that satisfies both themselves and their new society. This challenge is prefigured by the ring of Rutulians that watches and will remember the pair's fight, purposely invoked by Turnus in his plea to Aeneas.[9] The only certainty is that Aeneas' killing of Turnus will prompt a new set of commemorations. The inescapability of the past and civil war, on both a personal and social level, looms for Aeneas and the Trojans as well as for Vergil's Roman audience. While the *Aeneid* maps out the challenges involved in productively integrating the past with the future, it reveals that there is no easy route to follow.

[9] It is also foreshadowed by Aeneas' declaration, before his single-combat with Turnus is set to begin, that, with his victory, the Trojans and Italians will enter "into everlasting peace" (*aeterna in foedera*, 12.191).

Bibliography

Abbreviations of ancient and modern works follow the conventions set out in *L'Année Philologique*, the *Oxford Latin Dictionary*, and Liddell and Scott's *Greek-English Lexicon*.

Adams, J. N. 1982. *The Latin Sexual Vocabulary*. Baltimore.

Alcock, S. E. 2002. *Archaeologies of the Greek Past: Landscape, Monuments, and Memories*. Cambridge.

Anderson, W. S. 1957. "Vergil's Second *Iliad*," *TAPA* **88**: 17–30. Reprinted in Hardie 1999: **3**: 74–86.

Armstrong, R. 2002. "Crete in the *Aeneid*: Recurring Trauma and Alternative Fate," *CQ* **52**: 321–40.

Arthur, M. 1981. "The Divided World of *Iliad* VI," in H. P. Foley, ed. 1981: *Reflections on Women in Antiquity*. Philadelphia. 19–44. Reprint of 1981, *Women's Studies* **8**: 21–46.

Assmann, A. 2011. *Cultural Memory and Western Civilization: Arts of Memory*. Cambridge.

Assmann, J. 1992. *Das Kulturelle Gedächtnis: Schrift, Erinnerung und Politische Identität in Frühen Hochkulturen*. Munich.

2006. *Religion and Cultural Memory: Ten Studies*. Trans. R. Livingstone. Stanford University Press.

Austin, R. G. 1955. *Aeneidos Liber Quartus*. Oxford.

1964. *Aeneidos Liber Secundus*. Oxford.

1971. *Aeneidos Liber Primus*. Oxford.

1977. *Aeneidos Liber Sextus*. Oxford.

Bakhtin, M. 1981. *The Dialogic Imagination: Four Essays*. Trans. C. Emerson and M. Holquist. Austin.

1984. *Problems of Dostoevsky's Poetics*. Ed. and trans. C. Emerson. Minneapolis.

Bakker, E. J. 2008. "Epic Remembering," in E. A. Mackay, ed. *Orality, Literacy, Memory in the Ancient Greek and Roman World*. Leiden. 65–77.

Bal, M. 1997. *Narratology: Introduction to the Theory of Narrative*. Toronto.

1999. "Introduction," in M. Bal, J. Crewe, and L. Spitzer, eds. *Acts of Memory: Cultural Recall in the Present*. London. vii–xvii.

Bandera, C. 1981. "Sacrificial Levels in Virgil's *Aeneid*," *Arethusa* **14**: 217–39.

Baraz, Y. 2009. "Euripides' Corinthian Princess in the *Aeneid*," *CP* **104**: 317–30.

Barchiesi, A. 1984. *La Traccia del Modello: Effeti Omerici nella Narrazione Virgiliana*. Pisa.

1997. "Virgilian Narrative: Ekphrasis," in Martindale 1997: 271–81.

1999. "Suffering and Interpretation in the *Aeneid*," in P. Hardie: **3**: 324–44. Reprint of 1995, "Rappresentazioni del dolore e interpretazione nell'Eneide," *A&A* **40**: 109–24

2001. *Speaking Volumes: Narrative and Intertext in Ovid and Other Latin Poets*. Ed. and trans. M. Fox and S. Marchesi. London.

2002. "Martial Arts: Mars Ultor in the Forum Augustum," in G. Herbert-Brown, ed. *Ovid's Fasti: Historical Readings at Its Bimillennium*. Oxford. 1–22.

Bartlett, F. C. 1932. *Remembering: A Study in Experimental and Social Psychology*. Cambridge.

Bartsch, S. 1998. "*Ars* and the Man: The Politics of Art in Virgil's *Aeneid*," *CP* **93**: 322–42.

Bassi, K. 2005. "Things of the Past: Objects and Time in Greek Narrative," *Arethusa* **38**: 1–32.

Beard, M. 2007. *The Roman Triumph*. Cambridge, MA.

Behr, F. D. 2005. "The Narrator's Voice: A Narratological Reappraisal of Apostrophe in Virgil's *Aeneid*," *Arethusa* **38**: 189–221.

2007. *Feeling History: Lucan, Stoicism, and the Poetics of Passion*. Columbus, OH.

Bergmann, B. 1994. "The Roman House as Memory Theater: The House of the Tragic Poet in Pompeii," *The Art Bulletin* **76**: 225–56.

Berlin, N. 1998. "War and Remembrance: *Aeneid* 12.554–60 and Aeneas' Memory of Troy," *AJP* **119**: 11–41.

Berres, T. 1982. *Die Entstehung der "Aeneis."* Wiesbaden.

Bettini, M. 1997. "Ghosts of Exile: Doubles and Nostalgia in Vergil's *parva Troia* (*Aeneid* 3.294ff.)," *CA* **16**: 8–33.

Bews, J. P. 1987. "Philosophical Revelation and Its Function in *Aeneid* 6," in B. Anthony, ed. *Laurea Corona: Studies in Honour of Edward Coleiro*. Amsterdam. 91–8.

Beye, C. R. 2006. *Ancient Epic Poetry: Homer, Apollonius, Virgil, with a Chapter on the Gilgamesh Poems*. 2nd edn. Wauconda.

Biow, D. 1994. "Epic Performance on Trial: Virgil's *Aeneid* and the Power of Eros in Song," *Arethusa* **27**: 223–46.

Block, E. 1981. *The Effects of Divine Manifestation on the Reader's Perspective in Vergil's "Aeneid."* New York.

1982. "The Narrator Speaks: Apostrophe in Homer and Vergil," *TAPA* **112**: 7–22.

Blum, H. 1969. *Die Antike Mnemotechnik*. Hildesheim.

Booth, W. C. 1961. *The Rhetoric of Fiction*. Chicago.

Borges, J. L. 1964. "Funes the Memorious," in D. A. Yates, ed., and J. E. Irby, trans. *Labyrinths: Selected Stories and Other Writings*. New York. 59–66.

Bowie, A. M. 2008. "Aeneas Narrator," *PVS* **26**: 41–51.

Bowra, C. M. 1945. *From Virgil to Milton*. London.

Braund, D. and C. Gill. 2003. Eds. *Myth, History and Culture in Republican Rome: Studies in Honour of T. P. Wiseman*. Exeter.

Braund, S. M. 1997. "Virgil and the Cosmos: Religious and Philosophical Ideas," in Martindale 1997: 204–21.

Braund, S. M. and C. Gill. 1997. Eds. *The Passions in Roman Thought and Literature*. Cambridge.

Bright, D. F. 1981. "Aeneas' Other Nekyia," *Vergilius* **27**: 40–7.

Brockmeier, J. 2001. "From the End to the Beginning: Retrospective Teleology in Autobiography," in J. Brockmeier and D. A. Carbaugh, eds. *Narrative and Identity: Studies in Autobiography, Self and Culture*. Amsterdam. 247–80.

Buchheit, V. 1963. *Vergil über die Sendung Roms. Untersuchungen zum Bellum Poenicum und zur Aeneis*. Heidelberg.

Burnett, A. P. 1983. *Three Archaic Poets: Archilochus, Alcaeus, Sappho*. Cambridge, MA.

Cairns, F. 1989. *Virgil's Augustan Epic*. Cambridge.

Casali, S. 2004. "Nisus and Euryalus: Exploiting the Contradictions in Virgil's 'Doloneia'," *HSCP* **102**: 319–54.

2008. "The King of Pain: Aeneas, Achates and ἄχος in *Aeneid* 1," *CQ* **58**: 181–9.

Casey, E. S. 1987. *Remembering: A Phenomenological Study*. Bloomington.

Catto, B. A. 1989. "Vergilian Inversion of Lucretius in Anchises' Exposition of the Soul," *Vergilius* **35**: 60–9.

Ceauşescu, P. 1976. "Altera Roma: Histoire d'une Folie Politique," *Historia* **25**: 79–108.

Chatman, S. B. 1978. *Story and Discourse: Narrative Structure in Fiction and Film*. Ithaca.

Clausen, W. 1964. "An Interpretation of the *Aeneid*," *HSCP* **68**: 139–47.

1994. *A Commentary on Virgil, "Eclogues."* Oxford.

Clay, D. 1988. "The Archaeology of the Temple to Juno in Carthage (1.446–93)," *CP* **83**: 195–205.

Coleman, R. 1977. *Vergil: "Eclogues."* Cambridge.

Commager, S. 1981. "Fateful Words: Some Conversations in *Aeneid* 4," *Arethusa* **14**: 101–14.

Confino, A. 1997. "Collective Memory and Cultural History: Problems of Method." *American Historical Review* **102**: 1386–404.

Conington, J. 1884. *P. Vergili Maronis Opera: The Works of Virgil with a Commentary*. 4th edn. 3 vols. Revised by H. Nettleship. London. Reprinted with introduction by P. Hardie. 6 vols. Exeter. 2007–8.

Conte, G. B. 1986. *The Rhetoric of Imitation: Genre and Poetic Memory in Virgil and Other Latin Poets*. C. Segal, ed. and intro. Ithaca.

1992. "Proems in the Middle," *YCS* **29**: 147–59.

2007. *The Poetry of Pathos: Studies in Virgilian Epic*. Oxford.

Conway, M. A. 1995. *Flashbulb Memories*. Hillsdale.

Culler, J. 1977. "Apostrophe," *Diacritics* **7**: 59–69.

1980. "Fabula and Sjuzhet in the Analysis of Narrative: Some American Discussions," *Poetics Today* **1**: 27–37.

Currie, H. M. 1962–3. "The Sense of the Past in Virgil," *PVS* **2**: 17–32.

Detienne, M. 1996. *The Masters of Truth in Archaic Greece*, J. Lloyd, trans. New York.

Davis, N. Z. and R. Starn. 1989. "Introduction," *Representations* **26**: 1–6.

Dougherty, C. 2001. *The Raft of Odysseus: The Ethnographic Imagination of Homer's Odyssey*. Oxford.

DuBois, P. 1982. *History, Rhetorical Description, and the Epic*. Cambridge.

Duckworth, G. E. 1938. "The Chronology of *Aeneid* VIII–X," in *AJP* **59**: 135–44.

Dyson, J. T. 1997. "*Fluctus Irarum, Fluctus Curarum*: Lucretian *religio* in the *Aeneid*," *AJP* **118**: 449–57.

2001. *King of the Wood: The Sacrificial Victor in Virgil's Aeneid*. Norman.

Earl, D. C. 1961. *The Political Thought of Sallust*. Cambridge.

Eco, U. 1988. "An *Ars Oblivionalis*? Forget It!" Trans. M. Migiel. *Proceedings of the Modern Language Association* **103**: 254–61.

Edmunds, L. 2005. "Critical Divergences: New Directions in the Study and Teaching of Roman Literature," *TAPA* **135**: 1–13.

Edwards, C. 1996. *Writing Rome: Textual Approaches to the City*. Cambridge.

Elsner, J. 1995. *Art and the Roman Viewer: The Transformation of Art from the Pagan World to Christianity*. Cambridge.

Erll, A. and A. Nünning. 2010. Eds. *A Companion to Cultural Memory Studies*. Berlin.

Ernout, A. and A. Meillet. 1932. *Dictionnaire Étymologique de la Langue Latine: Histoire des Mots*. Paris.

Erskine, A. 2001. *Troy between Greece and Rome: Local Tradition and Imperial Power*. Oxford.

Falkner, T. M. 1990. "The Politics and Poetics of Time in Solon's 'Ten Ages'," *CJ* **86**: 1–15.

Fantham, E. 1999. "The Role of Lament in the Growth and Eclipse of the Roman Epic," in M. Beissinger, J. Tylus, and S. Wofford, eds. *Epic Traditions in the Contemporary World: The Poetics of Community*. Berkeley. 221–34.

Fantuzzi, M. and R. Hunter. 2004. *Tradition and Innovation in Hellenistic Poetry*. Cambridge.

Farrell, J. 1991. *Vergil's "Georgics" and the Traditions of Ancient Epic: The Art of Allusion in Literary History*. Oxford.

1997. "The Phenomenology of Memory in Roman Culture," *CJ* **92**.4: 373–83.

Faulkner, A. 2008. *The Homeric Hymn to Aphrodite: Introduction, Text, and Commentary*. Oxford.

Favro, D. 1996. *The Urban Image of Augustan Rome*. Cambridge.

Feeney D. 1983. "The Taciturnity of Aeneas," *CQ* **33**: 204–19.

1984. "The Reconciliations of Juno," *CQ* **34**: 179–94.

1986. "History and Revelation in Vergil's Underworld," *PCPS* **212**: 1–24.

1991. *The Gods in Epic: Poets and Critics of the Classical Tradition*. Oxford.

1997. "'Shall I Compare Thee . . . ?' Catullus 68B and the Limits of Analogy," in J. H. Gaisser, ed. *Catullus: Oxford Readings in Classical Studies*. New York. 429–46.

1998. *Literature and Religion at Rome: Cultures, Contexts, and Beliefs*. Cambridge.

2007. *Caesar's Calendar: Ancient Time and the Beginnings of History*. Berkeley.

Feldherr, A. 1995. "Ships of State: *Aeneid* 5 and Augustan Circus Spectacle," *CA* **14**: 245–65.

2000. "*Non Inter Nota Sepulcra*: Catullus 101 and Roman Funerary Ritual." *CA* **19**: 209–31.

Fentress, J. and C. Wickham. 1992. *Social Memory*. Oxford.

Fernandez, J. W. 1972. "Persuasions and Performances: Of the Beast in Every Body . . . and the Metaphors of Everyman," *Daedalus* **101**: 39–60.

Fisher, P. 2002. *The Vehement Passions*. Princeton.

Fitzgerald, W. 1984. "Aeneas, Daedalus, and the Labyrinth," *Arethusa* **17**: 51–65.

Fivush, R., Bohanek, J. G., Marin, K. and J. M. Sales. 2009. "Emotional Memory and Memory for Emotions," In O. Luminet and A. Curci, eds. *Flashbulb Memories: New Issues and New Perspectives*. New York. 163–84.

Flower, H. I. 2006. *The Art of Forgetting: Disgrace and Oblivion in Roman Political Culture*. Chapel Hill.

Fludernik, M. 2009. *An Introduction to Narratology*. New York.

Fordyce, C. J. 1961. *Catullus: A Commentary*. Oxford.

1977. *P. Vergili Maronis Aeneidos, Libri* VII–VIII. Bristol.

Fowler, D. 1997a. "Epicurean Anger," in S. M. Braund and C. Gill, eds. *The Passions in Roman Thought and Literature*. Cambridge. 16–35.

1997b. "Virgilian Narrative: Story-telling," in Martindale 1997: 259–70.

2000. *Roman Constructions: Readings in Postmodern Latin*. Oxford.

Fowler, D. and P. Fowler. 1996. "Literary Theory and Classical Studies," S. Hornblower and A. Spawforth, eds. *The Oxford Classical Dictionary*. Oxford. 871–5.

Fraenkel, E. 1945. "Some Aspects of the Structure of *Aeneid* 7," *JRS* **35**: 1–14.

1950. *Agamemnon: Edited with a Commentary*. Oxford.

Fratantuono, L. 2009. *A Commentary on Virgil, Aeneid* XI. Brussels.

Freeman, M. 2010. *Hindsight: The Promise and Peril of Looking Backward*. Oxford.

Gale, M. R. 2003. "Poetry and the Backward Glance in Virgil's *Georgics* and *Aeneid*," *TAPA* **133**: 323–52.

Galinsky, K. 1988. "The Anger of Aeneas," *AJP* **109**: 321–48.

1996. *Augustan Culture*. Princeton.

2003. "Greek and Roman Drama and the *Aeneid*," in D. Braund and C. Gill 2003: 275–94.

Gasti, H. 2006. "Narratological Aspects of Vergil's *Aeneid*," *Acta Classica* **49**: 113–20.

Gedi, N. and Y. Elam. 1996. "Collective Memory – What Is It?," *History and Memory* **8**: 30–50.

Genette, G. 1980. *Narrative Discourse: An Essay in Method*. Trans. J. E. Lewin. Ithaca.

Gill, C. 1997a. "The Emotions in Greco-Roman Philosophy," in S. M. Braund and C. Gill 1997: 5–15.

1997b. "Passion as Madness in Roman Poetry," in S. M. Braund and C. Gill 1997: 213–41.

2006. *The Structured Self in Hellenistic and Roman Thought*. Oxford.

Gillis, D. 1983. *Eros and Death in the Aeneid*. Rome.

Gillis, J. R. 1994. "Memory and Identity: The History of a Relationship," in J. R. Gillis, ed. *Commemorations: Politics of National Identity*. Princeton. 3–26.

Gotoff, H. C. 1985. "The Difficulty of the Ascent from Avernus," *CP* **80**: 35–40.

Goud, T. E. and J. C. Yardley. 1988. "Dido's Burning Effigy: *Aeneid* 4.508," *Rheinisches Museum* **131**: 386–8.

Gove, P. B. 1993. Ed. *Webster's Third New International Dictionary of the English Language, Unabridged*. Springfield.

Gowing, A. M. 2000. "Memory and Silence in Cicero's *Brutus*," *Eranos* **98**: 39–64.

2005. *Empire and Memory: The Representation of the Roman Republic in Imperial Culture*. Cambridge.

Grabes, H. 2005. Ed. *Literature, Literary History, and Cultural Memory*. Vol. 21. *Yearbook of Research in English and American Literature*. Tübingen.

Gransden, K. W. 1976. *Virgil: Aeneid Book* VIII. Cambridge.

Greene, T. M. 1999. "The Natural Tears of Epic," in M. Beissinger, J. Tylus, and S. Wofford, eds. *Epic Traditions in the Contemporary World: The Poetics of Community*. Berkeley. 189–202.

Grillo, L. 2010. "Leaving Troy and Creusa: Reflections on Aeneas' Flight," *CJ* **106**: 43–68.

Grimm, R. E. 1967. "Aeneas and Andromache in *Aeneid* III," *AJP* **88**: 151–62.

Gross, N. P. 2003/4. "Mantles Woven with Gold: Pallas' Shroud and the End of the *Aeneid*," *CJ* **99**: 135–56.

Gutting, E. 2006. "Marriage in the *Aeneid*: Venus, Vulcan, and Dido," *CP* **101**: 263–79.

Halbwachs, M. 1992. *On Collective Memory*. L. A. Coser, ed. and trans. Chicago.

Hamilton, C. I. M. 1993. "Dido, Tityos and Prometheus," *CQ* **43**: 249–54.

Hardie, A. 2007. "Juno, Hercules, and the Muses at Rome," *AJP* **128**: 551–92.

Hardie, P. 1986. *Virgil's "Aeneid:" Cosmos and Imperium*. Oxford.

1990. "*Forsan et Haec Olim Meminisse Iuvabit*." Review of E. Henry 1989. *CR* **40**: 263–4.

1993. *The Epic Successors of Virgil: A Study in the Dynamics of a Tradition*. Cambridge.

1994. *Virgil: Aeneid Book* IX. Cambridge.

1997. "Closure in Latin Epic," in D. H. Roberts, F. M. Dunn, and D. Fowler, eds. *Classical Closure: Reading the End in Latin Literature*. Princeton. 139–62.

1998. *Virgil*. Oxford.

1999. Ed. *Virgil: Critical Assessments of Classical Authors*. 4 vols. New York.

2012. *Rumour and Renown: Representations of Fama in Western Literature*. Cambridge.

Hardy, R. B. 1991. "The Uses of Memory in the Poetry of Vergil," unpublished PhD dissertation, Brown University.

Harrison, E. L. 1972–3. "Why Did Venus Wear Boots?," *PVS* **12**: 10–25. Reprinted in P. Hardie 1999: 4: 59–75.

1984. "The *Aeneid* and Carthage," in Woodman and West 1984: 95–115.

1986. "Foundation Prodigies in the *Aeneid*," *PLLS* **5**: 131–64.

1989. "The Tragedy of Dido," *EMC* **33**: 1–21.

Harrison, S. J. 1991. *Aeneid 10: Vergil*. Oxford.

1998. "The Sword-Belt of Pallas: Moral Symbolism and Political Ideology. *Aeneid* 10.495–505," in H.-P. Stahl ed., *Vergil's Aeneid: Augustan Epic and Political Context*. London.

Häusle, H. 1980. *Das Denkmal als Garant des Nachruhms: Eine Studie zu einem Motiv in lateinischen Inschriften*. München.

Heinze, R. 1993. *Vergil's Epic Technique*. Trans. H. and D. Harvey and F. Robertson. Berkeley.

Hejduk, J. 2009. "Jupiter's *Aeneid*: *Fama* and *Imperium*," *CA* **28**: 279–327.

Henry, E. 1989. *The Vigour of Prophecy: A Study of Vergil's "Aeneid."* Carbondale, IL.

Henry, J. 1873. *Aeneidea*. 4 vol. London.

Hershkowitz, D. 1991. "The *Aeneid* in *Aeneid* 3," *Vergilius* **37**: 69–76.

Herzog, R. 1993. "Aeneas' Episches Vergessen – Zur Poetik der *memoria*," in A. Haverkamp and R. Lachmann, eds. *Memoria: Vergessen und Erinnern*. Munich. 81–116.

Heubeck, A., S. West, and J. B. Hainsworth. 1990. *A Commentary on Homer's Odyssey*. Vol. 1. Oxford.

Hexter, R. 1990a. "What Was the Trojan Horse Made of? Interpreting Vergil's *Aeneid*," *Yale Journal of Criticism* **3**: 109–31.

1990b. "Sidonian Dido," in R. Hexter and D. Selden, eds. *Innovations of Antiquity*. New York: 332–84.

Hexter, R. and D. Selden. 1992. Eds. *Innovations of Antiquity*. New York.

Highet, G. 1974. "Speech and Narrative in the *Aeneid*," *HSCP* **78**: 189–229.

Hill, T. 2004. *Ambitiosa Mors: Suicide and Self in Roman Thought and Literature*. New York.

Hinds, S. 1998. *Allusion and Intertext: Dynamics of Appropriation in Roman Poetry*. Cambridge.

Hirsch, M. 1999. "Projected Memory: Holocaust Photographs in Personal and Public Fantasy," in M. Bal, J. Crewe, and L. Spitzer, eds. *Acts of Memory: Cultural Recall in the Present*. London. 3–23.

Hölkeskamp, K.-J. 2006. "History and Collective Memory in the Middle Republic," in N. Rosenstein and R. Morstein-Marx, eds. *A Companion to the Roman Republic*. Oxford. 478–95.

Hölkeskamp, K.-J. and E. Stein-Hölkeskam. 2006. Eds. *Erinnerungsorte der Antike: die Römische Welt*. Munich.

Hölscher, T. 2006. "The Transformation of Victory into Power: From Event to Structure," in S. Dillon and K. E. Welch, eds. *Representations of War in Ancient Rome*. Cambridge. 27–48.

Holt, P. 1979/1980. "*Aeneid* 5: Past and Future," *CJ* **75**: 110–21.

Hoppál, M. 1981. "Narration and Memory," *Fabula* **22**: 281–9.

Horsfall, N. 1981. "Virgil and the Conquest of Chaos," *Antichthon* **15**: 141–50.

1986. "The Aeneas Legend and the *Aeneid*," *Vergilius* **32**: 8–17. Reprinted in P. Hardie 1999. **3**: 265–77.

1987. "The Aeneas Legend from Homer to Vergil," in J. N. Bremmer and N. M. Horsfall, eds. *Roman Myth and Mythography*. London. 12–24.

1989. "Aeneas the Colonist," *Vergilius* **35**: 8–26.

1991. "Virgil and the Poetry of Explanations," *G&R* **38**: 203–11. Reprinted in P. Hardie 1999: **3**: 278–86.

1995. "Virgil: His Life and Times," in N. Horsfall, ed. *A Companion to the Study of Virgil*. Leiden. 1–25.

2000. *Virgil, Aeneid 7: A Commentary*. Leiden.

2003. *Virgil, Aeneid 11: A Commentary*. Leiden.

2006. *Virgil, Aeneid 3: A Commentary*. Leiden.

2008. *Virgil, Aeneid 2: A Commentary*. Leiden.

Hubbard, T. K. 1998. *The Pipes of Pan: Intertextuality and Literary Filiation in the Pastoral Tradition from Theocritus to Milton*. Ann Arbor.

Hunter, R. 1993. *The "Argonautica" of Apollonius: Literary Studies*. New York.

Irwin-Zarecka, I. 1994. *Frames of Remembrance: The Dynamics of Collective Memory* New Brunswick, NJ.

Jaeger, M. 1997. *Livy's Written Rome*. Ann Arbor.

James, S. 1995. "Establishing Rome with the Sword: *Condere* in the *Aeneid*," *AJP* **116**: 623–37.

Jenkyns, R. 1998. *Virgil's Experience: Nature and History: Times, Names, and Places*. Oxford.

Johnson, W. R. 1976. *Darkness Visible: A Study of Vergil's Aeneid*. Berkeley.

2005. "Introduction," in S. Lombardo, trans. *Virgil: Aeneid*. Indianapolis. xv–lxxi.

Joseph, T. 2010. "Tacitus' Repetition of Virgil's Wars at *Histories* 3.26–34," in J. F. Miller and J. Woodman, eds. *Latin Historiography and Poetry in the Early Empire: Generic Interactions*. Leiden. 155–69.

Keith, A. 2000. *Engendering Rome: Woman in Latin Epic*. Cambridge.

Kent, R. G. 1938. *Varro on the Latin Language*. Cambridge, MA.

Kepple, L. R. 1976. "Arruns and the Death of Aeneas," *AJP* **97**: 344–60.

Kirk, A. 2005. "Social and Cultural Memory," in A. Kirk and T. Thatcher, eds. *Memory, Tradition and Text: Uses of the Past in Early Christianity*. Atlanta. 1–24.

Kirk, G. S. 1985. *The Iliad: A Commentary, Volume 1: Books 1–4*. Cambridge.

1990. *The Iliad: A Commentary, Volume 11: Books 5–8*. Cambridge.

Knape, J. 1997. "*Memoria* in der älteren rhetoriktheoretischen Tradition," *Zeitschrift für Literaturwissenschaft und Linguistic* **27**: 6–21.

Knapp, S. 1989. "Collective Memory and the Actual Past," *Representations* **26**: 123–49.

Knauer, G. N. 1964a. *Die Aeneis und Homer: Studien zur Poetischen Technik Vergils mit Listen der Homerzitate in der Aeneis*. Göttingen.

1964b. "Vergil's *Aeneid* and Homer," *GRBS* **5**: 61–84.

Knox, P. E. 1997. "Savagery in the *Aeneid* and Virgil's Ancient Commentators," *CJ* **92**: 225–33.
Kristol, S. S. 1990. *"Labor" and "Fortuna" in Virgil's "Aeneid."* New York.
Küchler, S. and W. Melion. 1991. "Introduction," in S. Küchler and W. Melion, eds. *Images of Memory: On Remembering and Representation.* 1–46.
Kyriakidis, S. 1998. *Narrative Structure and Poetics in the Aeneid: The Frame of Book 6.* Bari.
Larmour, D. H. J. and D. Spencer. 2007. Eds. *The Sites of Rome: Time, Space, Memory.* Oxford.
Lee, M. O. 1979. *Fathers and Sons in Vergil's Aeneid: Tum Genitor Natum.* Albany.
Lefkowitz, M. R. 1991. *The Lives of the Greek Poets.* Baltimore.
Levi, P. 1988. *The Drowned and the Saved.* Trans. R. Rosenthal. London.
Lewis, C. S. 1949. *A Preface to "Paradise Lost."* Oxford.
Lincoln, B. 1982. "Waters of Memory, Waters of Forgetfulness," *Fabula* **23**: 19–34.
Lloyd, C. 1995. "The Evander-Anchises Connection: Fathers, Sons, and Homoerotic Desire in Vergil's *Aeneid*," *Vergilius* **45**: 3–21.
Lloyd, R. B. 1957. "*Aeneid* 3: A New Approach," *AJP* **78**: 133–51.
Lombardo, S. 2005. *Virgil: Aeneid.* Indianapolis.
Lowenstam, S. 1993. "The Pictures on Juno's Temple in the *Aeneid*," *CW* **87**: 37–49.
Lowrie, M. 2009. *Writing, Performance, and Authority in Augustan Rome.* Oxford.
Luminet, O. and A. Curci. 2009. Eds. *Flashbulb Memories: New Issues and New Perspectives.* New York.
Luria, A. R. 1968. *The Mind of a Mnemonist: A Little Book about a Vast Memory.* Trans. L. Solotaroff. New York.
Lynch, J. P. 1980. "Laocoon and Sinon: Virgil, *Aeneid* 2, 40–198," *G&R* **27**: 170–9.
Lyne, R. O. A. M. 1987. *Further Voices in Vergil's "Aeneid."* Oxford.
1989. *Words and the Poet: Characteristic Techniques of Style in Vergil's Aeneid.* Oxford.
MacDonald, R. 1987. *The Burial Places of Memory: Epic Underworlds in Vergil, Dante, and Milton.* Amherst.
Mack, S. 1978. *Patterns of Time in Vergil.* Hamden.
MacKay, L. A. 1957. "Achilles as Model for Aeneas," *TAPA* **88**: 11–6. Reprinted in P. Hardie 1999: 3: 87–92.
Mackie, C. J. 1990. "*Quisquis in arma vocas*: Turnus and Jupiter in the *Aeneid*," *Antichthon* **24**: 79–85.
MacLeod, C. W. 1982. *Homer: Iliad Book* XXIV. Cambridge.
Maltby, R. 1991. *A Lexicon of Ancient Latin Etymologies.* Leeds.
Martin, R. P. 1989. *The Language of Heroes: Speech and Performance in the "Iliad."* Ithaca.
Martindale, C. Ed. 1997. *The Cambridge Companion to Virgil.* Cambridge.
Meadows, A. and J. Williams. 2001. "Moneta and the Monuments: Coinage and Politics in Republican Rome," *JRS* **91**: 27–49.
Meban, D. 2009. "Virgil's *Eclogues* and Social Memory," *AJP* **130**: 99–130.

Miller, J. 1993. "Ovidian Allusion and the Vocabulary of Memory," *M&D* **30**: 153–64.

2009. *Apollo, Augustus, and the Poets*. Cambridge.

Miller, P. A. 1995. "The Minotaur Within: Fire, the Labyrinth, and Strategies of Containment in *Aeneid* 5 and 6," *CP* **90**: 225–40.

Mitchell-Boyask, R. 1996. "*Sine Fine*: Vergil's Masterplot." *AJP* **117**: 289–307.

Möller, M. 2009. "*attentio, intentio, contentio*. Ciceros Rhetorik als Theorie der Aufmerksamkeit." Habilitationsschrift, Heidelberg University.

Most, G. W. 2001. "Memory and Forgetting in the *Aeneid*," *Vergilius* **47**: 148–70.

Murnaghan, S. 1987. *Disguise and Recognition in the Odyssey*. Princeton.

Mynors, R. 1969. Ed. *P. Vergili Maronis Opera*. Oxford.

Nagy, G. 1979. *The Best of the Achaeans: Concepts of the Hero in Archaic Greek Poetry*. Baltimore.

2007. "Homer and Greek Myth," in R. D. Woodard, ed. *The Cambridge Companion to Greek Mythology*. Cambridge. 52–82.

Nappa, C. J. 2007. "Unmarried Dido: *Aeneid* 4.550–52," *Hermes* **135**: 301–13.

2010. "Catallus and Vergil," in M. Skinner, ed. A Companion to Catallus. Malden. 377–98.

Nelis, D. 2001. *Vergil's Aeneid and the Argonautica of Apollonius Rhodius*. Leeds.

Nora, P. 1989. "Between Memory and History: Les Lieux de Mémoire," *Representations* **26**: 7–24.

Norden, E. 1970. *P. Vergilius Maro Aeneis Buch VI*. 5th edn. Stuttgart.

1901. "Vergils Aeneis im Lichte ihrer Zeit," *Neue Jahrbücher für das Klassische Altertum*. 7: 249–82, 313–34. Reprinted as "Virgil's *Aeneid* in the Light of Its Own Time," in P. Hardie 1999: **3**: 114–72. Trans. H. Harvey.

Novara, A. 1986. *Poésie Virgilienne de la Mémoire: Questions sur L'Histoire dans L'Énéide 8*. Paris.

Nugent, S. G. 1992. "Vergil's 'Voice of the Women' in *Aeneid* 5," *Arethusa* **25**: 255–92.

Nussbaum, M. 1994. *The Therapy of Desire: Theory and Practice in Hellenistic Ethics*. Princeton.

Oakley, S. P. 2005. *A Commentary on Livy Books VI–X: Volume 3, Book IX*. Oxford.

Ogilvie, R. M. 1965. *A Commentary on Livy Book 1–5*. Oxford.

O'Hara, J. J. 1990. *Death and the Optimistic Prophecy in Vergil's Aeneid*. Princeton.

1996. *True Names: Vergil and the Alexandrian Tradition of Etymological Wordplay*. Ann Arbor.

2007. *Inconsistency in Roman Epic: Studies in Catullus, Lucretius, Vergil, Ovid and Lucan*. Cambridge.

Olick, J. K. 1999. "Collective Memory: Two Cultures," *Sociological Theory* **17**: 338–48.

Olick, J. K., V. Vinitzky-Seroussi, and D. Levy. 2011. Eds. *The Collective Memory Reader*. Oxford.

Oliensis, E. 2009. *Freud's Rome: Psychoanalysis and Latin Poetry*. Cambridge.

Onega, S. and J. A. G. Landa. 1996. "Introduction," in S. Onega and J. A. G. Landa, eds. *Narratology: An Introduction*. London. 1–44.

Orlin, E. 2007. "Augustan Religion and the Reshaping of Roman Memory," *Arethusa* **40**: 73–92.

O'Sullivan, T. M. 2009. "Death *ante ora parentum* in Virgil's *Aeneid*," *TAPA* **139**: 447–86.

Otis, B. 1964. *Virgil: A Study in Civilized Poetry*. Oxford.

Page, T. E. 1893. "Review: Translations of the *Aeneid* by Rhoades and Sergeaunt," *CR* **7**: 415–8.

Papaioannou, S. 2003. "Founder, Civilizer, and Leader – Vergil's Evander and His Role in the Origins of Rome," *Mnemosyne* **56**: 680–702.

Parry, A. 1963. "The Two Voices of Virgil's *Aeneid*," *Arion* **2**: 66–80.

Paschalis, M. 1986. "The Unifying Theme of Daedalus' Sculptures on the Temple of Apollo Cumanus (6.20–33)," *Vergilius* **32**: 33–41.

1997. *Virgil's Aeneid: Semantic Relations and Proper Names*. Oxford.

Pavlovskis, Z. 1976. "*Aeneid* V: The Old and the Young," *CJ* **71**: 193–205.

Perkell, C. 1997. "The Lament of Juturna: Pathos and Interpretation in the *Aeneid*," *TAPA* **127**: 257–86.

1999. "*Aeneid* 1: An Epic Programme," in C. Perkell, ed. *Reading Vergil's Aeneid: An Interpretative Guide*. Norman, OK. 29–49.

Port, W. 1962. *Sayings of Rammikar*. Chicago.

Pöschl, V. 1970. *The Art of Vergil: Image and Symbol in the Aeneid*. Trans. G. Seligson. Ann Arbor.

1975. "Die Templetüren des Dädalus in der *Aeneid*," *WJA* **1**: 119–33.

Primmer, A. 1994/95. "Das Tischprodigium im Rahmen der *Aeneis*," *WS* **107**/8: 397–416.

Purcell, N. 2003. "Becoming Historical: The Roman Case," in D. Braund and C. Gill 2003: 12–40.

Putnam, M. C. J. 1966. *The Poetry of the "Aeneid": Four Studies in Imaginative Unity and Design*. Cambridge, MA.

1981. "*Pius* Aeneas and the Metamorphosis of Lausus," *Arethusa* **14**: 139–56

1990. "Anger, Blindness and Insight in Virgil's *Aeneid*," in M. C. Nussbaum, ed. *The Poetics of Therapy: Hellenistic Ethics in Its Rhetorical and Literary Context*. Edmonton. 7–40.

1995. *Virgil's Aeneid: Interpretation and Influence*.

1998. *Virgil's Epic Designs*. New Haven.

Quint, D. 1982. "Painful Memories: *Aeneid* 3 and the Problem of the Past," *CJ* **78**: 30–8.

1989. "Repetition and Ideology in the *Aeneid*," *MD* **24**: 9–54. Reprinted in P. Hardie 1999: **4**: 117–57.

1993. *Epic and Empire: Politics and Generic Form from Vergil to Milton*. Princeton.

2010. "*Aeacidae Pyrrhi*: Myth and History in *Aeneid* 1–6," in B. Breed and C. Damon, eds. *Citizens of Discord: Rome and Its Civil Wars*. Oxford. 133–44.

Rea, J. A. 2007. *Legendary Rome: Myth, Monuments and Memory on the Palatine and Capitoline*. London.

Reckford, K. J. 1995/6. "Recognizing Venus. I, Aeneas Meets His Mother," *Arion* **3**: 1–42.

Redfield, J. M. 1994. *Nature and Culture in the Iliad: The Tragedy of Hector*. Expanded edn. Durham.

Reed, J. D. 2007. *Vergil's Gaze: Nation and Poetry in the Aeneid*. Princeton.

Rodgers, R. H. 1992. "*Quique Sui Memores Alios Fecere Merendo*: The Roman Reward for Public Service," *NECN* **19**: 24–7.

Rogerson, A. 2012. "Vegio's Ascanius: Problems in the Continuation of the *Aeneid*," *Classical Receptions Journal* **4**: 1–20.

Roller, M. B. 2004. "Exemplarity in Roman Culture: The Cases of Horatius Cocles and Cloelia," *CP* **99**: 1–56.

Ross, D. O. 2007. *Virgil's Aeneid: A Reader's Guide*. Malden.

Russo, J., M. Fernández-Galiano, and A. Heubeck. 1992. *A Commentary on Homer's Odyssey: Volume III, Books XVII–XXIV*. Oxford.

Rutledge, H. C. 1967. "Vergil's Daedalus," *CJ* **62**: 309–11.

1971–72. "The Opening of *Aeneid* 6," *CJ* **67**: 110–15.

Saylor, C. F. 1970. "Toy Troy: The New Perspective of the Backward Glance," *Vergilius* **16**: 26–8.

Scafoglio, G. 2008. "Sinon in Roman Drama," *CJ* **104**: 11–8.

Scarth, E. 2008. *Mnemotechnics and Virgil: The Art of Memory and Remembering*. Saarbrücken.

Scodel, R. 2002. "Homeric Signs and Flashbulb Memory," in I. Worthington, and J. M. Foley, eds. *Epea and Grammata: Oral and Written Communication in Ancient Greece*. Leiden. 99–116.

2008. "Social Memory in Aeschylus' *Oresteia*," in E. A. Mackay, ed. *Orality, Literacy, Memory in the Ancient Greek and Roman World*. Leiden. 115–41.

Segal, C. 1981. "Art and the Hero: Participation, Detachment, and Narrative Point of View in *Aeneid* 1," *Arethusa* **14**: 67–83.

Simpson, J. and E. Weiner. 2009. Eds. *The Oxford English Dictionary*. Oxford.

Shils, E. 1981. *Tradition*. Chicago.

Short, W. M. 2012. "A Roman Folk Model of the Mind," *Arethusa* **45**: 109–47.

Skutsch, O. 1985. *The Annals of Q. Ennius*. Oxford.

Small, J. P. 1997. *Wax Tablets of the Mind: Cognitive Studies of Memory and Literacy in Classical Antiquity*. London.

Small, J. P. and J. Tatum. 1995. "Memory and the Study of Classical Antiquity: Introduction," *Helios* **22**: 149–50.

Smith, A. 1997. *Poetic Allusion and Poetic Embrace in Ovid and Virgil*. Ann Arbor.

2005. *The Primacy of Vision in Virgil's Aeneid*. Austin.

Spence, S. 1988. *Rhetorics of Reason and Desire: Vergil, Augustine, and the Troubadours*. Ithaca.

1991. "Clinching the Text: The Danaids and the End of the *Aeneid*," *Vergilius* **37**: 11–9.

Stahl, H.-P. 1981. "Aeneas – an '(Un)heroic' Hero?," *Arethusa* **41**: 157–77.

1990. "The Death of Turnus: Augustan Vergil and the Political Rival," in K. A. Raaflaub and M. Toher, eds. *Between Republic and Empire: Interpretations of Augustus and His Principate*. Berkeley 174–211.

Stanford, W. B. 1962. *Homer: Odyssey XIII–XXIV*. 2nd edn. Bristol.

Stem, R. 2007. "The Exemplary Lessons of Livy's Romulus," *TAPA* **137**: 435–71.
Sumi, G. S. 2009. "Monuments and Memory: The *Aedes Castoris* in the Formation of Augustan Ideology," *CQ* **59**: 167–86.
Syed, Y. 2005. *Vergil's "Aeneid" and the Roman Self: Subject and Nation in Literary Discourse*. Ann Arbor.
Tarrant, R. 2004. "The Last Book of the *Aeneid*," *SyllClass* **15**: 103–29.
2012. *Virgil Aeneid Book* XII. Cambridge.
Tatum, J. 1995. "Aunt Elvie's Quilt on the Bed of Odysseus: The Role of Artifacts in Natural Memory," *Helios* **22**: 167–74.
2003. *The Mourner's Song: War and Remembrance from the Iliad to Vietnam*. Chicago.
Theodorakopoulos, E. 2004. "The Name of the Game: The *Troia*, and History and Spectacle in *Aeneid* 5," *PVS* **25**: 63–72.
Thomas, R. 1992. *Literacy and Orality in Ancient Greece*. Cambridge.
Thomas, R. F. 1986. "From *recusatio* to Commitment," *PLLS* **5**: 61–73.
1988. *Georgics: Virgil*. Vol. 1. Cambridge.
1999. "The Old Man Revisited: Memory, Reference, and Genre in Virg. *Georg* 4, 116–48," in R. F. Thomas, ed. *Reading Virgil and His Texts: Studies in Intertextuality*. 173–205. Reprint of 1992, *MD* **29**: 35–70.
Toll, K. 1991. "The *Aeneid* as an Epic of National Identity: *Italiam Laeto Socii Clamore Salutant*," *Helios* **18**: 3–14.
1997. "Making Roman-ness and the *Aeneid*," *CA* **16**: 34–56.
Trahman, C. R. 1952. "Odysseus' Lies (*Odyssey*, Books 13–19)," *TAPA* **6**: 31–43.
Vance, E. 1973. "Warfare and the Structure of Thought in Virgil's *Aeneid*," *QUCC* **15**: 111–61.
Van Dyke, R. M. and S. E. Alcock. 2003. *Archaeologies of Memory*. Malden.
Vernant, J. 1991. *Mortals and Immortals: Collected Essays*. F. I. Zeitlin, ed. Princeton.
Vervliet, R. and A. Estor. 2000. Eds. *Methods for the Study of Literature as Cultural Memory: Leiden 16–22 August 1997*. Amsterdam.
Wacht, M. 1996. Ed. *Concordantia Vergiliana*. Hildesheim.
Walter, U. 2004. *Memoria und Res Publica: zur Geschichtskultur im Republikanischen Rom*. Frankfurt am Main.
Watkins, C. 1990. "What Is Philology?," *Comparative Literature Studies* **27**: 21–5.
Weinrich, H. 2004. *Lethe: The Art and Critique of Forgetting*. Trans. S. Rendall. Ithaca.
Welzer, H. 2007. Ed. *Der Krieg der Erinnerung : Holocaust, Kollaboration und Widerstand im Europäischen Gedächtnis*. Frankfurt am Main.
West, D. 1974. "The Deaths of Hector and Turnus," *G&R* **21**: 21–31. Reprinted in P. Hardie 1999: 4: 381–91.
West, G. 1983. "Andromache and Dido," *AJP* **104**: 257–67.
West, M. L. 1966. Ed. Hesiod: Theogony. Oxford.
West, S. 1983. "Notes on the Text of Lycophron," *CQ* **33**: 114–35.
Wharton, D. 2008. "*Sunt Lacrimae Rerum*: An Exploration in Meaning," *CJ* **103**: 259–79.

Wheeler, S. M. 1999. *A Discourse of Wonders: Audience and Performance in Ovid's Metamorphoses*. Philadelphia.

White, P. 1993. *Promised Verse: Poets in the Society of Augustan Rome*. Cambridge, MA.

Williams, G. 1983. *Techniques and Ideas in the Aeneid*. New Haven.

Williams, R. D. 1960. "The Pictures on Dido's Temple," *CQ* **10**: 145–51.

1971. "Dido's Reply to Aeneas (4.362–387)," H. Bardon and R. Verdière, eds. *Vergiliana*. Leiden. 422–8.

1972. *The Aeneid of Virgil*. Vol. 2. London.

Wiltshire, S. F. 1988. *Public and Private in the "Aeneid."* Amherst.

Wiseman, T. P. 1984. "Cybele, Virgil, and Augustus," in Woodman and West 1984: 117–28.

Woodman, T. and D. West. 1984. Eds. *Poetry and Politics in the Age of Augustus*. Cambridge.

Wray, D. 2001. *Catullus and the Poetics of Roman Manhood*. Cambridge.

Wright, M. R. 1997. "*Ferox Virtus*: Anger in Virgil's *Aeneid*," in S. M. Braund and C. Gill 1997: 169–84.

Yates, F. A. 1974. *The Art of Memory*. Chicago.

Yerushalmi, Y. H. 1982. *Zakhor: Jewish History and Jewish Memory*. Seattle.

Zanker, P. 1988. *The Power of Images in the Age of Augustus*. Trans. A. Shapiro. Ann Arbor.

Zarker, J. W. 1967. "Aeneas and Theseus in *Aeneid* 6," *CJ* **62**: 220–26.

Zerubavel, E. 1996. "Social Memories: Steps to a Sociology of the Past," *Qualitative Sociology* **19**: 283–99.

Zetzel, J. E. G. 1989. "*Romane Memento*: Justice and Judgment in *Aeneid* 6," *TAPA* **119**: 263–84.

Index locorum

Index verborum

Index